Empowering Students to Write and Re-Write

Standards-Based Strategies for Middle and High School Teachers

Warren E. Combs

To Arnelle, a trusted partner in writing and in life

In memory of Warren D. Combs (1920–2001) and Norvin B. Norwood (1923–2009)

EYE ON EDUCATION
6 DEPOT WAYWEST, SUITE 106
LARCHMONT, NY 10538
(914) 833–0551
(914) 833–0761 fax
www.eyeoneducation.com

Library of Congress Cataloging-in-Publication Data

Combs, Warren E.
  Empowering students to write and re-write : strategies for middle and high
school teachers / Warren E. Combs.
     p. cm.
  Includes bibliographical references and index.
  ISBN 978-1-59667-123-2 (alk. paper)
1. English language—Composition and exercises—Study and teaching (Middle
school) 2. English language—Composition and exercises—Study and teaching
(Secondary) 3. Editing—Study and teaching (Middle school) 4. Editing—Study
and teaching (Secondary) I. Title.
  LB1631.C655 2009
  808'.0420712--dc22

                                                        2009016270

10 9 8 7 6 5 4 3 2 1

Production services provided by
Rick Soldin, Electronic Publishing Services, Inc.
Jonesborough, TN — www.epsinc-tn.com

Also Available from Eye On Education

Vocabulary at the Center
Amy Benjamin and John T. Crow

**Literacy Leadership Teams: Collaborative Leadership for
Improving and Sustaining Student Achievement**
Pamela S. Craig

**Active Literacy Across the Curriculum:
Strategies for Reading, Writing, Speaking and Listening**
Heidi Hayes Jacobs

Family Reading Night
Darcy Hutchins, Marsha Greenfeld and Joyce Epstein

**Formative Assessment for English Language Arts:
A Guide for Middle and High School Teachers**
Amy Benjamin

**Literacy from A to Z:
Engaging Students in Reading, Writing, Speaking and Listening**
Barbara R. Blackburn

Literature Circles that Engage Middle and High School Students
Victor Moeller and Marc Moeller

**Socratic Seminars and Literature Circles for
Middle and High School English**
Victor Moeller and Marc Moeller

Writing In the Content Areas, 2nd Edition
Amy Benjamin

Rigor is NOT a Four-Letter Word
Barbara R. Blackburn

Building A Culture of Literacy Month-by-Month
Hilarie Davis

**But I'm Not A Reading Teacher:
Strategies for Literacy Instruction in the Content Areas**
Amy Benjamin

About the Author

A former classroom teacher and university professor, Dr. Warren E. Combs has devoted his professional career to the application of best practices in the teaching of writing based on the conclusions of recognized research strands. He received the Ph.D. in English Education and Child Language Development from the University of Minnesota. As co-director of the *Timothy Road Elementary School Writing Project* with the late Bruce McNair, he developed frameworks for empowering students to learn to write, write to learn and experience grammar instruction in the context of the writing process. In 1986 he established Erincort Consulting, Inc. for publication of *Writing to Win* instructional resources to support his work with K-12 public and private schools as well as home-school associations.

Dr. Combs and his associate trainers work with over 250 schools in seven states, recognizing over 140 of them as *Exemplary Schools of Writing* in 2008. His practical instructional strategies resonate equally well with teachers of core academic, vocational, special education, ESOL and gifted students. Signatures of *Writing to Win* trainers include 1) demonstration of best practice in working with writing in classrooms of students as teachers observe, 2) action research projects with each implementation and workshops for writing coaches that empower local leaders to maintain increased student performance. To keep in touch with the realities of changing classroom venues, Dr. Combs works directly with several thousand students in class each year. He has authored several books and journal publications and is an invited presenter at several national and state conferences throughout the southeast and mid-west. He resides in Athens, Georgia with his wife and professional colleague, Arnelle. Their three children and three grandchildren have or are presently benefiting from the guidance of the *Writing to Win* frameworks of writing to learn and learning to write.

Contents

Free Downloads

Two types of materials are available free for bookbuyers on the Eye On Education website. Anyone who has purchased this book has permission to download and print them out.

You can access these downloads by visiting www.eyeoneducation.com. Click on FREE Downloads, or search or browse our website to find this book's page and scroll down for downloading instructions.

You'll need your bookbuyer access code: **EMP-7123-2.**

The following downloads are blank forms. Filled out versions of these forms can be found on the pages referenced below.

The following downloads are additional materials that are not included in the book. The page numbers refer to the pages on which these materials are discussed.

Introduction

*What we think, or what we know, or what we believe is, in the end,
of little consequence. The only consequence is what we do.*
John Ruskin

Revision is one of the exquisite pleasures of writing.
Bernard Malamud

This is a book about getting students to rewrite—really revise, completely on their own.

Revision does not have to be hard work. Malamud is right: *Revision is the one of the exquisite pleasures of writing.* When we teachers truly follow the conclusions of research in the teaching of writing, students do not have to be convinced or coaxed to revise.

"Don't have to be convinced to revise?" you asked, checking out the sides of my head for subtle evidence of alien life. You might turn to a fellow teacher and say, "Should we tell him?" Then you both unload your frustrations about getting your students to revise. You say that I have not met your students and that getting your students to revise is like pulling teeth. Actually, I know exactly what you mean. I have been where you are.

You see, I embraced the same thoughts for some time until I met Donald Graves in a writing seminar that he conducted for some of my students early in my career.

After he prompted us to write, wrote along with us and shared a vivid description of an old woman sweeping alongside a curb, I wanted to wad my writing up and toss it across the room. I saw my students making eyes at one another, clear signs of group despair. Graves knew exactly how we were responding because he moved immediately to the pleasure of revision. He said in reading his short piece aloud, he already had three things he wanted to revise, and he mentioned what they were. He told us to read our pieces aloud to a partner and see if the same thing happened to us. Amazingly, it did. He made only one comment **about** revision—that it was *as natural a part of writing as holding a pencil*. I believed him and saw no reason to doubt him even in the face of the majority of teachers who think otherwise and believe they have classrooms of living proof.

Not long after my conversion to the Graves form of revision, I started spreading his method with each new group of students and teachers I met. That's when I met Marge. She stood up towards the end of my presentation at a National Council of Teachers of English conference in Cleveland. She was so convinced that her kids in an inner city school not two miles away could not revise that she couldn't keep her seat. She was twice my age, matched my experience in the classroom times five, and she was good. "You seem like a smart young man, but if you are as smart as you sound then you will visit my fourth period class tomorrow and put a little walk behind your talk." The group laughed too loud for my comfort and way too many of them clapped in response.

The next day, I was in Marge's fourth period American literature class filled with swaggering boys larger than I and sullen girls in revealing attire. First thoughts told me I'd met my match. Fortunately, thanks to my inspired method for presenting writing, I had all the preparation I needed. Previously, Marge had shared the writing assignment with me, and I carried my handwritten first draft in my attaché case (remember those?) when the cab dropped me off in front of this downtown high school. I felt a little like the boy named David on his way to meet the Philistine, Goliath.

She introduced me as *Dr. Combs* to the group who was still milling about the aisles between desks in the room. I said, "What's going on?" in my coolest manner and sat on the edge of Marge's desk. My guess is that she never sat there herself because as I did, the move caught the attention of most of her students who glanced her direction and immediately quieted down.

"I have my first draft on your assignment; I wrote it late last night," I spoke softly holding my paper in the air for all to see. "So, get your drafts out, and let's get going; I'll read mine first."

"Hey, Doc, I can't find mine. I know I did it, but see?" A lanky tee-shirted fellow draped over the seat of his desk shrugged his shoulders and held empty hands palms up. I was experienced enough to recognize the bait for what it was and heard myself quip, "I'm really sorry. Hope you have a better day tomorrow" and looked away. After all, I had 24 other emerging writers to move on to revision!

As I read my first draft aloud slowly, I felt them all listen with intent. The lanky guy was sitting up straight and spoke, "You write that for real?"

"Uh-huh," I admitted and continued, still as softly as I heard Graves do that day. "It's just natural for people who read aloud what they write to think of extra words that they didn't put in the first time. In fact, that happened to me just now. This sentence and this phrase and this sentence here were parts where extra words just popped into my mind. It was kind of like magic." As I spoke I held up my draft and circled the parts that I mentioned with a red felt-tipped pen for all to see.

"So I'm going to put a number "1" by the circle I know I could write the 'most more about.' " (Although the term "most more about" is not preferred English grammar, it helps students understand what to do. See Chapter 8.)

I moved and spoke with intention without looking at the class. "There," I went on, "now, it's your turn to do the same. If you don't have a paper to revise, just listen really carefully and watch without saying a word. It's important that you do not say a word. You'll catch on just the same. This is really simple to do." Not a word about revision. Not a word about trying. There was only **do**.

To make a long story short, Marge's most incorrigible group revised right along with me as she sat there in amazement. They marveled at how I added crisp detail to my first draft since it seemed good enough to them already. Some of them shared their revisions. The shock of their peers was unmistakable. I do hope Marge took my cue and began writing with her students.

Now, especially if you are a teacher whose classes are filled with students who don't revise, it is time for a new direction. Let's look each other squarely in the eye and agree to stick together until we see your students give in to their tendency to revise that is as natural as holding a pencil. Since you are already reading *Empowering Students to Write and RE-write,* start with this book. It amplifies the revision section of my *Writing to Win©* resource guide for teaching the writing process. If you want a complete guide for prewriting, proof-reading or scoring final drafts, move to this companion publication (Combs 2005b).

In all of my work with students and writing, I keep four researched conclusions in mind. The first conclusion comes out of research in the teaching of writing. The other three emerge from the broader research of school improvement, assessment and brain-based studies.

1. Write with your students as a model for them to follow (*National Writing Project*). This includes writing an assignment

    a. before you assign it to make sure that it can be done in the time you allow for your students.

    b. along with your students as the leader in your community of writers.

2. Focus on nonfiction writing as assessment of what students are learning in your subject area or across curriculum (Reeves, *The Learning Leader,* ASCD).

3. Include student self-assessment of everything they write as an integral part of the writing routine in your class (Rick Stiggins, *Classroom Assessment for Student Learning*).

4. Take advantage of Prime I, II or III of brain activity in pacing student writing in class (David Sousa, brain-based studies).

    a. The first 5–7 minutes (Prime I) or last 5–7 minutes (Prime II) of a lesson for short writing.

    b. Twelve to nineteen minutes (Prime III) for longer, in-class writing tasks.

When I remember to follow these four conclusions simultaneously in working with students, I am always pleased with the results. This book is a collection of the vocabulary, the classroom routines and lessons, my invitations for students to write with me.

I call the first section, Chapters 1–4, *What revision is. . .,* which curiously concludes with a chapter on *What revision is not.* In this section, I admit my debt to teachers who were students of Flannery O'Connor, specifically a department of English teachers most of whom she trained when she was adjunct instructor of education in middle Georgia. In the first three chapters, their influence is so pronounced that I cannot adequately cite all their contributions separately, but my debt is great. The fourth chapter is equally important since distractions to natural and effective revision are powerful and widely accepted among students, parents and many teachers. These ideas arise from my own experiences with serious disruptions of the flow and power of authentic revision. When I learned to anticipate these disruptions, I disarmed them before they did their harm.

Chapters 5–14 make up the largest part of the book. Each chapter presents one or more revision strategies, invitations for students whom I meet to write with me. In this writing, I offer them as invitations for your students to write with you. Don't be put off by the scripted nature of these chapters. They detail for you strategies that work for me every time I call on them, with all manner of students. The precise word, the successful phrase, the meaning students readily understand came from years of tweaking strategies that needed to improve. So start with the scripts and begin your own plan for tweaking one phrase at a time until you have the strategy that works best for you with your students. Teaching writing and using writing to learn has been my only business for years.

By the way, these strategies will help your students create a mindset for revision whether you embrace the writer's workshop model or hold to more traditional tenets of teaching and learning. Remember Graves' foundational comment, *Revision is as natural a part of writing as holding a pencil.* Authentic revision is not ensured by adopting the writer's workshop model, nor is it doomed by adopting more traditional patterns of teaching and learning. The strategies I present are simple and concrete lessons, classroom born and classroom ready.

The final chapter, Implementing a Mindset for Revision, shows how revision is a recursive feature of each step of the writing process. Here I pay particular attention to helping students consider possibilities before making a choice at each step of the process.

Throughout the book, a Guide for Professional Learning Teams (PLT) appears at the end of six chapters in a sequence of six PLT sessions. If your school follows a model for professional learning communities or whole-faculty study groups, you already know the intent and design of the sequence. Even if your school has no such model, this guide is simple to follow. Directions for setting up teams of teachers to study this book together are found in the appendix. Completion of the study qualifies the participating teachers for two professional learning credits in most states. I provide pages for you to use in submitting a course portfolio for two hours of elective graduate credit in graduate schools of education. We provide the sequence for learning; you choose the timeline for implementing it.

Additional writing samples and extension of the concepts and skills in this book are on Eye On Education's website. Visit www.eyeoneducation.com, go to this book's page, and follow the links.

Empowering Students to Write and RE-write is the outgrowth of my experiences with classroom teachers throughout my career. My confidence in each strategy comes from countless observations in classes of students from the gifted to students with special needs. When one of them does not work for me or a fellow teacher, we simply revisit the four research conclusions on page xi and the fundamentals of effective revision found in the first section of this book. We always discover why. Then we return to the same students with the same strategy and watch it work with power and sustainability in their writing. It's my pleasure to share them all with you.

Here's to authentic writing!

Warren E. Combs

1

Revision Is Picturing Again— Voice, Pictures and Flow

There is no great writing, only great rewriting.
Justice Brandeis

I'm not a very good writer, but I'm an excellent rewriter.
James Michener

When it comes to the revision of writing, *the truth is out there,* and I speak of nothing extra-terrestrial. Book publishers have tapped professional authors and master teachers of writing to present their methods for getting students to revise. All of these authors present frameworks for revision that they have seen work. So why isn't the joy of revising writing among students in this country more widespread? Why do eager teachers still fill sessions on revision at conferences to overflowing?

The answer to these questions lies in the responsibility that these books on revision require of classroom teachers. The books fit into two large groups: one I'll call the direct instruction group and the other the workshop group. Both groups of authors define revision the same way. *Revision* derives from *re + vision* meaning to *look again.* Writers simply look back at their writing, and in so doing, see how to make their writing work better. Professional writers do this naturally and revising their way through each step of the writing process towards a final draft. Not so for most student writers who remain impervious to the many books published on revision.

The first group takes the path of direct instruction. These books on revision started appearing in the 1970s and 1980s and echo in standard textbooks of writing to date. Peter Elbow's *Power with Writing* and Kit Reed's *Revision* are representative of this group. I valued both of these books when I read them years ago. Reed lays the directives out in a comfortable manner like a kindly relative talking to the new writer in a fireside chat.

Your first thoughts are not necessarily your best thoughts.

It takes revision to turn a loss into a win.

Be your own toughest critic. (pp. 4–10)

Reed, and others like her, appear to assume that students are interested in revision or see a need for it in their writing. Teachers without self-motivated students have work to do to bring their students to a place that they can benefit from Reed's advice.

On the other hand, the authors from the workshop group begin by recognizing that student resistance to revision is real and in some cases, robust. They echo student comments like these from Heard's *The Revision Toolbox: Teaching Techniques That Work:*.

"But I like what I wrote the first time."

"You mean I have to change my writing?"

"I like it just the way it is!" (pp. 1–2)

Heard's book addresses these comments and suggests that teachers motivate their students to revise in subtle ways. Teachers need to allow students to talk through their feelings. They also need to show them how professional writers revise, get them hooked on reading good literature and spotlight revision in the writing process—all excellent ideas.

Both the direct instruction and workshop groups of authors offer solutions that require teachers to plan, assemble and present the motivation for getting students to revise. In short, the teacher's burden for motivating revision is monumental. In his foreword to the second edition of Nancie Atwell's *In the Middle*, Donald Graves writes, "Beyond such incredible student writing works a pragmatic, literate professional. The key word is *works*. Nancie works her tail off. The faint-hearted need not apply for this kind of teaching." (p. ix) That is a very different approach than I take in *Empowering Students to Write and RE-write*. A host of classroom teachers have helped me understand that it is possible to help students make sense of what they are learning through sound writing and thinking without the teachers working themselves to death. Teachers never should work 'harder' than students.

I revise my own writing as a model for students each time I prompt them to write and revise. I keep my writing in a portfolio and call on it again and again each time I meet a new group of students. My simple organization of portfolios keeps the task of prompting student writing enjoyable. When I see how energized students are by my straightforward, authentic writing, I experience energy myself, not exhaustion.

A note about modeling writing. Writing an assignment and sharing my writing before students write is just part of the definition of modeling writing. Equally important to me as a teacher of writing is writing along with students. Nothing, and I do mean nothing, distracts me from writing an assignment along with students. Oh, I get up for a 20- to 30-second conference with a student or two to help them along, but I always find my way back to my laptop to dash off my model writing in time to share if the occasion requires it, and I insist my host teacher write along with us. Administrators know that when they drop in on my demonstration lessons, they have committed to write with us, too. Whether I share my model aloud or not, I always project it briefly on the screen for students to see that I was writing, too.

Revision Defined

Revision means more than **looking again**; it is important to take the **vision** in revision literally.

Now I tell students to

> Look at the **vision** or **picture** that you saw in your mind when you wrote your first draft. Close your eyes if it helps you bring the image back. Now compare the picture(s) in your mind with the words on the page. Do the words fully describe the picture you see in your mind?

With this approach I find that the students engage themselves in the revision process readily and naturally. So students' understanding of revision occurs more in my **doing revision** with them instead of **talking about revision** to them. I acquired this important distinction from two English language arts teachers from Baldwin County, Georgia, who had this simple and natural way to revise down pat. Both attended a language studies for teachers course that I taught at the University of Georgia. They invited me to their school like many of my graduate students did, but for some reason, I followed through and observed them work in their classes. When they talked to their students about writing, I heard them use words like *voice* and *pictures* and *flow*. I did not hear terms like *style*, *content* and *organization* that to my mind were standard fare in the teaching of writing. I had to ask what this word-switching was all about.

In short, the teachers couched their approach to writing in a statement they credited to Flannery O'Connor who trained the veteran members of their department at a local teacher's college.

> *Voice, pictures and flow. That's all they need to know.*

It certainly had a nice ring to it, and I saw them use the terms effectively with their whole class and with students one-on-one. As these terms played out in their rooms filled with students, I saw students writing busily and seriously. One class was arranged with student desks in groups, an obvious workshop model. Another arranged students in straight rows with desks equidistant from the desks to the front, back and sides. Equally authentic writing emerged from each of these classrooms. Could a solution to an overall approach to writing be wrapped up in three everyday words—*voice, pictures* and *flow*?

The teachers had answers for these questions and more. "You see," one teacher opined, almost impatient with a question that she settled years before in her mind, "Miss O'Connor didn't mince words. She taught our department how to write and wrote with us until every member of the department wrote well. When I joined the department, the veteran teachers expected me to teach writing like they were taught. Something like on-the-job training. We all write with our students, and we and they help each other revise and improve our drafts. By engaging our students in revision this way, they become motivated to revise until some of their pieces are quite impressive. We help them publish their best writing in our school's *Rain Dance Review,* an annual anthology of student writing. The kids sell enough copies to pay for its publication and throw a big party. We're having a great time."

I was taken a little aback and asked, *So what's the underlying philosophy?* As a young professor, I knew there always had to be an underlying philosophy.

The response was equally simple, clear and easy to follow. "Miss O'Connor believed that the problem with U. S. American education was that teachers and students play the wrong game in the teaching of writing. They play *What does teacher want?*, a deadly guessing game for the students. It also frustrates the teachers and completely forfeits learning." My former student continued, "We tell our students that the game in our classes is different. We call it *What am I thinking?*" I saw what she meant by scanning her room. Her students were writing their own thoughts about what she had assigned. Out of the corner of my eye, I saw a student motion for her to come over to his desk.

One of your better writers? I inquired.

"Good heavens, no," she replied and excused herself. I followed her to remain within earshot, occupying myself with the students around the requested conference.

"I'm stuck," the student said quietly, "I'm trying to show my readers that Antonio is really a kind person inside, but his rude manners get in the way. Should I. . ." the student's voice trailed off into a couple of options he was considering that he wanted his teacher to help him choose. He was engaged. All his classmates were engaged. I remained in the class for over 20 minutes, and they all worked intently, oblivious to my presence.

A note on the game students play. At first, I treated the distinction between *What does teacher want?* and *What am I thinking?* as a needless digression. Then, as I saw some teachers fail to get authentic revision using a strategy they saw work for me, I realized the central role the instructional game *What am I thinking?* plays in effective and authentic revision. When students failed to revise as prompted, I saw in the behavior of the teacher that they had signaled that the game *What does teacher want?* was in play. One teacher moved about the room making comments, *How many times do I have to say not to write like you're text messaging?* Another added to the lesson prompt, *Remember our grammar lesson on vivid adjectives. I need to see at least five to eight in your first draft.* A third just monitored from the front corner of the room, standing with arms folded in front. In the absence of a teacher who sat writing intensely what he was thinking, the students got the clear signal that the instructional game of the day had reverted back to *What does teacher want?*

Back at the university, I put into practice what I had learned from these proponents of *voice, pictures* and *flow*. In classes where I saw little engagement, I used variations of the following script. The script worked every time. From time to time I change a phrase or two, but essentially the script mirrors those first classrooms of students intent on writing what they were thinking.

Script for helping students play *What am I thinking?*

> *Thanks, Ms. Smith for your kind introduction. Good morning students.*
>
> > [Good morning, Dr. Combs.]
>
> *Ms. Smith says that it's okay for me to write along with you and her this morning as we start a new draft like the one you will write for the state writing test. Is that right?*
>
> > [General agreement]
>
> *Before we start writing together, I want to make sure that we are all thinking about writing in the same way. Is that all right with you?*
>
> > [General agreement]
>
> *Fine, take out a clean sheet of paper and write the three words I'm writing on the board on the first, fifth and tenth lines.*
>
> > [I write *voice, pictures* and *flow* on the board with ample space between them.]
>
> *Here come three questions.*
>
> Question #1: *Write this question to the right of* **voice,** *the word on the top line. "Are there voices when you write?"*
>
> > [Everyone usually writes out the sentence fully; some ask if they are doing it the right way.]

Most often in classes I meet for the first time, no one risks an answer to this unusual question, so I add. *This is a question that needs to be answered. Someone tell me if there are voices when you write?* A range of typical responses.

> "Oh no, we're not allowed to talk when we write."
>
> "I don't know."
>
> "Oh yes, you can hear Ms. Howard's class talking through the walk right there."
>
> > [I don't challenge these perceptions, but rephrase the same question.]
>
> *How about voices you can hear when you are all alone without a person or TV within earshot?*
>
> > [Be patient until a student comes up with a version of I hear voices in my head. Sometimes students simply tap the sides of their head with their index fingers.]

I usually have a little fun with the right-responder and ask, *Who are the voices talking to?* When the student replies "me," I extend the fun with, *So are you saying that you talk to yourself when you write?* Since a titter in the class is likely to follow, I quickly conclude that all writers talk to themselves inside their heads when they write. There are special institutions for people who don't hear themselves think.

> Question #2: *Write this question to the right of the word pictures on line 5. "Are there pictures when you write?"*
>
> [Students are usually quick to respond "yes" this time, so I continue.]
>
> *So where is the picture when you start writing?*
>
> [I help them draw and fill in the three boxes on their own paper with my model on the board.]

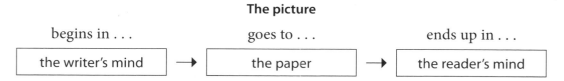

The picture

begins in . . .	goes to . . .	ends up in . . .
the writer's mind →	the paper →	the reader's mind

> Once students respond and fill in the boxes, I ask a final question about *pictures: So who is responsible for making certain that the picture in the reader's mind resembles the picture in the writer's mind?*
>
> [When the students agree that the writer is responsible, I know they are moving in the right direction.]
>
> Question #3: *Write the third question to the right after the word **flow** on line 10. "Is there flow when you write?"*
>
> [By this time, the students are talkative, ready to cite examples of *flow* and *lack of flow* in writing, "When you have to stop to figure some words out, the writing has stopped flowing."]
>
> *How right you are.*

When talking with teachers in my home state, I point out that **voice** corresponds to the writing trait of *style* on the writing rubric of the state writing assessment and accounts for 20 percent of the total score. The word **pictures** corresponds to the trait of *ideas* and counts for 40 percent of the total score. **Flow** corresponds to the trait of *organization* and counts for 20 percent of the total score. On the state writing rubric for many states, O'Connor is close to right. *Voice, pictures and flow. That's all they need to know.* In addition, these three words

- ◆ are easy for students to process.

- ◆ apply to all students (few students think they have *style*, but they all know they have a *voice*).

- ◆ keep them playing the instructional game, *What Am I Thinking?* instead of *What Does Teacher Want?*

I have looked through the writings of Flannery O'Connor to find the philosophy of *voice, pictures* and *flow* in print to no avail. Apparently, her student teachers picked it up from her teaching and demonstrations of how to teach. In *Mystery and Manners,* she mentions that when teachers try to help students revise, it is like the blind leading the blind. After all, we teachers cannot see what is in students' minds, and they cannot guess what we like.

A caveat. Next Monday you can use the above script to help your students shift from guessing what **you** want to writing what **they** are thinking. I assure you, however, that when your students return on Tuesday, they will be playing *What does teacher want?* once again. The game is deeply engrained in the ethos of U.S. American education. So be patient. Help your students shift back into playing *What am I thinking?* Eventually they show up in class playing the right game from the beginning. It is only a matter of time.

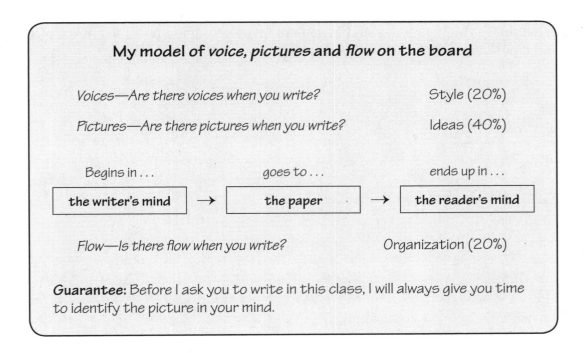

My model of *voice, pictures* and *flow* on the board

Voices—Are there voices when you write?   Style (20%)

Pictures—Are there pictures when you write?   Ideas (40%)

Begins in . . .   goes to . . .   ends up in . . .

| the writer's mind | → | the paper | → | the reader's mind |

Flow—Is there flow when you write?   Organization (20%)

Guarantee: Before I ask you to write in this class, I will always give you time to identify the picture in your mind.

Revision, then, is ***picturing again*** what you visualize when you started your first draft. All writers benefit from a picture in mind when they start writing. A clear picture from the beginning can ensure that the writing is well worth reading. Student writers of math problems need a clear picture of how to work the problem in their minds before they can expect to explain it clearly in writing. Science writers visualize the setting, execution and conclusion of a lab experiment before they can describe it in writing adequately. History students must picture events of the past clearly before they share them with an audience.

Language arts students must picture memories before they capture them in writing. They must also visualize character, plot and settings in literature before they explicate selections convincingly. Career and tech students visualize their lab and other practical experiences in classes before they can convince their teachers they are ready to work on their next class project. This book is filled with strategies for helping students **picture again** what they were picturing at the beginning. These strategies can do their work best when students begin their writing with clear pictures in their minds. They also help students develop a clearer picture of their emerging thoughts as they revise.

❮ Looking Back

In your response journal, describe two ideas of value to you about using the terms *voice, pictures* and *flow* to help students focus on the productive instructional game, *What am I thinking?*

❯ Looking Ahead

What things coming up in your curriculum invite you to use terms like *voice, pictures* and *flow* that you have met in this chapter?

2

Identifying the Voice, Pictures, and Flow in Writing

Make a movie behind your eyelids.
Nancie Atwell

We know that all writing has **voice** that arises from the writer's unique choice and arrangement of words. It has **pictures** that arise from the ideas and mental images of the writer. It also has **flow**, a movement from idea to idea or part to part in the writer's thoughts. These terms help focus more on **what the students are thinking** and less on **what their teacher wants** them to write. Of course, effective teachers set expectations that guide students' presentation of their thoughts. When a teacher sets an expectation of an expository essay, the students need to present an expository essay, but the ideas in the essay arise directly from what the students are thinking. Students may be asked to write on assigned topics, in required modes or *genres*, to specified audiences and for stated purposes. Still, the thoughts and presentation of those thoughts are their own.

Unfortunately, in many classes where I demonstrate best practice in writing, students rush to please me without exploring their own personal thoughts on a writing task. For example, one time I projected a description of a strict dress code that included school uniforms for students and asked them to write a paper to their principal that explained their opinion of the new code. I read my model of a draft that eagerly embraced this new, much more rigorous code. I then prompted students to brainstorm possible responses to the topic and choose the one they could write the most about. I gave them time to jot list their ideas, work on arranging them a bit and start explaining their thoughts to their principal in writing. Most of the students started writing, but three hands went up immediately. As I moved from student to student for 30-second conferences, I heard.

"What exactly do you want me to write?"

"How do you want me to start this?"

"Do you mean I need to write what you read to us?"

My response to each was roughly the same. *I want you to write what you hear your mind saying about the new dress code described on the board. Start with what you thought first when you read the topic with me. Then keep letting your pencil jot list the ideas that you hear from your mind.* When I saw that one student still misunderstood, I knew she was distracted by competing thoughts in her mind, so I added, *Everybody's mind is thinking about more than one thing at a time, so try this. Turn the volume up on what your mind is thinking about this new dress code, and turn down the volume on everything else you are thinking.*

These students' questions were honest, the students absolutely serious. They deserved equally honest and serious answers. I intended my standard response to be serious, and most often it worked. Students said. "Oh, all right." or "That's straight," and started accessing their thoughts about the assigned topic. Some students, like Charlie, needed more help so I moved to a trusted routine.

Impromptu Conference in Writing

Teacher	Charlie
Where have you heard about school uniforms?	"My cousins in Nyack wear them."
Oh, so your mind can picture those uniforms?	"Yeh."
So does their experience help you make up your mind about school uniforms in general?	[a pause] ". . .I guess it does."
What's your mind saying?	[squirming in his seat] "They are definitely not for me."
That's the voice in your mind you need to listen to. Write several sentences about how you made up your mind; that's your introductory paragraph. Then start explaining the reasons why your mind is made up for good. Do you have 1, 2 or 3 reasons for your opinion?	[pause] ". . . two, or maybe three."

As I made the last comment, I helped him write on an organizer I provided the class for prewriting:

Introduction: I never think about school uniforms, but my cousins have to
wear them.
Uniforms aren't for me
Reason 1   Mom and dad don't have the money
Reason 2   My clothes work fine
Reason 3   Who wants to look like a robot?

Not a bad start for someone who was distracted by what he thought I wanted him to do just moments before. Amazingly, many students try to write exactly what they think we want them to write and, in so doing, put their own thoughts on hold. They seem to be saying, "Just tell us what to write and we'll do it." They are unaware that they stopped writing and have entered the world of that perilous guessing game, *What does teacher want?* When I first started working with young writers, I thought all of their questions required me to step up and help them by doing exactly what they asked me to do: tell them exactly what to write. After all, that was what they asked me to do, right? I finally learned that the best thing for me to do was help them get inside their minds and learn to trust their own thoughts.

This is the routine that works for me. You are welcome to start with it, but you will develop your own version that works better for you, one that fits your teaching style and the prevalent learning styles of your students. Most simply, the routine must treat students honestly and move them back to writing about their own thoughts instead of guessing what would impress you.

There is yet another group of students embracing the game of *What does teacher want?* with negative results. These students actively seek out what individual teachers like in student writing. They ask peers who have taken a class from a teacher they have just been assigned, "What did you have to do to get an A on your biology research project?" Remarkably, these students readily accept what they hear. Once students take courses from teachers, they are obviously experts whose advice can be accepted by novices with eager ears.

"Ms. Torcelli falls big time for long paragraphs."

"Get a pocket thesaurus. Doc Kravitt loves big words—the longer the better."

"They don't call her 'Five-paragraph Fultz' for nothing."

"Write short sentences in this class. Two run-ons and you get F."

It has taken me most of my career, but I learned to set expectations of topic, genre, purpose and audience without divulging my preferences for ideas, style, organization or mechanics. For sure my preferences are well defined, but no one will discover them from reading this book or my comments on student writing. I have weaned myself from the need to micromanage the writing of others. At one time, I needed to write copious notes in the margins of students' papers, suggesting that they expand this point, that they rearrange that point and move one part to another location. I learned the hard way that when I indulged myself in directing the revision of students' writing, they turned their papers over to me; **their** writing became **my** writing. I don't do that anymore. My students deserve better, and so do all students.

Even when I help student writers in much need of help, they know that they remain in charge of their writing. I have enough to do to keep my own unbuttoned writing habits in check. By letting students watch me keep my writing in tow and improve it, they will pick up pointers on how to make their writing work. My job, however, does not stop with modeling authentic writing. If all I do is model good habits of the writing process, there's still a chance that students will try to follow my model too closely.

So what else will it take for students to wean themselves from guessing what they think I want? How do I keep our expectations from becoming one-liners like the advice of one student to another? Actually, I have already begun the answer to these questions and ones like them.

- First, I introduce the concepts of **voice**, **pictures** and **flow** like I presented in chapter one.

- Then I keep the discussion about student writing focused on these three concepts. When students understand voice in writing the way I use it, they know I am talking about a process inside their heads. They know that pictures in their writing start in their heads, and no one but they can see the pictures until they take the time to write the details of those pictures on paper or a computer. They also realize that the best words for them to use to make their thoughts flow are in their minds. We just need to help them identify them and become confident in using them.

- To keep the focus on *voice, pictures* and *flow* every time students write in class, I include a share-and-respond routine.

  ◊ Journal writing: When I prompt students to write a journal entry, they write for five to seven minutes, two or three of them share aloud, and several peers comment on the *voice, pictures* or *flow* in the shared writing.

  ◊ Essay writing: When I prompt students to write a first draft, they write for 15 to 18 minutes, one or two share aloud, several peers comment on the writing.

  ◊ Prompted revision: I teach students a mini-lesson on revising body paragraphs that I see all of the students need, they revise for 12 to 15 minutes, 1 or 2 share aloud, and several peers comment on the writing.

The point is belabored, I know. But it took me years to figure out that students sharing with students immediately after a writing task was as important as the writing task itself, maybe more important. Share-and-respond routine specifies roles both for those who share and those who respond.

- **The sharing student** reads her writing aloud **verbatim**. Oh, she may add an omitted word or delete a repeated word for clarity, but otherwise she reads word- for-word. Two extremes in sharing are not permitted:

  ◊ A student who writes a sentence or two, then talks on and on about his thoughts

  ◊ An articulate thinker who writes at some length and then self-consciously condenses her thoughts into a terse, vague summary

♦ **The responding students** listen intently to the sharing student read aloud and agrees to respond in one of two ways:

◇ A couple students mention something strong about the writing they have just heard (using the words *voice*, *pictures* and *flow*, for example).

◇ A couple students ask questions about the writing.

The sharing starts with the class as a whole group, then moves into small groups once students are conditioned to response that are specific and constructive.

An experience with a group of students new to me shows what I mean. After introducing the terms **voice**, **pictures** and **flow** to eighth-graders at Columbus Middle Grades Academy, I prompted them to write about themselves as writers in a journal entry. I gave them their first sentence, *I am _____, the writer.* If I were meeting them in a course in family and consumer science, band, algebra, chemistry or history, they would have written about themselves as a person versed in the content of those courses: *I am _____, the nutritionist, the conductor, the mathematician, the chemist* or *the historian.*

I read them a model of how I responded in writing to *I am _____, the writer* my first time. I asked them to listen carefully for evidence of **voice**, **pictures** and **flow** in my writing; I would call on some of them for their response when I finished reading.

I am Warren, the writer from the northwestern U.S. I never met a published author while I grew up out in Washington and Idaho. Oh, I recall that Ernest Hemingway traveled to Sun Valley to end his own life, but no one actually taught me much about being a writer. If someone did, why don't I have better memories? I mostly recall writing on assigned topics. There was Ms. Rock, second grade, who traced over my misshapen letters in green lead. In seventh grade I admired my English teacher, Mrs. Rachel, but was completely confused when she crossed out half of the eight robust adjectives that I used in the opening sentence of a personal narrative. Then there was Miss Baker. She always graded me an A/B for content/mechanics. Never saw anybody's paper with an A in mechanics. A few years back when I helped mom clean out her attic, I found a senior research paper titled "The Art of Gentlemanliness: the life and times of Sir Walter Raleigh." As I read it that day, even then it smacked of the controlled tone and style of The World Book Encyclopedia. Yes, I'm Warren, the writer, not because of how I was taught, but because of the 1000s of K–12 students each year who listen to me read my writing, who laugh, smile or question my writing, but most of all, keep the writer in me alive.

I asked for a response, prompting students to use their three new terms for writing as they respond. I pointed to the words **voice**, **pictures** and **flow** on the marker board and turned to field the response of the students.

- ♦ I saw the A and B at the top of all of your English papers.

- ♦ I could see those teachers marking up your writing with colored pencils.

- ♦ Your writing flowed from second grade to the present.

- ♦ I felt your voice coming through; you were sarcastic at first. Then you mellowed out at the end when kids enjoyed your writing.

Sometimes I have to work to elicit the responses, but the work is not hard. I ask

- ♦ What specific words in my writing brought a picture to your mind?

- ♦ What gave you a hint of my voice?

- ♦ What made my writing flow? Or did it?

Then I stopped talking and started jotting notes in the margins of my journal entry.

Next it was the students' turn. I asked them to write back at me. Many of them wrote in the manner that I modeled; a goodly number wrote about themselves as writers in a completely different way. I set concrete expectations—5 to 7 sentences, every one about themselves as writers, in six minutes. I wrote along with them, seated at the front of the room, writing intensely for all to see. Ms. Crooks, the host teacher, followed my lead, writing with great focus at her desk. I learned long ago that my moving about the room to monitor student writing disrupted. The same thing is true for any adult in the room.

After six minutes, I asked students to finish the sentence they were writing. To make certain that the sharing was productive, I asked for a show of hands for all those who *wrote at least 5 to 7 sentences and felt their writing begin to flow.* From the group of raised hands, I encouraged, with some cajoling, three volunteers to read their own writing aloud.

> **Note.** Sharing aloud is not for students who write fewer than the expected length of text that did not flow; it is a time for noticing strengths in writing and asking questions about the art and craft of the writer. Sharing aloud is a privilege to be earned, not a requirement that embarrasses reluctant readers or permits clownish student behavior.

I clarified the rules for sharers and responders from pages 12–13. Since this class was new to my routine, I got a student to listen for the **voice**, a second to look for *pictures* and a third to comment on the **flow** of the first writing shared. See what I mean in this average class of eighth-graders.

Angelo   I am Angelo, the writer. I hate wrighting because after your finish writing your nuckels start to hurt, then your fingers. And they feel like it wants to fall off and then after all that your head starts to hurt you. Then you have to go and get the aspirin and take two of those nasty bitter things and to top if off you have to do more homework after that. Why I hate wrighting because you feel pain in your body after your day of wrighting is over plus you have mom and dad giving you a lecture about wrighting and compare your wrighting to your older sister like I wanta be like her.

—special needs student

Teacher   *Thanks, Angelo. This is the first time I've heard you read your writing. Tell me, was this typical writing for you?*

Angelo   Not really. I like to correct the mistakes before I read it out loud.

Teacher   *Interesting* [a standard response that actually projects interest]
Someone tell Angelo what you notice about his writing?

[silence. . .so I continue] *What three words have we discussed that are found in all writing?* [I look at Tameka who agreed to comment on the pictures in the first shared entry.]

Tameka   Oh yeh. Pictures. Angelo's writing made me picture his body pain—his knuckles and fingers and other body part. [several students snicker]

Carlos   I heard his voice at the end when he said, "Like I want to be like her." That's real attitude. Nice, Angelo.

Teacher   *Anyone else notice something about Angelo's writing?*

Thomas   He made me picture taking nasty aspirin. I could see him making this weird face and maybe shaking his head. He does that, you know.

Teacher   *I did, too. So you're saying that the strength of Angelo's writing is the pictures his words made you see? Everyone agree?* [consensus] *Well, we'll keep our minds open when we hear from him again. Who's next?*

Two student volunteers read aloud one after another. I asked the class to write each student's name and jot down how each used **voice**, **pictures** or **flow** in their writing. After each student shared, I repeated my standard teacher-response routine of asking whether this was typical writing for them.

Nicole   Well, for starters, she's turning fourteen tomorrow, 9/4/95. Her name is Nicole Raquel Hardaway, and she's been writing ever since she could hold a pencil. It's me!!! I love to write because it expresses things I find too hard to say out loud. Writing lets me visually see my thoughts on paper, and trust me, I think of lots of things in a day. Writing keeps me focused; when the writing utensils are in my hand, I am just thinking out of my head and my hands are assisting it. I write when I'm alone or something is in my mind, but mostly at school. Writing to me is better than personal therapy.

—above average student

Tyekerri   I'm Tye, the writer. Writing is not all that important to me. In fact, I hate writing. I don't know why, I just do. Sometimes I think to myself, realizing why I don't like writing, really because it takes up too much time. That's how I feel about writing. Many teacher say that writing will makeover your vocabulary, but I still look at writing as a waste of time. Even though Ms. Crooks, not just Ms. Crooks, but all my teachers tell me that I need to write, I do it for myself, meaning that I do write because I have a choice of passing or not passing. Really, I want to pass so I do it for my own good.

—average student

Teacher   *So there you have it. Three journal entries, all with voice, pictures and flow. Each of them has more of one than the others, or do they? What do you think?*

A lively discussion ensued. Like other classes I met for the first time, these students effortlessly analyzed and talked about their peers' writing. Within ten short minutes, the majority of students agreed that Angelo's writing tilted toward the **picture** in writing. Nicole's writing definitely tilted heavily towards **voice**; it contained the drama and expression they all expected from her writing. An animated speaker, she let the animation come through in her writing. Tyekerri's writing was the most difficult to pinpoint, but the group ended up agreeing that the **flow** was its most notable feature. Her thoughts moved from logical reason to the next step in thinking through why she had strong feelings about writing. No surprise registered among the students; Ms. Crooks couldn't, and didn't, hide hers. She had never heard this chatty group stay on task for so long.

Last year, I visited the ninth-grade physical science class in an established *Writing to Win* site. The young teacher, an assistant football coach, introduced me to his class of 27. I greeted the students and bragged on their teacher's rigorous journal routine. In response, the teacher asked if he could introduce his class to me. I knew I was in for a treat.

*Everyone who is a **picture** writer stand up so Dr. Combs can see who you are.*

About one-third of the class stood up to the left of their desks. They shook their heads "Yes" when I asked if this were really true. I asked if creating word pictures came easily to them or if they had to work at it. This response was about 50–50. They all agreed that they felt best about their writing when it was filled with crisp, descriptive details.

I had a good idea of what was coming next; fewer than one-third of the students stood up as **voice writers**. A little over one-third stood up as **flow writers**. Their teacher quipped that his afternoon class was full of **voice writers.** Interesting! Although this was the first time I'd met a class in this fashion, it was not the last.

It doesn't seem that the identification of **voice**, **pictures** and **flow** in writing can be this simple, but it is. **Style**, **content** and **organization** are paper-based words; they don't ensure a connection with students' thoughts. **Voice**, **pictures** and **flow** are mind-based words that describe processes of the mind. Using these three words activates students' minds and supports their writing in ways not possible for words that describe features of writing on paper.

❰ Looking Back

In your response journal, describe two ideas about how the author helped students become comfortable with analyzing and commenting on each other's writing.

❱ Looking Ahead

What things coming up in your curriculum invite you to help your students become confident users of *voice*, *pictures* and *flow* in talking about their writing and the writing of others?

3

Crafting the Pictures and Voice in Writing that Fit Your Mind

I wish that introducing terms like **voice, pictures** and **flow** in writing transformed all student writing into sweetness and light. It does not. On my return visit to classrooms, the writing may have slightly more evidence of these elements, but just slightly so. Funny, isn't it, since students so quickly embraced writing from clear **pictures** or ideas in their minds? When they saw no clear pictures, they wrote about the unfocused ones until clearer ones appeared. They felt great talking about their writing **voice.** They said **flow** really help them understand how writing worked.

So why does the lack of obvious change remain in their writing? Well, if we believe learning theory and practice, and I do, we know that it takes six to eight exposures to a new concept before it becomes an indelible part of the way learners think. So, on to a second way of exposing the power and workings of **pictures** and **voice** in this chapter; I deal with matters of **flow** in writing in chapter 6.

Writing about Pictures that Your Audience Already Possesses

Sometimes teachers ask students to write to an audience who already knows the topic well. Physical science students change one feature of an experiment on physical change and report their results to fellow student scientists. Family and consumer science students stitch a seam using a different attachment on their sewing machine and report to their classmates. Math students present information that they met in a bar graph in an alternate graph of their choice and explain how it affects the information. Students in English class narrate an imagined visit to their hometown by the characters in a short story they read.

Professional writers have audiences who come to their writing with pictures of characters and settings already placed clearly in their minds. In *Harry Potter and the Sorcerer's Stone,* J. K. Rowling described her main characters and the places around Hogwarts, their school away from home. She painted indelible pictures of Harry, Hermione and Ron. In the remaining books of the series, she needed only mention their names and how a year had changed their appearance in the narrative; her adoring audience pictured them clearly.

Sportswriters treat their audiences in like manner. Sports fans know the people and places of their writing as well as or better than they do. Your writing and the writing of your students need to adjust to the audiences they meet. Assume you are writing to friends or people with whom you share interest in your local high school baseball team. In writing about a game-ending hit to the hometown fans, you never think of writing. . .

> Antonio Stiles, the sixteen-year-old pitcher on a team of nine baseball players for Huron Senior High School, held a standard-sized stitched baseball stretched over his head in his right hand with his cowhide mitt designed for catching balls held high as a tight cover. As he stood atop a mound some 15 inches above the playing field, he raised his left knee to eye level, toe pointed deliberately to third base. He pumped the ball down to his belt buckle, then up into a windup and straight over home plate in front of the opposing batter some 90 feet in front of him. Carlisle swiftly swung his 32-inch, 36-ounce bat of titanium composite metal from atop his right shoulder, level around about chest high over the five-pointed white plate. The bat connected with the 79 miles/per/hour pitch square in its center, and the ball reversed direction in a flash, high over the pitcher's head, then over the second baseman's outreached glove designed for fielding the ball, and finally. . .

Not to readers who were diehard baseball fans! They would yawn and put your writing aside. Worse yet, some would be offended that you treated them like know-nothings. They picture high school pitchers versus batters clearly. They demand *Skip the details that are like every other pitch in baseball, and give me just the facts that make this pitch unique.* Your writing would read more like this.

> Two out and three on in the bottom of the ninth. The Howlers are down by three; the pinch-hitter, Carlisle, waits for the pitch, his bat circling with power above his shoulder. Stiles gets set, winds up with the runners in motion, and hurls a fastball number high that Carlisle reads and launches high and deep, deep, deep into centerfield over Myer's head and into the stands for a homerun, a game-winner that brings this hometown crowd of 3500 to its feet in thunderous response. The Howlers defend their state title, 5 to 4 with a dramatic finish! Unbelievable!

In the second description of this play, the writer omitted the fielder's mitt, a bat, a mound, a baseball or the positions of the players on the teams. He included only the features of this pitch and this hit that contributed to the outcome of this game. The writer knew what was in the minds of his audience. He moved quickly to the only details that his audience needed to picture them exactly as he saw them in his mind.

Creating New Pictures in the Minds of Your Audience

Every time we write, we must consider our intended audience and ask one question,

Are you familiar with the pictures in my mind that form my writing?

If the answer is "no," we must estimate how detailed our writing needs to be. Since we cannot really know for sure, we need to write more details than we think we need. It's not bad to include a few more details than necessary. It is disastrous to provide even fewer details than the audience needs.

Matching writing to the needs of an audience is a skill that can be taught. The simplest way I teach the concept is with **Sentence Expansion,** a journal strategy from *Writing to Win© Journal for Writing Across the Curriculum*. It has a long tradition of helping students flesh out the details in their writing. Use **Sentence Expansion** as a mini-lesson for helping students revise a first draft, not as an isolated task out of the context of writing. I'll show you what I mean.

Go with me to McDowell County High School, North Carolina. When Mr. Turner showed me the first drafts of his students' expository essays, I introduced **Sentence Expansion** to them as a mini-lesson before I prompted them to revise. Their first drafts were clearly devoid of clear pictures for any potential audience. By the end of the 75-minute block, these tenth-graders had expanded a simple sentence, then beefed up the descriptive power of their own writing.

The conversation with the class went like this:

Combs	[holding up first drafts that they recognize as theirs] *Good morning, I am proud to meet the writers behind the first drafts that I have recently read.*
Students	[sighs and exchanging glances]
Combs	*I'm quite serious; your exposition of topics gives me hope that your generation is serious about maintaining what is good about the United States of America. They show extensive interest and understanding of U.S. American history as well as current issues of our day. I'm eager to help you make these pieces of writing ones that make you proud. Is that okay with you?*
Students	[signs of obvious buy-in from the majority of students]

Since these were tenth-graders, I launched into an abbreviated introduction of **voice**, **pictures** and **flow** and how these words impact their performance on their state's writing assessment that they would take in the following year. Then I continued.

Combs	*Look at the simple, four-word sentence that I have placed on the board (p. 22). Anyone see a picture of what I saw when I wrote it for you to see.*
Students	[sighs and exchanging glances before a student speaks] We have no clue what picture you saw. We'd just be guessing.
Combs	*Quite true. So what needs to happen?*
Three students I selected.	Adjectives. Yes, like descriptive modifiers. Additional sentences that describe a full picture. [Good, they remembered my introduction]
Combs	*True again, so where can we add such modifiers?*
Student	Before nouns.
Combs	*Could we not add modifiers before "rode" and "to" and after "school"?*
Students	[After silent consideration, most of the students agreed that we could add descriptive modifiers before and after each of the four words in this lackluster sentence.]
Combs	*Let me get this straight. You are saying that writers, people like you in this room, return to their first drafts and consider adding details before and after every word?*
Students	[considerable pause, then] Sometimes. If we need to. [I saw Mr. Turner roll his eyes in my peripheral vision.]
Combs	*So the problem is not that you cannot think of anything to add. The problem is deciding where of 600 places in a 600-word essay to add the needed, vivid details. Right?*
Students	[widespread agreement]
Combs	*Remember, I read your first drafts as a member of your audience, and I declare that you really do need to add vivid details to many of the possible places in your first drafts. I am convinced that you see clear pictures of your topics in your minds, but as a reader, I'm out of the loop. I saw very few if any clear pictures of the ideas you were explaining in your drafts.* 　　*But not too fast. We need to help this sorry four-word sentence on the board before I turn you loose on your drafts.*

Sentence Expansion

List three to five words/phrases at each point in a sentence. Then add as many of them to the sentence while maintaining grammatical sense.

Boys	rode	to	school

I showed an example of the following four-word sentence expanded by a group of high school students I'd met earlier.

Boys	rode	to	school
the	silently	on their bikes	Huron Senior High	on 16th Avenue
five freshman	from Detroit	with care	find the culprits at their	through downtown Dearborn
on March 1	of Hellcomb	like trained monkeys	deliver pizzas to their	in the driving rain
without a word	who remained	absent mindedly	the	at last
over-weight	selected by their coach	skillfully		after they set off the security alarm
Buff		crowded in a taxi		

The earlier students created two possible sentences expanded with a minimum of one word/phase from each list. The easiest combination that makes good sense is a sentence from the first word/phrases from each list.

> The **boys** silently **rode** on their bikes **to** Huron Senior High **School** on 16th Avenue.

A more descriptive sentence comes from using several words/phrases from each list.

> Without a word the five buff **boys** selected by their coach **rode** skillfully on their bikes to deliver pizzas **to** their **school** in downtown Dearborn in the driving rain.

The earlier students created a third sentence, adding any words that they liked to create the longest single sentence possible without running into trouble with grammar or meaning. Three students read their creations to the whole class. The remaining gave thumbs down and a short "buzz" when a sentence became two sentences, meaningless or ungrammatical. Since I announced special recognition for the student who added the most words to the four-word sentence provided, the task unleashed students' syntactic prowess. The two longest were 59 and 38 words.

> At the stroke of midnight in the dark blackness, the **boys** hopped on their skateboards and **rode** over steps and park benches, cement walls and garbage cans and stuff along the way and around the town [some students buzz] until they wore themselves flat out [all students buzz] **to** the parking lot at Central Middle **school** and they [buzz again] left a ton of litter behind them. 59 words

> After cleaning out Miss Pitts' attic for three hours, the exhausted 9th-grade **boys** from the Lancaster High School Key Club **rode** crowded into the back seat of a taxi **to** their **school** just in time to accept the coveted annual service project award [applause]. 38 words

The class recognized the trouble in the first instantly. The second student gave evidence of syntactic control and emphasized the importance of the moment by building up to the "coveted annual service project award" as a fitting end to an anecdote, a little story completed within a sentence. One classmate asked him how he wrote such a great sentence in such a short time. His response was classic, "Probably because I was there." There was no question that he understood. **Even in a contrived writing exercise, it** was **best to write from clear pictures already in his mind.** The first student found this out the hard way. He readily admitted that he made his sentence up, creating a picture as he went that clearly grew out of control.

Mr. Turner's class was ready to move through *Sentence Expansion* with gratifying enthusiasm. Twelve minutes later, the group celebrated Robert's winning, longest, grammatically correct, expanded version of the sentence, *The boys rode to school.*

> Early Monday morning, **the** seventeen good-looking, red-neck high school **boys** slowly **rode** straight from the Flats and past the bait shop in a caravan of customized cars and trucks **to** McDowell County Senior High **School** to learn important lessons from Mr. Turner [applause]. 33 words

Conclusions drawn from this task: ask students to admit what they have learned about the skill of revising their writing to help it match with the needs of a possible audience. Some ideas about revising sentences from students included these:

- ◆ You can add words before and after each word in a sentence. . .for your audience.

- ◆ Sentences of 25 to 30 words or longer can still make good sense.

- ◆ Very long sentences are not always run-on sentences.

- ◆ Some phrases can be added in different places in a sentence: *straight from the Flats* and *early Monday morning* could appear in several places. [A teachable moment for adverb phrases!].

- ◆ *Sentence Expansion* is a good way to make your sentences say more in your writing.

- ◆ You can make a complete word picture in one sentence.

Moving on to their first drafts, the students followed these set expectations.

- ◆ Circle 15 to 18 phrases in your first draft that make a clear picture return to your mind.

- ◆ Place the number one by the circle that you could write the most more about.

- ◆ Continue numbering 7 to 9 more phrases that you could write the most more about.

- ◆ On a clean sheet of paper, place the number of each phrase, and *Jot* down vivid, descriptive details to use in each phrase.

- ◆ *Blend* the descriptive details into your first draft.

Students reached these expectations of a strategy that I formally present as *Jot & Blend* in fewer than 15 minutes, leaving time for several of them to share their revisions with others. The consensus of the group was that there were many more than 8 to 10 phrases in their first drafts that needed additional descriptive details. I left those ambitious expectations for them on a later paper. To be sure, they were all surprised at how much the increased description of 8 to 10 phrases in first drafts buoyed the reach of their drafts toward a potential audience.

Here's a typical student's first draft followed by his revision. In his second paragraph, Robert circled the top four phrases that he could write the most more about.

First draft of The History of Moonshine

After about 120 years, moonshine in the United States became the first illegal whiskey. Stills were still in operation, but the moonshine wasn't as good as it was back in the 1790s. Most moonshiners diluted their shine to make more of it, the more shine the bigger the profit, which meant food on the table for families of some of the shiners. Because making shine was not a hobby or a way to make extra cash, it remained a necessary way to survive for many. It was a way to get through the [1] Civil War, through [2] World War I, through [3] World War II and even the [4] Great Depression.

On a separate sheet of paper, he jotted down vivid details of how the makers of moonshine saw each event. Since he wrote the details on a separate sheet of paper, he was not constrained by the lack of room in margins and between the lines of his first drafts.

REVISION (on a separate sheet of paper)

1. Civil War was a bloody, really not necessary war that killed hundreds of the shiners' friends, family, and neighbors.

2. WWI took customers and friends from the shiners. They helped the U.S. fight for the good of the countries like France and Britain against the German empire.

3. WWII put pictures of Japanese bombs that covered the Hawaiian sky and sunk U.S. battleships in the shiners' minds. They sold shine to people who worked in war factories to fight against the Japanese.

4. The Great Depression was one of the worst things that could happen to southern country towns. It killed as many people as a small war. In small towns shiners were about the only people who had a way to make money.

In a conference with a peer-consultant, Robert blended in the above details into his second paragraph.

Revised draft of The History of Moonshine

. . . Because making shine was not a hobby or a way to make extra cash, it remained a necessary way to survive for many. It was a way to get through the Civil War, a bloody, really not necessary war that killed hundreds of the shiners' friends and family and neighbors. Moonshine helped the children of shiners through World War II whose customers and friends helped the U.S. fight for the good of countries like France and Britain against Germany. Moonshine helped shiners through World War II that pictured Japanese bombs in the Hawaiian sky and sunk U.S. battleships. They sold shine to people who worked in war factories to fight against the Japanese. And it even made shiners survive the Great Depression that killed as many people as a small war. Shiners were about the only people who had a way to make money in their home towns.

These four additions helped Robert see that he had a full second paragraph. So he indented and continued his revised draft in three more paragraphs that explained how moonshine 1) fit the annual cycle of farmers, 2) led to the birth of NASCAR and 3) continued its manufacture into the 21st century.

Writing with a Voice that Engages Your Audience

There are many concrete strategies for isolating the pictures in writing and conditioning students to use words that push the pictures into the minds of the waiting audience. Isolating voice in the same way is a completely different matter, and I learned to rely on modeling as the primary tool for delivering instruction in writing voice or style. Take my example for modeling ironic voice for middle and high school students in a persuasive essay that argues a personal opinion.

As with all good persuasive writing prompts, I start with a Yes/No question that contains a blank for me and students to fill in with topics of our own.

Are _____ Really Necessary?

I lead with a model first draft titled *Are Little Brothers Really Necessary?* that recalls a relationship easy for adolescents to relate to. I tell the students that I attempt to

- ♦ establish my credibility on the issue in the first paragraph.

- ♦ provide two or three vividly described reasons for my opinion in the body.

- ♦ help the audience agree with me in the final paragraph.

First Draft of Are Little Brothers Really Necessary?

As the father of 16- and 20-year-old daughters and a nine-year-old son, I feel particularly well equipped to answer the question, *Are Little Brothers Really Necessary?* Some welcomed and some endured experiences have helped me answer with an unconditional yes. As I look back on the last ten years of fatherhood, my position is firm. Families with older sisters and younger brothers are the epitome of healthy and optimal U.S. American family life. Three examples show you exactly what I mean.

If it weren't for littler brothers, older sisters would never learn what it means to be afraid. Our little brother came by creating fear naturally. On a campsite in the middle of the moonlit night, little brother, Taylor, set about waking his older sisters in a fashion to be remembered. No, he didn't shake their arms or tickle their feet. Such ploys were much too ordinary. Instead, an ice-cube pressed against her cheek helped older sister, Cortney, open her eyes to a close-up of dangling frog legs dripping pond slime. Her screams, flailing arms and legs brought the pup tent down as little brother kept the frog close for the benefit for all, save, alas, the innocent frog itself. Now, that's real fear.

If it were weren't for little brothers, older sisters would never learn the value of messed up hair. For two or three years, the biggest arguments around our backyard pool centered around the same incessant report— Taylor messed up my hair. Good heavens, couldn't they see that as long as they complained, the bearer of messed up hair prevailed. On-going incidents of spraying hoses and surprise tackles on the edge of the deck amazed me to no end. It seemed that as long as the sisters needed to learn, little brother was willing to teach. It was over two years before I saw teenage friends meet the big sisters who stood proudly with hair matted down with chlorinated water as if to say, "I'm just here luxuriating by the pool."

Most important, if it weren't for little brothers, older sisters would marry far too soon. How often had I seen a sister stride up from downstairs with uncharacteristic grace in a newly pressed outfit and aroma guaranteed to turn every head, asking, "Has anyone seen Mike?" When pressed, little brother finally quipped with arms raised in protection, "I told him you weren't here. How was I to know?" Then there were years of misinterpreted *phone messages. Without a doubt, if it weren't for little brothers, older sisters would marry at much too early an age.*

If it weren't for little brothers, older sisters would never know that there were human beings that ate a big lunch, then stopped by a friend's house for granola cookies, PBJ sandwich and milk before striding into the house and asking "When will dinner be ready?" In fact, without little brothers, older sisters would never to be ready for a long life in relationship with that unusual creature, the human male. Little brothers are really necessary.

Now came the critical discussion. I asked them, *Do I really value little brothers? Did I convince you that little brothers have real value? If so, why did the reasons seem to work? Did dangling frogs, messing up hair and misinterpreting messages have value?* Students usually reached consensus after testing out comments like, "You're joking, You're not saying what you mean," and "I don't think you believe little brothers are necessary." They saw that an ironic voice did appear to say one thing, but mean something quite different. They realized that they have the ability to be ironic and that writing helps them control their ironic voice in socially acceptable ways.

When I modeled ironic voice in my writing, I helped them isolate the voice in their writing. When I helped them succeed at manipulating their writing in order to be ironic, they saw what it meant to work with their writing voice. Ninth-grader Rachael and seventh-grader Billy demonstrated how students at various levels approached irony in their writing voices.

First draft, Is Writing in Class Really Necessary?

Three years ago, teachers in Walton County Schools started requiring all of us students to complete writing assignments in class. By this time, I have sat quietly and completed my assignments dutifully. My fellow classmates and I obediently turned them all in. Yet we saw no real benefit for the teachers or students much at all. Writing in class is absolutely unnecessary.

When we students write in class, we see our other class work turn into dreaded extra homework. Extra homework eats into valuable phone time that could be spent on finding out who is on the outs in our social group or who is about to break up with who. Extra homework eats into alone time that we could spend listening to Hip-Hop or recording ourselves on funny talk-show routines. If you aren't convinced by the plight of all my friends and classmates, read on.

When I have to write in class, I use up time that could be spent in creating masterpiece doodles, imagining the plot of my new movie, *Nightmare on Writing Street, Part VI,* or observing students and teachers for my master novel. Everyone knows that my next publication is guaranteed to set me and my family up for life.

Besides, writing in class causes noticeable and long-lasting physical and mental damage. It increases the sizes of calluses on the fingers of your pen hand. Sitting on hard chairs for long hours causes misalignment of the spine and huge doctor bills. Brain scientists conclude that trying to think of something to write on demand has caused lasting brain damage in teens.

There you have it. I rest my case against writing in class. Don't you think our lives would be better in the long-run if we didn't have to write in class? If you don't oppose in-class writing yet, I can't help you much. It means you don't care about teens' social life, their futures or unnecessary medical bills. All I have left to write is "Heaven help you!"

Like other teens, she talks to friends and family, saying one thing, but meaning another. Now she knows that doing so in writing is a matter of writing voice.

A much younger Billy comes alive after he heard me read my model about little brothers.

First draft, Is Humor Really Necessary?

I am 13 years old and a funny guy. I know I can answer the question, "Is Humor Really Necessary?" Yes, humor is necessary. If there was not any humor, we couldn't laugh.

If it wasn't for humor, there would be no Eddie Murphy to star in Beverly Hills Cop movies or Bowfinger. We'd miss the fun of seeing how Eddie dresses up like women and other people you wouldn't believe. We wouldn't be able to laugh at the old-timey Curly, Moe and Larry films or Audra Levi when she talks on Kids Beat.

If there was no humor, we wouldn't be able to laugh when Fred and Barney got into trouble on the Flinstones. We couldn't laugh when Kady told on Michael and Claire in My Wife and Kids.

There would be no red-neck jokes for Jeff Foxworthy to make up. What would Chris Rock or Jon Stewart do for a living? Think of all of the comedians out of work. What a sad world this would be without humor. Humor is necessary to make people laugh and keep their lives happy. So smile, America, and tell a joke!

Although Billy doesn't achieve ironic voice, he does write more than his teacher had seen him write in a single draft before. And he achieved the level of **telling** his audience about his humor; that's only one step away from **showing** them with descriptive details. Maybe he has begun a period of writing for his audience as the funny guy that he is.

So revision is reaching an audience with clear pictures and authentic voice, something all students need to practice each time that they show up at school. At home with friends and family, they use what sociolinguists call a *restrictive* language register regardless of their socioeconomic situation. Before their school days begin, everyone they meet knows them well and shares the mental pictures of experiences and ideas important to them. When they arrive at school, they run head on into a language environment that requires an *elaborative* language register, one with which none of them have had much experience.

So this chapter presented two simple tasks that students with widely differing skills enjoy. Each task moved students definitely towards a mindset where they said "not yet" about their first drafts. They had yet to find the right words, at least *not yet*. When we provided them with the time, their quest for finding the right words began. After all, it was clearly an inside job, one that they handled for themselves inside their own heads.

A Bonus

Are _____ Really Necessary? is just one of number of questions that work well in prompting students to explain and defend strong personal opinions in persuasive essays. On this book's page on www.eyeoneducation.com, you will find several more persuasive prompts that guarantee engaged and elaborative student writing.

❮ Looking Back

In your response journal, describe two ideas of value about writing drafts that reflect the pictures and voice in the writer's mind.

❯ Looking Ahead

What things coming up in your curriculum invite you to use these ideas of crafting pictures and voice that accurately reflect the writer's thoughts?

4

What Revision is Not

Do not put statements in the negative form.
And don't start sentences with a conjunction.
If you reread your work, you will find on rereading that a
*   great deal of repetition can be avoided by rereading and editing.*
Never use a long word when a diminutive one will do.
Unqualified superlatives are the worst of all.
If any word is improper at the end of a sentence, a linking verb is.
Last, but not least, avoid clichés like the plague.

William Safire

I know. I know. The definition of revision so far in this book is remarkably slim and disarmingly simple: three words, two with only one syllable. But I'm convinced that they are enough. In fact, including more in the classroom of developing writers is counterproductive and potentially harmful as William Safire playfully illustrates. So I extract five topics that teachers and textbooks often include in their work with revision:

◆ The *very good* habit of responding to students who share their writing aloud

◆ Proofreading

◆ Systematic conferencing with all students

◆ Peer-revision forms

◆ Student writing that needs revision the most.

Bear with me, though. The lessons of this chapter were a long time in coming to me, and you will likely agree that the points are well taken. They arise from my classroom experiences and observations in sixth- to twelfth-grade classrooms once I left the university setting. These five topics began as part of my toolkit for teaching revision and helping students revise, and they now lie where I know they belong: in some other part of the curriculum or off with all the missing socks we have learned to live without in our lives.

Exclude the "Very Good" Habit

This robust habit of mine—saying a variation of **very good** in response to students' reading their writing aloud in class did not go gently into the night. I blame it on my course, Introduction To General Methods Of Secondary Education. Don't we blame a truckload of grief on *that class?* What teacher hasn't said, *I didn't learn a practical thing about teaching until I walked into my own classroom and closed the door.* My professor actually allowed me to spend hours on a project that I titled *101 Ways to Say "Very Good."* Armed with a trifold project board, I marched into class and talked at length to a class of uncritical sophomores. I had just misunderstood a prerecorded interview with Thomas Harris, who eventually published his philosophy in his book, *I'm OK, You're OK.* I knew I was onto something momentous, a strategy that resulted in students' feeling really good about themselves, no matter what. That was my take on Harris' message back then.

Today, I see far too many teachers caught in the *very good* bind. Rushed for time like me, they haven't created anything better to say and know to keep public responses upbeat. In truth, saying *very good* to all writing does a number of things, none of them very good for either students or teachers.

- *Very good* quashes student response. When teacher say *very good,* no student dare have anything to add. The teacher approves; obviously, end of discussion.

- *Very good* does not respond to the thoughts of the student. Only a response to the ideas of the writing validates the writer and the writing itself.

- *Very good* models a general and vague response, the kind of response we want our students to avoid in their responses to one another.

- *Very good* feels just like the abrupt dismissal that it is to the student. Since it is used after all students' writing, it rings of insincerity.

I remember thinking there were advantages to a brief, consistent public response.

- When more students read aloud, teachers hear more writing in class and therefore can spend less time out of class reading student writing.

- It kept me from going negative in my response to a students' writing when the writing needed a lot of help.

- Rapid reading with positive feedback for all makes for an upbeat classroom atmosphere. A good time is had by all.

So let's wrap this up. *Very good* is out of here. There is no logical place in an effective writing routine for *very good* as the primary public teacher response. *Very good* is a red flag that the teachers have retreated to the game of *What does teacher want?* The students get the clear message that their thinking and writing are fine as they are or that they are not important at all. Their teachers miss the opportunity to talk with them about their thoughts. Their ideas wither from lack of attention.

In chapter 2, I presented a substantial teacher-response model for students using *voice, pictures* and *flow* productively. I found a second model when I observed a math class in

Bridgewater, South Dakota. Ms. Byington's students were studying four ways of graphing an equation, and they had to select the one graph that had no focus and explain in writing why that was the case. When she saw that the students were finished writing, she called on three students to share; Alex was first. When he finished, she directed the class with, *Someone mention something **strong** about Alex's explanation.* Two students commented on the flow of his ideas. She directed the class a second time, *Someone ask Alex a **question**.* At this point, several students him about specific points in his explanation. It was clear that Alex's understanding of what he wrote improved with the interaction of his peers. Now, I offer the **Strong-and-Question** response model everywhere I visit. Each time I use it, the students respond in ways that impress me. Surely, there are other alternative response-models to the vacuous and repetitive *very good.*

Exclude Proofreading

Proofreading or editing is one aspect of revision. Every book I've read on composition and rhetoric admits as much. As a practical matter for students of all grade levels and abilities, separating proofreading from other aspects of revision in a class lesson is absolutely necessary. When I allow students to correct errors at the same time they try to improve their ideas, style or organization, they correct errors and slight the other improvements. Proofreading is an on-the-paper job; revision is an inside-the-head job. So proofreading is the topic of another book, and many such books exist. Jeff Anderson's *Mechanically Inclined* is one of the more enjoyable reads. For the simple **Proofing Strip** strategy I use for proofreading, visit www.eyeoneducation.com, go to this book's page, and follow the links.

In my mind and for the sake of young writers, I move to a simple distinction. **Revise first** or intermediate drafts; **proofread final** drafts. Think about it. Proofreading first drafts expends unnecessary effort. Errors corrected in a first draft often reoccur in the next draft, and new errors always appear. In classes of students, it is efficient use of time to wait until the final draft and correct the errors just once. This is not to say that students should be stopped from correcting errors as they revise. On the contrary, any error corrected at any step of the writing process is an error corrected—and an improvement to the writing. Students do more and better revision when teacher expectations exclude the correcting of surface errors.

Exclude Hands-On Conferencing with Student on Every Piece of Writing

I believe in conferencing with students. The three students in chapter 2 who could not get started deserved a quality conference of the length needed for them to start trusting their thoughts and moving them forward in writing. The most important teacher skill of conferencing, however, is discerning when *not* to conference. Conferences timed when students show obvious uncertainty serve an important purpose. Ones imposed on students who are self-propelled in a productive direction can distract, disrupt or derail their progress.

Conferences present situations that are always touch-and-go for students. Consider the situation: an older articulate adult who holds the power of the grade over the student sits next to the student. The temptation for the adult to suggest and the student to follow the suggestion without thinking it through is strong. Writing programs that tout conferencing promote questioning strategies that are for the most part productive and valuable. Some strategies are of uncertain value, and it's not always easy to separate the good from the bad. I've watched a demonstration of a student-teacher conference at which a noted expert asks of a student, *Have you ever considered doing X with your writing?* or *What do you think about doing X?* These suggestions sound innocent enough. Unfortunately, at their base, students interpret such questions as camouflaged versions of one question: *Have you ever thought about writing your thoughts the way I would?* At such a point, students have shifted back into playing the game, "What does teacher want?"

Hands-on Conferencing in Writing that Distracts

Teacher (pencil in hand)	Student (pencil in hand)
Teacher sets the agenda	
Let's talk about your main idea? Did you mean _____?	Student hesitates long enough that the teacher rewords a possible main idea, and the student accepts it. (Student writes what he hears the teacher say.)
Where are your related details?	Student hesitates, then accepts the help of the teacher in identifying related details.
Have you ever considered doing X to your writing?	Student writes down X in the margin.
What do you think about doing X?	Student writes down X in the margin.

In a few short minutes, a student has willingly given up ownership of her writing and followed the lead of her teacher. In the rush of a school day, students can feel the hurry of their teachers' questions and follow what they think their teachers want them to do. A hands-off conference keeps the ownership in the hands of the students.

Hands-off Conferencing in Writing That Works

Teacher (no pencil)	Student (pencil in hand)
Student sets the agenda	
Tell me the main idea of this draft in your own words?	"Dressing wrong for the occasion can be a big problem."
What went well in this draft?	"The little stories I added as examples in my essay."
What picture should I have in my mind at this point [pointing to a short paragraph]?	"You should see a man that is too dressed up in a gym full of people working out."
Really, that picture didn't reach my mind.	"Doesn't he act surprised to you?"
I don't see him act any way.	"I could add 'looking around with his mouth open.'"
That helps.	"I see what I need to add." [writing what he said in the margin]
Jot the key words down. Add more to make them fit on the final draft.	"OK, is my writing getting good?"
It is, and it will get better and better with changes like this one.	
What voice should I be hearing?	"You should hear an angry and disappointed voice because the man is disappointed. I need 'shakes his head.'" [writing in the margin]
What is a plan for the rest of the draft?	"Adding enough details so readers see my pictures and hear the right voice."
What can I help with?	"I'm good; I see what I need to do."
I wasn't sure what this concluding sentence means: "So be careful what you wear."	"I meant that you should remember that the right thing to wear depends on where you are going. If you need to call ahead to find out the dress for the activity, call right away. Call even if you think you already know. It is the only way to be sure you won't be embarrassed."
Wow, that is a lot more to add. Can you remember to write it out fully?	"I'll do it now."
Go for it. Here's to good writing!	"Thanks."

The writer concludes the conference. "I'll do it now" is a request to let him revise. This second sample conference feels entirely different than the first. I know; I've been in both kinds, and conferences like the first sample are no fun; the student sits until the hurried teacher acts.

The second conference took no more time than the first, and the student knew from experience that **his** thoughts were the focus of the conference. There is little room in the teacher's script for "you" comments or questions that make the student feel interrogated. When I see that the writing of a number of students needs the same kind of revision, I move to a small-group or whole-group activity.

Written Teacher Commentaries

As an alternative to systematic conferences, I recommend, with a caveat, teacher commentaries as a vehicle of guiding individual students in revision. Write two or three short sentences that go the heart of what students can revise to meet the expectations of the assignment. Without simplicity and clarity, written teacher commentaries can become as heavy a burden for the teacher as a rigid schedule of conferences. See my description of First Draft Response Forms in chapter 14. The written commentary simply reminds the students to consider using some revision strategies previously introduced in class. The response to the first draft is simple, graphic and directive, but it leaves the thinking and revising up to the students.

Suggestions for Revision from Peer-Revisers

Peer-revision seems to be a buzzword for the last couple of decades, and I promote it in a specifically defined way in chapter 12. Here's the caveat: avoid peer-revision in which students trade first drafts and make unguided suggestions on how to revise. I find this spin on peer-revision as ineffective as conferences with students mindlessly following their teachers' suggestions. The rule of thumb: responses from peer-revisers are helpful when the peer remains a reader, a member of a potential audience, not a competing writer. When peer-revisers slip into the writer's place and start revising the draft, they over-step the bounds of their task. In *The Craft of Revision*, Don Murray defines test readers (peer-revisers) in this way:

> It is easy to get readers, hard to get good readers who can help us improve
> what we have written. . . .Those who are not great help respond in terms of the
> book they want to write or the book they imagine I should write, not the book
> I am writing or can write. (pp. 34–35)

Too many of the peer-revision forms available on the Internet or published in national textbooks include items that ask readers to take on the role of the writer. These forms set readers up to suggest what they would do if they were the author, a task that needs to remain outside the responsibility of the audience. From a center that trains teachers in the art of teaching writing, a ***Peer Response Sheet*** moves the reader to the responsibility of the authors in 3 of 10 items.

Derek Bok Center for Teaching and Learning, Harvard University

Peer Response Sheet

Writer _____   Reader _____

RECORD YOUR RESPONSES TO THE FOLLOWING QUESTIONS EITHER IN THE SPACES BELOW OR ON SEPARATE SHEET(S) OF PAPER.

Remember, you are not being asked to evaluate the paper; you are being asked to respond to it with an eye toward **helping the writer improve it.**

6. Identify places that need better transitions and make suggestions.

7. List at least two ways in which the essay could be improved.

10. Ask of the essay "so what?" after you finish reading. Write a sentence or two paraphrasing the point of the paper, answering the question, "in what way(s) is this interesting, surprising, intriguing, etc.?" If the paper lacks a "so what," point that out and discuss the possibilities.

Two of nine items on a response form that cross the line of peer-revision for a problem-solving experiment on a science website.

4) What are the limitations of each solution? If the author does not mention possible limitations, suggest at least one limitation of each solution.

9) Examine one paragraph in the essay. How many **be** verbs does the author use in this paragraph? Rewrite one or two sentences replacing be verbs with action verbs.

All of these items are mixed in with valuable items that help the peer-reviser stay in position as a member of the potential audience. Items that prompt peer-revisers to take the reins of the writer are out of the purview of revision.

Finally, research on the value of peer-revision is mixed, especially in grades 5–12. From the ERIC Clearinghouse on Reading, English and Communication Digest #8, Andrea Herrmann notes that studies of the effects on peer suggestions for revision are as likely to show negative as positive effects. This is enough for me to use extreme caution in the use of ready-made peer-response forms.

Not all the studies of peer reaction show unqualified positive effects on revision, however. Some studies suggest negative consequences as well. Gere and Stevens (1985) [concluded this from study of] a fifth-grade writing class. A case study of four children with low, average, and high abilities in writing (Russell, 1985) . . . indicated that in revising, **poor writers were dependent on the questions of other students** [emphasis added]. Another case study conducted with college freshmen (Berkenkotter, 1983, 1984) . . . revealed that the students' attitudes toward assistance from their peers varied considerably, as did the writers' approaches toward revision. An experimental study (Rijlaars-dam, 1987) looked at peer feedback among 11 classes of eighth-grade students in eight Dutch schools. The control group received teacher feedback; the experimental group received peer feedback. . . [with] no differences between the two.

Herrmann notes that peer-response proves to be highly effective with writers of elementary school age.

Exclude Student Writing that Needs Revision the Most

Finally, revision should not include student writing that is most in need of revision. Like many other U.S. Americans, I grew up thinking that revision was for bad writing, writing that didn't work, writing that needed help. The "revise everything you write" requirement of many writing courses accepts this view without question. Common sense, however, holds that some writing is just not worth revising. The writing or the topic should be abandoned, and the writer should work with other writing that shows more promise.

In all courses of writing, I prompt students to write a minimum of three first drafts in a *genre* of writing before they select one to revise and take to the end of the writing process. It doesn't cross my mind to ask the students to select the draft that needs the most help, nor does that possibility occur to the students. Instead, we all agree that the one of three drafts to revise is the one that they could write the "most more about" or the one that they think has the most promise. That just makes common sense. (Although the term "most more about" is not preferred English grammar, it helps students understand what to do. See Chapter 8.)

Starting multiple texts in a *genre* and completing one in a four- to eight-week block satisfies the standard of any state department of education. Long ago, Donald Murray established that it is better for students to work through the writing process thoroughly fewer times in a course than to hurry through the complete process on many occasions.

So *Empowering Students to Write and RE-write* focuses on keeping students' minds focused on the ideas (pictures), style (voice) and organization (flow) of their writing, not giving them

- flat and cursory responses like *very good* to their writing regardless of its quality.
- the tasks of proofreading errors of conventions and revision of content at the same time.
- hands-on teacher conferences that present suggestions students feel obliged to follow.
- peer-revisers who take over their writing.
- tasks to revise drafts that need the most help.

❰ Looking Back

In your response journal, describe two things that are excluded in the author's definition of revision that were of value for you as a teacher in your present courses.

❱ Looking Ahead

What comes up in your curriculum that will benefit from a definition of revision that excludes ideas like those mentioned in this chapter?

Empowering Students to Write and RE-write
Session Guide #1 for Professional Learning Teams

Responding to

Introduction

    Chapter 1: Revision is picturing again—*Voice, Pictures, Flow*

    Chapter 2: Indentifying the *voice, picture*(s) and *flow* in your writing

    Chapter 3: Crafting the *pictures* and *voice* in writing to represent your mind

    Chapter 4: What revision is not

Before joining *Professional Learning Team (PLT) Session #1*

Write your response to these items in your journal.

1. In two or three sentences, explain the difference between teaching ***about*** revision and ***doing*** revision with students.

2. Describe the classroom experience in which you helped your students understand how *voice, pictures* and *flow* relate to their writing.

Exemplars

Read through the writing that your students have created since you introduced them to the terms *voice, pictures* and *flow*. Select and share with your PLT some writing that may serve as examplars of those features.

Discussion questions for *PLT Session #1*

1. How important is the distinction, teaching ***about*** revision and ***doing*** revision (introduction)?

2. What is the advantage of using *voice, pictures* and *flow* with student writers instead of *style, ideas* and *organization* (chapter 1)?

3. How can you make the point that students still need to understand and use terms such as *style, ideas* and *organization* in discussions about writing (chapter 1)?

4. What did you do to help your students become comfortable with using *voice, pictures* and *flow* in responding to the writing of peers (chapter 1)?

5. What suggestions do you have for your colleagues whose students are not comfortable with the concepts *voice, pictures* and *flow* in writing (chapter 2)?

6. Some teachers have noted that journal entries and first drafts place students in one of these three profiles:

Picture-writers: students who are fluent elaborators of details in their writing

Voice-writers: students whose writing presents novel or fresh expressions and tells the audience a good bit about the writers themselves

Flow-writers: students whose freewriting and first drafts show clear signs of logical organization

Do you see a benefit in using these categories for you to look at students' writing and let students learn about themselves as writers (chapter 2)?

7. How can you help students know when to create new pictures in the minds of their readers and when they can prompt readers to access clear pictures already in their minds (chapter 3)?

8. Why do you think it is important to exclude proofreading when you are trying to help students become confident revisers (chapter 4)?

9. What besides proofreading needs to be excluded from revision (chapter 4)?

Building a Professional Learning Portfolio

An important part of a professional learning experience is documenting its benefits. For that we suggest a portfolio of artifacts related to your growth as a teacher who is becoming comfortable with helping your student *do* revision. A suggested table of contents includes:

- ♦ Your personal response journal with two entries for each chapter of *Empowering Students to Writing and RE-writing*

- ♦ Samples of student revision that show increased understanding of a course concept

- ♦ Examples of revision in your own writing

- ♦ Description of the ideal routine for requiring students to return to a first draft and revise it for accuracy and completeness

- ♦ Description of revision strategies you rely on most often

- ♦ Description of how you adapt revision strategies from this book

- ♦ Revision strategies developed or discovered outside of this book.

5

Kindling Innate Writing Abilities

Language learning has a biologically organized schedule.
Jean Aitchison

The acquisition of language is maturationally controlled,
emerging before it is critically needed.
Eric Lenneberg

A chapter on innate writing abilities is essential; but please, let's not conduct a debate here about nature versus nurture in the teaching of writing. I have endured several of those debates, and there are no winners; the opponents talk right past one another. Back in the mid-1970s at the University of Minnesota, linguist Noam Chomsky and my colleague Professor McCorquodale addressed a forum with robust applause from students for each side of the debate. Throughout the last century, high school debate clubs tossed the topic about in competitions around the globe. What we do know from this debate is that human beings arrive in life prewired with some innate abilities to speak and write, to use re-combinable units of language to create meaning. Experiences of all kinds (nurture) kindle genetic features (nature). Whole philosophies of teaching and learning, such as Montessori, Steiner-Waldorf and Paideia, hypothesize when certain experiences best kindle innate abilities. What we don't know for sure is which part of writers' skills result from which group of forces. One thing is clear, however, the innate ability to write, and thus the potential to write understandably well, is possible for every student. That's why I must begin this chapter with a teacher's comment that represents an all-too-common misunderstanding of the human innate ability to write.

"I enjoyed your session, but you don't know my students," said a teacher who stayed after a session on designing student writing projects across the curriculum. "They don't have any experiences. Their parents are non-readers; they are at least three grade levels behind. They don't even know the difference between nouns and verbs."

That's right, I replied with hesitation to a description of students I hear often. *I have not met your students; this is my first visit to New Orleans; however, many students I teach are from non-reading homes judged several grade levels behind on reading tests. It is curious that your students haven't had experiences. They'll be the first I know who haven't. They aren't restrained or quarantined, are they? And nouns and verbs? I have trouble with that, too. Give me a word out of context, and I think, 'could be a noun; could be a verb.' We U.S. Americans have a history of using nouns as verbs and verbs as nouns. Some linguists say that's what makes English the language of the globe.*

My new acquaintance wasn't used to being misunderstood, but she was kind as she continued, "You know, they don't have a family car; they log hours in front of a TV; they've never been out of our county;, and a trip to them is a ride in a neighbor's van to Wal-Mart."

Well, my last visit to Wal-Mart was quite an experience, I replied, *and I have enjoyed many an experience on TV.*

I'm afraid she gave up on making me understand and accept her view of her students whom I never did meet. I have, however, met a good number of teachers who paint a similar picture of their students. I have met some of their students, but I don't see what they see. What I found were students who wrote little when prompted to write about a trip to the beach or camping in the mountains. For sure, they hadn't done either, but anyone who is mobile with a moderate pulse and connections with a few other people has experiences. Granted, they may not be experiences that fit typical writing prompts; they may not be experiences that show much promise, but the problem is not experiences, but our approach to helping students present those experiences.

Marge, whom you met in the introduction of this book, had a group of students who hid behind claims that they had nothing to write about. A single visit from a person who looked beyond their mindsets and expected them to write and to respect the right of others to write moved a handful of them off of their excuses and into their minds to write what they were thinking.

The Marge experience helped mold my philosophy of getting students to write. Early on, I became convinced that students need not **know** much **about** writing in order to write. ***Know-about*** knowledge of skills is greatly overrated in our culture, especially when it comes to teaching students to write or use writing to explain what they know across the curriculum. This is quite puzzling since there are so many times in our lives and the lives of our students that we don't expect extensive ***know-about*** knowledge.

We don't require ***know-about*** knowledge of children as they begin to acquire oral language. Who among us even thought of requiring a two-year old to identify nouns or verbs before we accepted and responded to their first utterances? Yet, they learn to use language for their and our benefit. Who remembers requiring a lesson on pedal propulsion before we let our children mount their first bikes? Or water dynamics before they tried to swim?

No, we celebrated the first utterances with, *Martha, he said, "Daddy shoe" and patted my shoe! I heard it! He said it!* We also walked and ran along side of the first bike with a teetering form atop, back and forth in the back yard to exhaustion before our children turned to us, shouting, "I'm riding! Dad, I'm riding!" and promptly ran into a bush or chair. And in shallow water, we coach, *You can do it, swim to me. I'm right here,* and we backed up in the water to let our children dog paddle to us as long as they stayed afloat. We did not use the excuse that they can't swim because they have had few experiences. That was a given and we moved on from there to help them swim. So why are U.S. Americans in the habit of not expecting **know-about** knowledge of skills **except** when it comes to writing?

What all students need to know in order to write:

> They need to understand the writing prompt. They need to accept its limitations and consider the possibilities within their minds and experiences when no limit is stated.

At first, this requires walking through the writing topic prompts with students, explaining them as you go until students understand the typical patterns that they follow. They need to know that topics may state a situation or context, an issue, purpose, task or audience. If one or more of these elements of a topic prompt is not mentioned, the students are free to specify that element for themselves.

Elements of a writing topic prompt:	Brainstorm possibilities	Choose
Situation or context **I**ssue **T**ask **P**urpose **A**udience	If a context is not stated, students are free to brainstorm possible contexts of their own in their minds or from their experiences.	When students have several possibilities in mind, students choose the one that they can write the most about with confidence.

The mnemonic, SITPA, helps me and students remember all the possibilities to consider when we write. In responding to an assigned writing topic prompt in class, SITPA helps students discover precisely what their teachers want. In the following topic prompt for tenth-graders in family and consumer science class, a teacher stipulated all five elements for writing.

Elements of a writing topic prompt:	Sample topic prompt	Brainstorm possibilities	Choose
Situation or context	Quality health care in the U.S. helps people live longer.	No possibilities here. I accept this situation.	
Issue	Your school could benefit from the talents of these senior citizens who live longer.	Different specific talents and expertise of seniors in our town	The talents and expertise I know the most about
Task	Write a plan that offers a solution.	Different specific plans	Pick a plan I can explain and my audience will accept.
Purpose	Convince audience to accept your plan for using these people's talents.	Specific persuasive strategies that we have studied in class	Use strategies that appeal to my audience.
Audience	Your school administrators	Specific features of administrators	Appeal to administrators' good nature.

Even though all elements are specified in the prompt, students still have a wide range of choices for four of the five elements. They must accept only the situation as stated; otherwise, they can consider possibilities from their own observation and experiences.

Sample topic prompt	Brainstorm possibilities		
	Juanita	Thomas	Lakisha
Quality health care in the U.S. helps people live longer.	No possibilities here. I accept this situation.		
Your school could benefit from the talents and expertise of these senior citizens.	babysitter cook cleaning landscaper bus driver	legal help family assistance health advice guest speaker	Motivation after-school aids tutors host field trips
Offer a solution to the problem of unused talents of seniors.	seniors will work for less money than employees volunteers	create a group of volunteers	write a grant to pay minimum wage ask for volunteers pay with store discounts
Convince your school administrators to accept your plan for using these people's talents.	people are hard workers and not ready to stop Ms. Carlisle is the one who makes the decisions.	funding from the United Way Show how students will manage the volunteers	student write the grant in FACS Mr. Todd will be impressed that students did the paper work.

It is little surprise that Juanita is a second-generation Hispanic student. You can prob-ably believe that Thomas' mother is a lawyer, and Lakisha's parents are both teachers. The experiences of the three students are different, their ideas different; none of their thoughts show obvious impediments to writing an essay that meets state or national standards. When students understand the elements of a topic prompt and their freedom to brain-storm possibilities for each element, they feel empowered. This is even more so the case when the elements of a writing topic prompt are not all specified. The students have even more power of choice.

Take the example of a prompt typical of writing assessments for middle grades students.

Elements of a writing topic prompt:	Sample topic prompt	Brainstorm possibilities	Choose
<u>S</u>ituation or context	The passages you have read in this test booklet involve people with strong character traits	No possibilities here. I accept this situation.	
<u>I</u>ssue	People need strong character traits to face many challenges	Specific challenges I face: peer pressure, fitting in, home curfew, absent parents	I can write the most about peer pressure.
<u>T</u>ask	Write a paper	Specific character traits that middle school students need: free-write feelings, listen as much as you talk, think the best of others, perseverance,	I can explain perseverance and free writing the best.
<u>P</u>urpose	Explain the importance of strong character traits	Modes of writing that best explain each trait	I'll tell a story about "perseverance" and describe a vignette of "free-writing" to show how I face peer pressure.
<u>A</u>udience	My classmates	Specific classmates who have trouble with peer pressure, too.	I'll write to four classmates in science class.

So when we give the students a writing topic prompt without specifying the five elements, we are giving them incredible freedom [and challenge] to brainstorm and choose. That's a good thing when they understand and appreciate that freedom. It's not so good when they don't. I observed a middle school class with this topic on the board:

> Describe how to make a peanut butter and jelly sandwich.

That's it. No audience, no task, limited purpose and no issue to speak of. Such a prompt, selected by many teachers in my years of observations, assumes that students know the joy of brainstorming possibilities of SITPA and choosing the best of the possibilities for an audience that they want to reach. Too often unspecified elements of a prompt lead to writing filled with vague statements and abrupt conclusions. When undirected by a prompt, students revert to using the restrictive language register of their family and personal lives.

Even in classes where teachers bring in an unidentified object in a paper bag and ask students to *Reach in the bag, feel around and guess what the bag contains. Without saying a word to anyone, describe the contents in writing without naming it so that others can guess the contents, too.* While this assignment captures the attention of students with ready imaginations, it does not compel most students to create engaged writing.

When teachers provide SITPA, students are able to do the following:

1. Focus their thoughts until they picture their ideas clearly.

2. Listen to what their minds say about these clear pictures.

3. Jot down the best words that they hear in their minds in lists, clusters, webs, maps or sketches.

4. Arrange the parts and choose a starting point that helps their thoughts flow.

They are ready to accept invitations to write with you throughout each step of the writing process. In chapter 6, I demonstrate how to invite students to prewrite with you in a way that develops a mindset for revision. In chapters 7–13, I present a variety of ways to prompt students to return to their first efforts and improve them. In chapter 14, I present tools for talking with students about their final drafts and preparing them for future expectations. Even though revision is most often a task seen as a response to first or intermediate drafts, it is important to keep students' minds open to brainstorming possibilities and making choices from among those possibilities at each step of the writing process.

❰ Looking Back

In your response journal, describe two ideas about innate abilities and the *SITPA* table that you found valuable as a teacher in courses that you presently teach.

❱ Looking Ahead

What things coming up in your curriculum invite you to adopt or adapt the *SITPA* strategy?

6

Prewrite with Me

Before beginning, prepare carefully.
Marcus Tullius Cicero

Begin with the ending in mind.
Stephen Covey

Creating a mindset for revision moves seamlessly from analyzing a topic prompt into pre-writing. With the mnemonic Situation-Issue-Task-Purpose-Audience (SITPA) in chapter 5, we prompted students to consider the situation, issue, purpose, task and audience before they started to write. Now it is time to help them brainstorm the possible ways to respond to those prompts.

If you are thinking, *What does prewriting have to do with creating a mindset for revision?* I understand exactly why. I remember asking the same question. Actually, prewriting has more to do with later revision than I ever imagined. Prewriting provides writers with a scaffold from which all of their later thoughts flow in a prepackaged draft for readers to enjoy. The crucial role of prewriting in writing reminds me of my only visit to a podiatrist. These medical practitioners hold that when we correct problems in our feet that the rest of the body has a better chance of increased health. When foot problems go unaddressed, health issues throughout the rest of the body go unexplained. Of course, a chiropractor starts with the spine, claiming that realigning vertebrae is the key to a healthy lifestyle. In the study of all aspects of human behavior, scientists agree that there are root causes of life's successes and problems. Problems later in the writing process can often be traced back to prewriting. Consequently, the degree to which students succeed in revising first drafts is in large part determined by the quality of the possibilities they consider and the choices they make in prewriting.

This is very different from traditional presentations of revision. In colorful posters on classroom walls provided by major textbook publishers, revision appears as one step in the writing process. Students learn that revision comes after the first draft and before the final draft. It includes at least one sweep of revision strategies, and it could include more, depending upon the scope of the writing task and the commitment of the writers. Revision so defined may produce nice posters and charts, but this definition fails to capture the full scope of revision and reduces its power.

Revision for even beginning writers can occur naturally in each step of the writing process, from prewriting to publication. It recurs as writers move from their first thoughts to their final presentation, and by the testimony of writers like Leo Tolstoy, for some time thereafter. Tolstoy claimed that he never read his own books lest he think of a better way to write them. We less-published writers know the feeling; we never feel like what we write is quite the way we want it. Revision is a continual state of mind, a healthy, normal one. Students need our help in realizing that their writing will never reach perfection, and they never need to put themselves under that kind of pressure.

Therefore, when students prewrite with a mindset for revision (brainstorm possibilities and make choices about them), their writing is off to a sound beginning. The following figure shows how considering possibilities and making choices (revision) occurs at every step of the writing process.

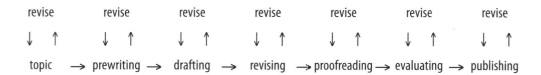

Some prewriting strategies make the path of later revision obvious and viable; others make no path at all or one so clear that it constrains the writers and their thoughts.

Prewriting that Increases the Need for Revision

Two habits of prewriting that increase the need for later revision come to mind. The first is cursory or scant prewriting typical of students who write as little as possible during the prewriting task. Students who do not see the need for prewriting say many different things, but their comments boil down to essentially two reasons for not prewriting.

Reason for not prewriting	Teachers' response that solves the problem
"Prewriting is too much trouble and not worth the effort."	*Oh, I'm sorry I must not have made it clear. Solid prewriting increases the chance that you and others will enjoy what you write.* [A corollary: *With little prewriting, there is little writing to enjoy later*].
"I already know what I want to write about."	*You are absolutely right. You knew what to write about once you read the topic prompt. Prewriting is all about <u>how</u> you present your writing to others.*

Both of these reasons miss the point: prewriting is as essential a part of writing as drafting, revision, proofreading or publishing. In fact, it is the step of the writing process that writers return to at every other step to keep their thoughts on target. To start writing without a firm foundation is like building a house without one. Housing contractors will not do it. They know that houses without firm foundations do not last. Writers follow suite; they set a firm foundation when they write.

The second kind of prewriting that increases the need for later revision is freewriting. A number of writing programs prompt students to start exploring their thoughts with freewriting, calling them quick writes or silent writes. These aren't bad techniques in themselves. They mirror the habits of noted professional writers who start their novels by freewriting: F. Scott Fitzgerald, Thomas Wolfe and Beverly Cleary all admit the value of free-association prewriting. In school, however, starting with freewriting just delays the inevitable need for creating a plan, especially in *genres* other than narration. Writers have to settle on a main idea and project how they will go about presenting that idea in their writing. Too often students who freewrite immediately after reading the topic prompt think that the freewriting is the prewriting. Most often it is not. Read through the quick write below and the wandering of thoughts is quite obvious. While freewrites can be enjoyable reading, it is impossible to determine where these writers' thoughts are headed. Few would describe ninth-grader Casey's freewriting in a health class as foundational for any future writing assignment. Her ideas taxi, but three minutes does not permit lift off.

In this writing the reader will get to know about dental hygiene. The reader will learn what I know about dental hygiene. A few causes for bad dental hygiene is not flossing. Not flossing can cause plaque buildup between the teeth and cause breakdown on the teeth that could make your teeth rot. You should floss daily maybe after every meal at least once a day. Most people does not even floss once a day. Another cause is not brushing, probably one of the biggest reasons. There is no doubt if you don't brush you won't have teeth. Nobody wants to be walking around without teeth. If you do not brush your teeth you will not have good dental hygiene [time for quick-write called].

The writing needed to continue, but more important, the writer needed to focus on presentation of "what I know about dental hygiene." After a 3-minute quick-write, Casey still needs to return to square one and brainstorm and jot list thoughts about the total presentation. I have found it equally hard to identify indications of effective prewriting in the quick-writing of many students. The quick-write focuses students' thoughts, but the real work of prewriting has yet to be done.

Many professional writers tout frequent and extensive freewriting as a valuable prewriting strategy; several cite their daily journals as sourcebooks for all that they write. Professional writers don't have homework in science, health, math and social studies like student writers do. In classrooms focused on standards-based curricula, more efficient ways to prewrite in class trump the time-demanding exploratory freewriting.

Prewriting that Deadens Sensitivity to Revision

Another group of prewriters run into problems because they have been taught a standard technique for responding to topic prompts. The most obvious example is the five-paragraph essay.

Title	Why *iPhones* are better than the new *Blackberries*
Introduction	*I will show you three reasons why my iPhone is better than my best friend's new Blackberry Storm*
#1	*iPhones provide a larger screen.*
#2	*iPhones interface more simply with other technologies and the Internet*
#3	*iPhones will stay current longer.*
Conclusion	*I've shown you three reasons why. . .*

Whereas this plan seems to work well enough for persuasive writing as illustrated above, it runs into problems when it is imposed on topic prompts that require students to explain a cause-and-effect relationship, a compare-and-contrast relationship of two or more items, a problem-solution connection or a narrative of a simple story. Armed with such a simple formula, I have seen students pen with confidence, "In this paper I'm going to explain to you three reasons why Thanksgiving at grandma's farm was so exciting. . ." The narrative continues in three truncated parts that make the readers wonder why the writer felt compelled to convince them that the experience was exciting. Why not convince us as we experience grandma's farm vicariously through your words?

Formula writing has been around since the teaching of composition began in U.S. public schools in the 1890s. Even today, some teachers and administrators tout it as the responsible way to help marginal writers create a plan for packaging their thoughts. Unfortunately, students who "need" the formulaic scaffold resist giving up a prop when their teachers say it's time to move on. Since the formula worked once, they see no reason to discard it. If they did, what else would they use?

In response to widespread use of formulaic writing among students, some state departments of education released standard rubrics for assessing writing that deducts points for writing by formula. By Georgia state law, students must write a first and final draft that meets state standards for promotion to grade 9 and graduation from high school. The trait of organization on the state rubric—the *Analytic Scoring System*—accounts for 20 percent of students' score on the grade 8 and 11 state writing assessments. State department raters are trained to score formulaic writing a "1" or "2" for organization. Students whose writing scores a "1" for organization would be hard pressed to meet the overall state standard for the writing assessment.

Organization =

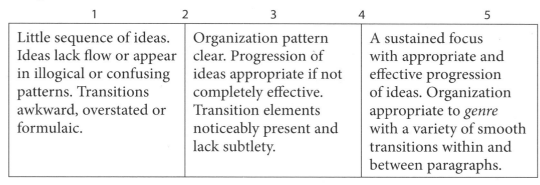

1	2	3	4	5
Little sequence of ideas. Ideas lack flow or appear in illogical or confusing patterns. Transitions awkward, overstated or formulaic.		Organization pattern clear. Progression of ideas appropriate if not completely effective. Transition elements noticeably present and lack subtlety.		A sustained focus with appropriate and effective progression of ideas. Organization appropriate to *genre* with a variety of smooth transitions within and between paragraphs.

Prewriting for *Voice, Pictures* and *Flow*

The shortcoming of both the underdirected quick-writes and the overdirected formulas for prewriting is their inattention to the standards of good writing. Neither approach assures that students' ideas become **pictures** for the readers to access, that their style emerges from the writing with clear **voice** and that the organization ensures a seamless **flow** of their thoughts instead of aimless meandering or jerky cascading from point to point.

Since the major reason students fail to meet standard on state writing test is that they write off-topic or off-genre, I insist on consistent use of the *Writing to Win*© **Assignment Page** and **Advance Organizer** everywhere I go. I offer these two instructional tools that require students to write out their thoughts fully as they prewrite. Our action research studies show that completed **Assignment Pages** and **Advance Organizers** boost students' scores on tests of written expression significantly for elementary, middle and high school students.

Now, I don't mean to be offensive, but I meet a number of teachers who look at these two instructional tools and say, "We already do that. We don't have any trouble getting our students to prewrite; prewriting is not the problem." Well, let me introduce you to three schools whose teachers said the same thing but agreed to a test of these strategies exactly the way that they were designed. I include a Georgia high school, middle school and elementary school that were all part of a 2007–2008 trial study of *Writing to Win*© *Working Portfolios* that required students to use these tools fully.

> Terrell County High School is a 90–90 school with a goal of becoming a 90–90–90 school.* The students have steadily shown improvement in performance over the years, some years exceeding 90 percent proficiency on the English Language Arts graduation test but never in the corresponding test of written expression. Ms. Coleman, the eleventh- grade English teacher, noted that the Working Portfolios for Students gave students a concrete and easy-to-understand strategy for responding to writing on demand in a test situation.

---

*Douglas Reaves defines a 90–90–90 school as one that includes a student body that is 90% poverty, 90% minority and 90% proficient on all independent assessment tests.

Apparently, the ***Assignment Page*** and ***Advanced Organizer*** gave all students a way to make sure that they wrote on the topic as prompted. None of the students who failed to meet the standard wrote off-topic, a first for the school.

Georgia High School Writing Test	2005	2006	2007	2008
Pass rate of 1st time test takers	78%	71%	90%	92%

The performance of Grade 8 students at Twiggs County Middle School see-sawed just below or just above the state average on the state writing test using the *Writing to Win©Management System* until the state changed the standards assessed. In 2007 no longer could students choose to respond to a prompt in the narrative genre that they all had mastered. Instead, students received a writing topic prompt that required them to respond by writing either a persuasive or expository essay. Student performance reached an all-time low on the 2007 test; it was a small consolation that eighth-graders statewide scored considerably lower. The school opted to participate in the trial of *Working Portfolios* with their 2008 eighth-graders who turned in a mean score that is significantly improved over the 2007 performance of similar eighth-graders.

Group	2007	2008	Change
Twiggs County Middle School students	42.5%	65.7%	+23.2%
State of Georgia	70.1%	77.0%	+6.9%

In the fall of 2007, my office received a call from the principal of Tiger Creek Elementary School and learned of the 16 percent gap in achievement between grade 5 students of veteran teachers of writing and those of teachers new to teaching writing. Tiger Creek joined the group of schools testing out the *Writing to Win Working Portfolios.* Two teachers in their second year of teaching writing employed the portfolios in the expository *genre* with the following results. Not only did the students of these beginning teachers of writing outperform the fifth graders from 2007, they posted a pass rate just 2 percent below that of their peers in classes taught by veteran teachers of writing. The achievement gap was closed.

Teacher	2007	2008	Change
Beginning teachers of writing	52%	76%	+24%
Veteran teachers of writing	68%	78%	+10%

The Assignment Page

The *Assignment Page* is simple enough. It requires students to write out their thoughts about a topic prompt in complete sentences that cover the traits of writing that all good writers consider before they write: a clear understanding of the topic of the writing, a specific audience, a purpose, an appropriate tone and the standards for judging their final drafts. The written responses document the fact that, indeed, the students had considered the prompt thoroughly.

Writing Prompt
A classmate of yours has started falling asleep in class. Write a paper to your fellow student that describes fully several causes of falling asleep during the day. Include examples and details so that the he/she understands your explanation fully.

Note how completely the teacher models what she expects of her students on her *Assignment Page*. What I like about this teacher's model is that it represents authentic adult thought. No student will be tempted to copy this teacher's model; that registers as *un-cool* in the minds of students. I used to write at the level of the students I taught, respond in a way that I expected them to respond. It didn't take me long to realize that students didn't expect me to write thoughts like theirs any more than I expected them to write thoughts like mine. The game that works for teaching and learning in schools is *What am I thinking?*, whether at the pen of students or teachers.

The Assignment Page* – 1st Draft #1

Self-checked score _20_

The topic assigned to me	I need to explain what a student of mine must try in order to quit falling asleep in my class.
Audience: Who am I writing to?	I actually will picture Harold, a student of mine years ago, who slept and failed Georgia studies.
The purpose of my writing (genre)	My purpose is to explain changes that will help him get serious about learning Georgia history.
Tone: serious, humorous, asking, demanding. . . . (two descriptive words)	I'm going to be humorous this time; last time when I was dead serious, Harold didn't get my point at all and continued to sleep away.
How will my final draft be evaluated?	A student, and then I, will score my final draft using the rubric found on page 23 of the working port folio.
Title of Final Evaluation Form	The rubric is titled "Explain A Cause."

For the assignment page, EARN 20 points by writing a complete sentence for each of these five items.

*An Expository Writing Cycle: a working portfolio for students, student materials for Writing to Win, Phase II, 2008, p. 5

In a pilot study of the use of these 24-page working portfolios,* the power of student self-assessment mentioned in Chapter 1 (Stiggins *et al.,* 2007) was reaffirmed. For completing the **Assignment Page**, students award themselves up to 20 of the 100 points possible for writing a first draft. When students saw the expectation highlighted at the bottom of the page, they filled out each line on the **Assignment Page** completely, their time spent in prewriting decreased and their productivity increased.

Conferencing for issues on *The Assignment Page*

Teacher (no pencil)	Student (pencil in hand)
Focus: Student inflated his self-assessment of the assignment page.	
I see no sentences on this assignment page, and yet there's a "20" at the top of the page. Can you tell me how that happened?	I wrote good answers.
They may be, but the expectation is clear. I see no beginning capital letter, no end punctuation, subject-verb pairs, so let's see, no points on the assignment page.	I don't see why I have to write sentences?
Oh, I'm sorry to mislead you. You don't have to write sentences, but you need to assess your work accurately. Let's see. Zero sentences = zero points, right?	[. . . a pause, a sigh, and the student begins writing additional details to each response to create complete, informative sentences and a self-assessed 20 points.]

---

* The pilot study included 19 Georgia public schools with 5,300 students from grades 2 through 12 from August 2007 through April 2008. Results from several schools are reported in *Report of Action Research Focus Studies,* Athens, Georgia: Erincort Consulting, Inc., 2009.

The Advance Organizer

The *Advance Organizer* follows on the heels of the *Assignment Page* in the recommended routine of the *Writing to Win©Management System*. Completing the *Assignment Page* and *Advance Organizer* in about fifteen minutes, students are conditioned to respond to writing topic prompts within the time constraints of most state and national tests. Take this example of a character sketch prompted as an expository essay. When students meet the expectations of the *Character Sketch Advance Organizer*, they have well-developed ideas (*pictures*) that draw them back to their prewriting as they write organized and informative first drafts. Note the expectations highlighted in the bar at the bottom of the *Advance Organizer*.

A model from my own writing responds to this writing topic prompt.

> **Writing Prompt.** Write an essay that explains how a person in American history has influenced America either in a positive way or a negative way. Give specific details supporting your ideas to help the reader understand your point of view.

To respond to this topic prompt, I selected the *Character Sketch Advance Organizer*. I knew from the prompt that the expected *genre* was not persuasive because of the word *explain* and the phrase *understand your point of view*. I was not asked to convince anyone of my point of view, just to help them understand it clearly and easily. I wrote a caption of the topic at the top of my *Advance Organizer*.

Note the brainstorm section. Since I listed eight possible characters before I chose Abraham Lincoln, the other seven stared at me from the top of the organizer in the event that my jot lists about Abe stalled. I have seen and encouraged many a student to ditch a topic from their brainstorm list that was not jot listing well and revise their jot list by starting with another topic. The brainstorm list helps them organize and revise their thinking from the early moments of prewriting, some of the most crucial moments, especially when students are writing under the pressure of time constraints.

A person who influenced American history for good or for bad

Advance Organizer for **Character Sketch**

BRAINSTORM: Think about an assigned prompt, then list up to six characters that come to mind. When you picture the first character, write a name or phrase that will help you remember it. Picture and list at least five more characters before you select one about which to write. You may include groups of living beings (such as tigers, Eskimos, heroes).

1. Bill Gates
2. George Washington
3. Abe Lincoln
4. Elvis Presley
5. MLK
6. Rosa Parks
7. Oprah Winfrey
8. Christopher Columbus

Thesis: Abraham Lincoln is the US President who has had the most positive effect on most groups within the U.S. of America today

JOT LISTS: Circle the character (or group of characters) that you picture best in your mind from the brainstorm list. Jot list phrases that fit the character in the following columns, features that you notice first when you see or remember the person. List common behaviors like eating, walking, talking, sleeping, breathing—the distinctive ways that your character does what most characters do.

External Features	Internal Features		Typical Behaviors
tall lanky frame	self-educated	→	studied law books by cabin fire
full black beard	inner motivation	→	ran and lost elected office
dark, wavy hair	pensive	→	Photographs
tall black top hat	courageous	→	Emancipation Proclamation
tight white shirt	indecisive	→	long time to start civil war
black tuxedo	honest	→	
long pointed nose	perseverance	→	didn't give up when losing war;
			lost elections; lost children
	dedicated	→	to Mary Todd; US Constitution
	orator	→	Gettysburg address

Circle three typical internal features and the corresponding typical behaviors that you picture the best in your mind and write a full paragraph about each. Use details from the other column to create a full description of each typical behavior.

For the *Advance Organizer,* EARN 30 points by completing every line on this page. Use only vivid words and phrases. NO sentences.

A second way that brainstorming starts the recursive process of revision is in the construction of the introductory paragraph. Following the productive game of *What am I thinking?*, I prompt students to draw a huge circle that includes the topic prompt that they have abbreviated at the top of their **Advance Organizer**, their brainstorm list and thesis. Since the first thing they do after reading the topic prompt is create a brainstorm list and try out a thesis, I suggest that they summarize these thoughts as an introduction to their first draft. I hear myself saying, *Explain your first thoughts on the topic that led you to the focus of your selected topic.* What better way to achieve authentic writing?

The next time I used the topic prompt, I ended up writing about Alexander Hamilton from a different brainstorm list.* This time I had to revise my list. As I wrote the first few sentences of my introduction, I consulted my list and noted that Benedict Arnold didn't fit the flow of my thoughts in writing the first paragraph. So I inserted the second president of the U.S. and a detail that I'm not certain actually applies. Anyway, it read smoothly and was accepted by several audiences without question.

Introductory Paragraph

America's history is filled with interesting and important people who had influenced the U. S. of America in its first two decades. One was George Washington, who affected the office of President like no president since. Another, John Adams showed that power moved from one elected person to another. There is little evidence that he left his mark in any other way. Others like Thomas Jefferson, Ben Franklin and Thomas Paine lived very public lives, and their impassioned speeches echo in voices of American students today. There is one founding father, however, whom I believe is the most influential of all. He created framework of the American federal government, a sound federal treasury and a stock exchange that financed the westward expansion to the Pacific Ocean. His name? Alexander Hamilton.

The Advance Organizer is a straightforward strategy for getting students started in drafting their thoughts. It conditions them to trust their thoughts by brainstorming several possibilities. Once they choose the best of the possible topics brainstormed, they can move with confidence to engage a potential audience and compel them to read beyond the first paragraph.

---

* Each time you use the same writing topic prompt, vary your response to it. Your model for writing will stay new and fresh, and you will find yourself growing in the understanding of the subject matter you teach.

A person who influenced American history for good or for bad

Advance Organizer for **Character Sketch**

BRAINSTORM: Think about an assigned prompt, then list up to six characters that come to mind. When you picture the first character, write a name or phrase that will help you remember it. Picture and list at least five more characters before you select one about which to write. You may include groups of living beings (such as tigers, Eskimos, heroes).

1. *George Washington*

2. *Benedict Arnold*

3. *Thomas Paine*

5. *George Washington*

6. *Thomas Jefferson*

7. *Alexander Hamilton*

Thesis: *A little mentioned early American leader may have been the most influential.*

JOT LISTS: Circle the character (or group of characters) that you picture best in your mind from the brainstorm list. Jot list phrases that fit the character in the following columns, features that you notice first when you see or remember the person. List common behaviors like eating, walking, talking, sleeping, working, playing—the distinctive ways that your character does what most characters do.

External Features	Internal Features	Typical Behaviors
military uniforms	*organized* →	*created a framework for a federal government*
slim erect posture	*personal distance* →	*marriage of convenience; outside relations*
black patent shoes	*serious* →	*premeditated most decisions*
fair features	*financial genius* →	*designed a federal treasury*
thin long nose	*pro free enterprise* →	*developed the first national stock exchange*
high flat forehead	*quiet, ambitious* →	*planned his future under the radar*
long hair ponytail	*opportunist* →	*married into the wealthiest ny family*

Circle three typical internal features and the corresponding typical behaviors that you picture the best in your mind and write a full paragraph about each. Use details from the other two columns to create a full description of each typical behavior.

For the *Advance Organizer,* EARN 30 points by completing every line on this page. Use <u>only</u> vivid words and phrases. NO sentences.

Benefits of Prewriting

A group of teachers new to using the **Assignment Page** and **Advance Organizer** for pre-writing mentioned these benefits:

- ◆ Provides a specific direction for starting a first draft that can apply to any topic
- ◆ Helps students focus on what they are thinking
- ◆ Gives confidence to ill-confident students
- ◆ Nonwriters need it
- ◆ Stimulates all levels of students
- ◆ Scaffolding activity that can apply to all modes and *genre* of writing
- ◆ Scaffolding gave students the freedom to use it but did not require them to stick to it rigidly.
- ◆ Helps students with too many thoughts control them
- ◆ Appears very structured, but produces authentic writing
- ◆ Provides an alternative to students who use patterned introductions like, "In this paper I'm going to. . ."

❮ Looking Back

In your response journal, describe two ideas about empowering students re-write during prewriting that were valuable for you as a teacher in courses that you presently teach.

❯ Looking Ahead

What things coming up in your curriculum invite you to adopt or adapt the **Assignment Page** and the **Advance Organizer** that you have met in this chapter?

Empowering Students to Write and RE-write
Session Guide #2 for Professional Learning Teams

Responding to

Chapter 5: Kindling innate writing abilities

Chapter 6: Pre-write with me—The *Assignment Page* and *Advance Organizer*

Before joining *Professional Learning Team (PLT) Session #2*

Make sure you have written your response to these topics in your journal.

1. In two or three sentences, create a writing topic prompt that kindles innate writing abilities in students for a course you teach.

2. Describe the classroom experience in which you helped your students understand how to move seamlessly from reading a writing topic prompt to prewriting.

Exemplars

Read through the prewriting of your students that follow the suggestions in *SITPA,* the *Assignment Page* and *Advance Organizer.* Select some of them to share with your PLT that may serve as exemplars of prewriting that meet or exceed state or local standards. Bring your own personal prewriting that you used as an effective model for your students to follow.

Discussion questions for *PLT Session #2*

1. How important is a specific strategy like *SITPA* for analyzing writing topic prompts (chapter 5)?

2. How is it that prewriting contributes to creating a mindset for revision (chapter 6)?

3. Explain what is meant by the recursive nature of the writing process (chapter 6)?

4. Explain a disadvantage of prewriting that increases the need for later revision (chapter 6).

5. How can prewriting that reduces the need for later revision be detrimental (chapter 6)?

6. How and when is the *Assignment Page* a necessary part of prewriting (chapter 6)?

7. Explain fully the two essential features of an *Advance Organizer* (chapter 6).

Compiling *Professional Learning Portfolios*

Bring the artifacts that you have gathered to include in your *Professional Learning Portfolio.* Share your ideas for creating your portfolio and listen to the portfolio plans of other teachers.

7

Revise Words and Phrases with Me
An Introduction to Revising First Drafts

But words are things, and a small drop of ink,
Falling, like dew, upon a thought, produces
That which makes thousands, perhaps millions, think.
Lord Byron

One must be drenched in words, literally soaked in them, to have the right ones
form themselves into the proper patterns at the right moment.
Hart Crane

The Introduction

I introduce revision of first drafts to most students at the level of words and phrases, following a systematic framework of *invite, model, revise, reflect* and *learn*. As the teacher I invite students to write, then model a specific revision strategy for them. Students and I then revise our own writings independently. Then students reflect on the strategy they have practiced, and everyone involved in the process learns new insight into how writing works. The editor's note in the margins marks our progress through each revision strategy as invite, model, revise, reflect and learn.

Invite   *you to look at your first draft to understand the need for the strategy of the day.*

Model   *the strategy in adult writing to help you picture the process of the strategy.*

Revise   *along with me using the specific strategy I modeled for you.*

Reflect   *on what we have all revised*

Learn   *how the strategy improved our writing.*

This framework of revising first drafts extends Donald Murray's invitation to "write with me" in *The Craft of Revision*. Leaders in the teaching of writing advise teachers to write models for students and to write along with their students, but *Empowering Students to Write and RE-write* fleshes out the details of lessons in revision that make it simple to follow through on that advice.

All writers write first drafts for themselves, but few students write with this awareness. It seldom helps for me to tell them. They have to experience it for themselves. So my introduction to revising first drafts goes like this:

> *You have written first drafts, and from up here, they all look pretty good. Who did you write them for?*

> "You" and "Our teacher." [the most likely responses]

> *Are you sure? Do you mean to say that the first draft is ready to present to me or your teacher for a grade?*

Discussion about this question rarely leads to consensus. Half of the class is ready to be rid of the assignment and hand it in. Others think that their drafts have errors that need to be corrected. A student or two usually say something about changing the wording of their drafts. Clearly the majority of the class is not focusing on the thoughts from which they wrote their drafts, so I start from the beginning.

> *Anyone know what the word **revision** means?*

> "Correct mistakes," "Improve the writing" or "Do the paper over." [After these typical responses, I ask the question again.]

> *No, I mean it. No guessing. Someone define the word **revision, like in a dictionary**. It seems to have two parts to me. What are the two parts? Who wants to take a stab at it?*

I write REVISION on the board in all capital letters and ask them to do the same on the top of their notebook paper.

A student comments, "The two parts are RE- and -VISION." [I place a slash between the E and the V.]

> *So, what do the two parts mean? Someone start with the first part.*

> "RE- means over. It means do again. It means you do your paper over again."

> *Okay,* I agree, *so what have you already done in your first draft that you can "do over again." Did you correct errors in your first draft, so you correct them again?*

Classes reject this notion, but have little to offer in its place. Hearing no comments, I continue,

> *What's a vision? What does vision have to do with writing a first draft?*

The light dawns on a student or two. "You have a picture in your mind when you write your first draft," they say in different ways. Then all the class agrees as several recall their introduction to the terms **voice**, **pictures** and **flow**.

So, then, are you saying that revision is re-picturing in your mind what you were thinking when you wrote your first draft?

Why would you want to do that?

A student understands and says, "You look back at what you pictured in your mind so you can see if your first draft paints that picture for others."

Then the first draft isn't for other people. If it isn't for other people, who is the first draft written for?

Several students respond, "First drafts are written for the writer." Class consensus is achieved.

So does anyone still believe that first drafts are written for teachers?

Good, so you in your roles as writers are the only ones who presently see the pictures beneath your first drafts. Now we can revise!

Teachers are to lead students to knowledge of specific revision strategies that help their drafts become accurate and complete explanations of what they are thinking. For too long, revising first drafts has overwhelmed teachers, but especially students. When students are overwhelmed, but agree to revise anyway, they respond in one of two ways. They

◆ trivialize the task, attempting to save face, afraid to admit that they really don't know what to do. Two students may ask to be partners and agree to write "this looks good to me" on each other's drafts. Others may giggle or dismiss the task, overtly avoiding the possibility of failure by not trying, or so they think.

◆ exaggerate the task, letting emotions run wild with anxiety, asking questions of themselves, their peers and especially their teachers without consulting their own thoughts about their writing: "What do we do? Where do we start? How much is enough? Why revise it at all?"

All of these questions evaporate in the wake of well-tuned revision strategies like those that teachers have helped me create and hone over the years. These strategies satisfy two criteria of best practice in learning: student choice and universality. All of them require students to make specific decisions about how they will revise. They also apply to all modes and genres of writing and to students of all abilities and learning styles. For more than two decades I have watched these strategies empower students from the most marginal to the most talented of writers.

Humor me for three comments; the first one serves as a reminder.

◆ Revision of first drafts is an inside-the-mind task. It is impossible for read-ers to offer significant help in directing the revision of writers to any specific degree. A discerning teacher prompts students to **brainstorm possibilities** from among several revision strategies taught, then **choose** the best one(s) for a specific draft. When teachers make specific suggestions, the writing of the students becomes the teacher's writing. I meet far too many students willing to share their first drafts and turn the responsibility for revision over to me. "What should I do?" "This is bad, isn't it?" Such questions remind us that student writers gain no benefit from guessing what we teachers like.

♦ Students need to revise in a way that spotlights their revisions and gives them a concrete sense of accomplishment. Revising with a pen of a color that contrasts with the color of their first draft is all it takes. I issue students red pens and tell them that there is magic in them. *When you read your first draft with a red pen in hand, extra words pop back into your mind. Red pens are the best tool for jotting down those words and blending them into your first drafts.* In classes where students start adding red words and phrases to their sentences, they experience the sensory lure of spreading red on papers throughout the classroom. As they see red words spread across their first drafts and those of peers around them, they are motivated to ride the wave of vivid details and notes as it rolls over the classroom.

♦ Choice of revision prompts emerge from a quick read of the students' first drafts. Most simply, teachers read first drafts to determine whether the students need to attend to revision at four different levels.

Level 1	Words and phrases	Chapters 7, 10 and 11
Level 2	Sentences	Chapters 10-11
Level 3	Paragraphs	Chapters 8 and 13
Level 4	Whole drafts (essays, poems, stories)	Chapters 9, 12 and 14

Sometimes the first drafts of most students need revision at the same level, especially the first time you prompt revision. Later you will see that your students' drafts need revision at more than one level, so prompt them at the appropriate levels in small groups.

With all of this said, I invite you to start where I did several years ago, climbing the steep learning curve of helping students revise in a way that fit my teaching style and the changing learning styles of 21st-century secondary students. Each chapter details one or more revision strategies following the sequence of *invite, model, revise, reflect* and *learn*. If you don't feel confident to choose a revision strategy to start with, try the strategies out in the order presented. Over a period of years, you develop comfort in prompting strategies at each level and confidence in discerning when to use each of them.

> **Note:** You might start with Level 1—Words and Phrases (Chapters 7, 10 and 11) with your students and find that these strategies supply all of the help that you and your students need. Level 1 strategies suffice for some lab reports in science, technology and trade classes as well as abstracts of research articles in courses across the curriculum.

> **Caveat:** Oh yes, follow the scripts. I taught all of these revision strategies unsuccessfully several times before I got them right with the help of many classroom experiences. I know following scripts can be constraining, but the scripts will save you all of the time that I took to figure them out. Once you see how much revision the scripts elicit from students, you will be glad you used them. Later you may choose to tweak a detail here or there to maintain and boost the quality of student revision.

Revise Words and Phrases with Me

In prompting students to revise first drafts on topics across the curriculum, I ask them to **jot** down details, more than they need, throughout the draft and return later to **blend** them into the words around them—this strategy I call *Jot and Blend, which* is so accessible to students and applies in some degree to every first draft. In these two examples, students wrote first drafts that I prompted with the *Jot and Blend* strategy. Jeremy, a middle school student in a life science class, defines the habitat of the white-tailed deer.

> A deer habitat has trees, bushes, vines, and grasses. Deer eat all of these. Plants have to be scattered around so a whole area is usable. Deer need a variety of plants to stay alive. They need different plants in different seasons. Some plants give them cover or camouflage.
>
> Plant succession is the natural change of plants on a site during the year. When people disturb the land, it sets succession back. When they let the land rest, succession improves the habitat. Deer management involves two things, habitat management and population management. Habitat management is more important than population management because you have to have habitat before you can have deer. Bottomland areas make the best deer habitats. They support two to four times as many deer as upland areas. Population management has to deal with all of these things.

Lakisha, a ninth-grader in family and consumer science class, writes.

> The rules for matching colors are simple to follow. First, pick a pattern as the basis for a room. It must have two or more colors and follow a color scheme. Then choose three colors that match the pattern. Make sure one is dark, one medium and one light. Use the light color as background on the floors, walls and ceilings. Put the medium tone on the largest piece of furniture. Add the dark color as an accent on pillows, vases or frames. Remember the Law of Chromatic Distribution: As areas reduce in size, the chromatic intensity can be increased. Using less of a bright color makes it look brighter and highlights it. Too much intense color irritates the observers because their eyes have no place to rest. Balance small areas of intense color with large areas of neutral ones.

As I read these first drafts, I saw students dutifully completing their assignments, but I feel uninvolved in what they were writing. They covered the topics well enough, but their writing frames their new knowledge uncertainly; both drafts need details of color, shape and activity. I prompted them with a *Jot and Blend* revision strategy.

_____ Lesson for *Jot and Blend* _____

Jot and blend details with me. Our minds are remarkable organs. When we reread one of our first drafts, extra words and phrases pop up in our minds. They are already there, but they haven't come out for us to use. That's why we all have red pens in hand right now. So read each sentence of your first draft one at a time. As the details appear, jot them down above the place they belong in each sentence. Don't worry about making all the details fit just yet, just jot them down. Let your pen try to keep up with your mind. You can blend details in the details when you create your final draft.

Here's what I mean. Ms. Michaelson of Dakota Valley High School, South Dakota, sketched the character of a carved stature outside the door of the Jackpot Gambling Saloon. Here's how the draft read without the details.

> His pupils widened as he strained to size up a potential enemy. Zeke's eyes narrowed and cut to the right as he shifted his frame to his right leg. The movement dislodged the holster from his left hip. It slid down and rested against restless fingers. If there was to be a shoot-out today, Zeke would be ready.
>
> Zeke Merriwether was the epitome of the old western gunslinger. His hat, curled at the edges from sweat and sun, crowned a mop of black curls.

INVITE

MODEL

A shirt topped with vest and bandana, framed hands poised over loaded six-shooter. He was the perfect killing machine.

However, it wasn't always this way. In a former life, this cowboy was a different man, decidedly less violent. The softness at the corners of his mouth hint at the pain that backs the toughness. It is a pain borne from the murder of his young bride by bandits.

This tragedy is what fuels Zeke. It is what drives him this day to lean against this bar to wait to take out the last of his wife's tormentors. Or, at least that's the story as I imagine it looking at the wooden statue standing in the courtyard of the Jackpot Gambling Saloon in Mitchell, South Dakota.

We all see a picture that Ms. Michaelson imagined, but let's read it again with the descriptive details blended in and talk about the difference.

His **coal-black** pupils widened as he strained **against the darkness** to size up a potential enemy. Zeke's eyes narrowed and cut to the right as he shifted his **hefty** frame to his **jean-clad** right leg. The **subtle, cat-like** movement dislodged the **worn, leather** holster from his left hip. It slid down and rested against **five twitching**, restless fingers. If there was to be a shoot-out today, Zeke would be ready.

Zeke Merriwether was the epitome of the old western gunslinger. His **ten gallon** hat, curled at the edges from **a briney mix** of sweat and sun, crowned a mop of black curls. A **mustard yellow** shirt topped with **leather** vest and **red** bandana, framed **gloved** hands poised over loaded six-shooter. He was the perfect killing machine.

However, it wasn't always this way. In a former life, this cowboy was a different man...**confident and manly to be sure, but** decidedly less violent. The softness at the corners of his mouth hint at the pain that backs the toughness **of his soul**. It's a pain borne from **the horror of** the murder of his young bride by **a rouge band of** bandits.

This tragedy is what fuels Zeke. It is what drives him this day to **suck on his cigarette and** lean against this bar to wait to **pounce on and** take out the last of his wife's tormentors. Or, at least that's the story as I imagine it looking at the **chiseled,** wooden statue standing in the courtyard of the Jackpot Gambling Saloon in Mitchell, South Dakota.

Response of students to these two readings vary, but essentially, they see the two as a difference between a movie in black and white versus one in color. The details blended into the draft color, emotion, suspense and authentic life experience that Ms. Michaelson may have seen from the beginning. Now they are all in the writing for the audience to experience. Zeke comes alive. The details added 49 words to a frame of 209 words, an average of over four words per sentence.

Setting concrete expectations for *Jot and Blend*: I specify the amount of revision I expect from students in *jotting and blending* details in their first drafts: add an average of 2 to 3 words per sentence. To students it sounds like a reachable goal; it helps them pace their revision time. Yet when they reach the expectation, they have added a considerable number of details (a 20-sentence draft yields 40 to 60 added details) and earned themselves a target ⊙ (⊙ = 85 points). Significant revisions beyond these expectations earn students the + (+ = 100 points).

In response to a model like Ms. Michaelson's, Lakisha and Jeremy jotted descriptive words and phrases in some sentences and not others. That's how it should be. The ***Jot and Blend*** strategy prompts, but doesn't require, students to consider adding details to each sentence. Jeremy's 45 red (bolded here) words, blended into his 137-word draft about deer habitat made a 32% increase in word quantity that in turn made a clear difference in the quality of the pictures that readers see. Since he added over three words per sentence, he self-assessed his revision a plus (+).

A deer habitat has **healthy** trees, **berry** bushes, **leafy** vines, and **patches of green** grasses. Deer eat **some of** all of these. Plants have to be scattered around **fully** so a whole area is usable **for a deer population that is on the move.** Deer require a variety of plants to stay alive. They need different plants in different seasons. Some plants **like privet, rhododendrons or juniper hedges** give them cover or camouflage.

Plant succession is the natural change of plants on a site during the year. When people disturb the land **by tilling, burning or moving it,** it sets succession back. When they let the land rest, it improves the habitat. Deer management **increases succession when it** involves two things, habitat management and population management. Habitat management is more important than population management because you have to have **a healthy and full** habitat before you can have deer. Bottomland areas **with low limbs and vines and lush ground cover** make the best deer habitats. They support two to four times as many deer as upland areas. Population management has to deal with all of these things.

Lakisha added these words to her draft with similar results.

> The rules for matching colors are simple to follow. First, pick a pattern **like a geometric, paisley or floral one** as the basis for a room. It must have two or more **primary or contrasting** colors and follow a color scheme **in the pattern**. Then choose three **other** colors that match the pattern. Make sure one is dark, one medium and one light. Use the light color as background on **carpets, wall paper or woodwork in** the floors, walls and ceilings. Put the medium tone on the largest piece of furniture **like a hutch, dining room table, a sofa, bookcase or entertainment center**. Add the dark color as an accent on **scatter or prop-up** pillows, **stylish** vases or **striking** frames. Remember the Law of Chromatic Distribution: as areas, **sections or objects in a room** reduce in size, the chromatic intensity can be increased. Using less of a bright color makes it look brighter and highlights it. Too much intense color irritates the observers because their eyes have no place to rest. Balance small areas of intense color **of reds, blues or greens** with large areas of neutral ones **like beige, khaki or taupe.**

The short first draft reminded Lakisha of the rules for matching colors, but it had yet to connect with readers who had never taken a family and consumer science class. With the 52 red words (bolded here) added to only 12 sentences, she reached a wider audience to describe how the Law of Chromatic Distribution helps a person match colors in a design scheme.

Note how differently the students employed *Jot and Blend*. Billy peppered his draft with a balance of adjectives and prepositional phrases like Ms. Michaelson's model. Lakisha, however, expanded her first draft largely with prepositional phrases inserted after the nouns they modify. The *Jot and Blend* strategy reconnected the writers to their thoughts and the extra words and phrases began to flow. This first revision experience moved both students well on their way to becoming more engaging writers across the curriculum. Although we led with a revision strategy that focused on quantity (number of sentences and number of words added), the additions improved the quality as well.

I modify my invitation to *Jot and Blend* with students whose first drafts are already fairly descriptive. This tenth-grader writes a persuasive essay, trying to convince his class-mates to take a hypothetical journey back with him in a time machine that permits them to spend a day in a time period of their choice. In Taylor's second paragraph, he addresses the down side of visiting the 1970s. In the third paragraph, he is on to luring his audience into traveling back to that long ago 20th-century decade.

The only negatives about the 1970s that I could think of were truly insignificant compared to the problems of today. Poor technology was the cutting edge for those years. The Vietnam War occurred on the other side of the world. So in hindsight, the only things that could be construed as negative were the things that we would most likely never become involved with.

The 1970s marked a change from the Beatles to Led Zeppelin. Music was become a huge industry because of the teens who gulped it up. The live music of Led Zeppelin is a good enough reason to visit the 70s. Led Zeppelin kept in its stranglehold of musical perfection. Led Zeppelin's music transcends the sound barrier and connected with each and every person who listened to it.

Taylor's Revision

1. **Vietnam War was brutal, destructive and immensely controversial around the world, but it** occurred on the other side of the world.

2. from **the soft and easy rhythms of** the Beatles **to the hard, difficult opuses and cadenzas of** Led Zeppelin.

3. **Music was shifting into the mainstream society as a teenage generation searching for an identity devoured it.** [replaces gulped it up]

Note that this essay is anything but spare in its detailed description of the 1970s. Taylor does not need to add details to most of the sentences in his draft. There are, however, patches of sparse descriptions scattered about the draft. For this reason, I modified the invitation to this writer and six other students in his class like him.

> *Read your first draft and circle 10 to 12 words or phrases that you can write more about. Then number 6 to 8 of the circles that you picture best in your mind. Add vivid words or phrases that enrich the description of the circled parts. Make other changes that improve your readers' understanding.*

Taylor does precisely this. He creates 15 circles and jots details down for 7 circled phrases. He rewrote the entire sentence about the growing impact of the music industry. His peer-reviser felt that his revisions improved his first draft. No doubt they did.

The **Jot and Blend** applies to less confident writers than Taylor. Circling parts of their writing before they **Jot and Blend** provides the extra step for students who say "I can't think of anything to add." Austin, a student with special needs, wrote the following draft with details blended in. He then let me read his first draft aloud, and I stopped to let him add in the red word for the class to hear and approve

> My writing is about sports because it something [I always love.] Did you see the game Sunday where the Falcons beat the Chargers 22 to 16? These are the land of games that I love to watch. That is my goal to do and go to the NFL. As a matter of fact I am a major sports fan. Now you see me trying to go to high school. My older sister too. It was the last time I saw her. We have to move with our other famly because it has time for us.

His teacher remarked with surprise at the increased detail that Austin inserted into his draft even though the details came in additional sentences instead of words and phrases.

The first time you use **Jot and Blend** invite some students to share their additions aloud with the class. Walk around the room as the students revise in search of good examples of effective jotting and blending. In the following share-response routine, I kick-start the participation of volunteers for this important piece of the writing process.

> *How many of you felt the red words began to flow out of your mind as you jotted them down in your first draft?* [A third of the students eventually raise their hands].

> *Good, that means you have made promising revisions that are worth sharing.*

I help two students agree to read their drafts aloud, then I address the class, *Just a minute, now, you have important jobs, too. You all listen well to what Alex reads so you can tell him*

- ♦ if his additions fit his first draft
- ♦ whether he needs to write more, less or that his additions are about right.

Since the class cannot see Alex's first draft with the red revisions, I partner with him: he reads his first draft aloud, stopping at each addition for me to read. When we complete about a page of revisions, I ask the class:

- ♦ *Did the red words that I read in Alex's draft fit his draft?* [count the raised hands]
- ♦ *Raise your hand if you think that Alex needs to add even more red words to his first draft.*
- ♦ *How many say that he wrote too much already?*
- ♦ *How many say that his additions were just about right?*

It is important to poll the class with these points in this order. It is equally important to tally the response on the board for Alex and all to see.

Name	Add more	Too much	About right	Teacher's summary of the response of the class
Alex	14	0	9	*The class likes what you've added, but they need more of your good, vivid details. Can you circle places where pictures can be enhanced?*
Theresa	7	0	18	*The class likes your revision the way it is, but you need to add a few more vivid details. Can you mark a place or two to add descriptive details?*
Antonio	21	0	4	*You've got the class going on the details. Now you need to really turn the vivid details on. More details to what you have added and details in more places. Do you see what to do?*
Cortney	4	4	17	*The class thinks you've added too much, sometimes too little. As you blend in the details decide which needs more and which needs less. Do you understand the class's advice?*
Total	45	4	48	

Antonio has the most additional revising to do, but he just needs to add more of what he was prompted to do in the first place. Most first-time revisers are like Antonio; they add a little to see if it gets them by. Cortney has the biggest task. Fortunately, she has the most revision already invested in her first draft and can return to assess each addition.

On subsequent uses of *Jot And Blend*, students share their additions aloud in groups of three. One person reads his first draft aloud, a second reads the red words, all three decide which of the details need to be blended in effectively.

Student Self-Assessment for *Jot and Blend*

Students complete their reflection of the *Jot and Blend* strategy by assessing the degree to which they met your stated expectation for their revision. For an expectation of 2 to 3 words/sentence, students count the number of their sentences and multiply by 2 and by 3 to see how the target meets the expectation for a specific first draft. In a 20-sentence first draft, the expectation is 40 to 60 words blended into their draft. If they have added words within that range, they assess themselves a target ⊙ (⊙ = 85 points). If they added fewer words, they self-assess a bar ▱ (▱ = 70 points). More words permits them to self-assess a plus + (+ = 100 points).

The above chart of student responses has helped students I've met draw conclusions about the *Jot And Blend* strategy:

♦ Almost every sentence needs details.

♦ Every draft worth writing is worth revising. [a quote from the teacher]

♦ **Jot and Blend** helps us write what we meant to write the first time.

♦ The more you add to your writing, the easier it is to understand.

♦ Some details you add don't improve your writing.

♦ Jot extra words for every sentence; decide whether to blend them all in or not.

Conclusion: Wrap up the session with a statement that all can embrace fully.

> *All first drafts can benefit from revision. The easiest revision to use is adding details. Jot down all the details that come to your mind, then decide which to keep and blend those into your final draft.*

❮ Looking Back

In your response journal, describe two ideas about the *Jot And Blend* revision strategy valuable for you as a teacher in courses that you presently teach.

❯ Looking Ahead

Describe two places that you can use the *Jot and Blend* strategy or a variation of it in your coming curriculum.

8

Revise Body Paragraphs with Me

When your writing is filled with detail, it has a lot more impact.
Ivan Levison

Don't say the old lady screamed. Bring her on and let her scream.
Mark Twain

An excited group of eighth-grade science students eagerly went to work on the advance organizers for an *Explaining a Process* essay. With their collaborative partners, they brainstormed five to six changes in the earth's surface from which they selected the one that they could best present to their classmates. They moved quickly because their teacher told them that once they called out the physical change they selected, he would remove their choice from the list available to the class. Student pairs announced their choice like kernels of popping corn until the choices disappeared from the front board. I saw the partners move on to jot list specific points about their selected topics as a guide for writing their first drafts. Some of them discussed the order of their lists before they closed their books and wrote their first drafts.

After the energetic and engaged prewriting, I was surprised by the first drafts. As I moved around the room, I saw drafts emerge that touched on all of the points of partners' jot list, but touched them and moved on. Most of the drafts covered a lengthy process with little engaging detail. The drafts were fine for an audience that already knew about the process of a changing surface of the earth. These first drafts were ripe for the revision strategy **Circling Pictures Sentences**.

I have learned never to go negative at this point no matter how accurate a negative review is. I simply say, *Today, we're going to revise body paragraphs.* Then I attempt to be playfully accurate. *Most of your drafts start at the beginning of your report, and you apparently do not come up for air until you conclude with the completion of your selected physical change. You try to include everything that happens in the process. No part is treated with more emphasis than another.*

Here are other examples of drafts ready for the revision strategy of **Circling Picture Sentences.**

♦ AP history students turn in their first weekly abstracts of published articles that amount to an unwieldy sentence summary for each paragraph, leaving out no parts of the source while emphasizing none.

♦ Industrial arts students turn in their descriptions of how to run a digital lathe that reads more like the manual than an invitation to try out the procedures.

♦ The resource students describe a meaningful summer day that reads like a dawn-to-dusk journal entry, only several times as long.

♦ English students begin their critiques with a plot summary of the movie version of *The Great Gatsby* that swells into three pages of meticulous details, overpowering any critique that appears later.

What do you do? You return to the fundamentals of writing. Ask students who they wrote their first drafts for and wait for them to get the answer right. Some will say "For myself," and, with patience on your part, all of them will reach the consensus that they, indeed, wrote their first drafts for themselves. When they all agree, they can focus their attention on *pictures* in their writing that their audiences will need. You will see substantial revision appear. They are ready to dive inside their heads where their authentic thoughts lie. It's just a matter of time.

_____ Lesson for Circling Picture Sentences _____

Circle Picture Sentences with me. I looked over your first drafts, and I know how you feel. I prompted you with a large topic and your drafts covered it all. You touched it from start to finish, and the drafts are long. We wrote our first drafts for ourselves, and now we return to discover a better way to present our thoughts about the topic. Some of our most important ideas receive just a few words.

So here's the deal. I'll circle picture sentences in a recent draft of my own writing, and you do the same. I'll do what comes next, and you can follow me. We will talk about what we have done later, and you can explain why this is an important strategy for making your writing better in every class that you write.

Here's a first draft that I wrote about getting to know my new family.

My three children now call this rabid outdoorsman Grandpa Bud, but long before that, to me he was just Bud, the loving, but directive patron who undertook project after project to make an outdoors-type out of me, the city boy engaged to be married to his first-born daughter. The first project that he undertook? Helping me learn to love ice fishing. He had laid out all the gear that he, his two sons and I needed to survive four days in sub-zero temperatures on a northern most lake in Minnesota. As I pulled up into the circular drive of his house on the Mississippi River, his short stocky frame appeared from the garage in a coverall snowmobile suit, eager to help me fall victim to the lure of the wintry wilds of the snowy north.

I was already quite excited by the unknown—ice fishing in Minnesota with a new family, especially the brothers to replace the one I'd lost. And the excitement coming from them, Ryan, Arlen and Bud, was just as high as mine, the first sign that they were planning a little fun at my expense. The first few miles in the pick-up pulling a trailer full of camping, traveling and fishing gear was filled with raucous and rapid talk.

By the time Bud pulled our rig onto the bank of Otter Bay at Lake Orr's east end, things all took a different turn. The excitement had waned; the six-hour drive with four grown men sitting side-by-side in a pick-up had taken its toll; Bud's exciting stories of earlier trips no longer trumped the discomfort of four guys too close for too long. ① Outside of the truck in the raw brisk air, reality set in. I walked up on a large rock at the edge of the bay and stretched my arms high and then wide. No signs of life for as far as the eye could see. . . .

(For a complete draft, visit www.eyeoneducation.com,
go to this book's page, and follow the links.)

I placed a "1" by the circle beginning *The excitement had waned. . . .* I could write the "most more about" this sentence (see below), and I knew why. It was the first evidence of the fun these three guys were planning to have at my expense, and it wasn't in my first draft. How could I have left it out? I read my addition to circle #1 for the assessment of my audience.

A note on *most more about*

A number of ELA teachers questioned the revision prompt:

Place a "1" by the circle that you can write the most more about.

Most more about, they contend, is not preferred English usage (or "grammar"); it is redundant word choice. Maybe so, but other prompts I have used for this strategy do not help students identify the best sentences to revise and form new body paragraphs. I have tried prompting students with *place a "1" by the circle that*

> *you like the best.*
> *you picture the best in your mind.*
> *you think needs to be expanded.*
> *makes the best topic sentence for a new paragraph.*
> *you can write more about.*
> *you can write the most about.*

None of these lead to expansions that improve the first draft most of the time. The fourth revision prompt, especially, leads students to questions about topic sentences and avoids revision altogether. I have learned by trial and error, mostly error, that *write the most more about* best leads students to identify picture sentences to expand successfully into body paragraphs. So I continue to use *most more about.*

The excitement had waned; the six-hour drive with four grown men sitting side-by-side in a pick-up had taken its toll; Bud's exciting stories of earlier trips no longer trumped the discomfort of four guys too close for too long. **Stuck in the middle with little brother Arlen for the distance, I had squirmed, turned to the right, then the left, put my arm around Arlen to the right, then driver Bud to the left. I was fit to be tied and wondered why we were just sitting perched atop the bank.**

"Let's get some air," I coaxed with a shift of my hips.

"Hold your horses; I've got to park this rig. Hang on," Bud quipped with a planned grin and let the pickup and trailer begin rolling down the steep bank to the lake. My city-slicker eyes saw us picking up speed with nothing to stop us from rolling headlong into the icy lake to our watery graves. Arlen remembers that I opened my mouth wide in horror, *emitted not a sound, but grabbed his leg so hard he thought I'd cut off the circulation. When the pick-up leveled out safely atop the thickly frozen ice, I realized what happened at my expense. I turned on the younger guys with fiery eyes. "You're gonna pay for this," I barked, as they jumped out the passenger side and sprinted across the lake with me in pursuit until we all slowed of exhaustion and agreed that they had pulled off a good one.*

My heart and breathing settled down as I stood outside the truck, and reality settled in. [return to the first draft]

After reading my revision, I asked two questions of the class. The first was *Does this addition fit in this place in my draft?* The students said that it did. I called on three to explain why and heard three good reasons for me to keep this addition in the revised draft.

- ◆ It lightened up the tone of the narrative.
- ◆ You said the brothers were planning a little fun at your expense, but you left out the fun until now.
- ◆ The addition showed us how you become brothers.

The second question was, *Is my addition too long, too short or just about right?* About two-thirds of the class raised their hands for *just about right;* the other third felt it was too long. They all thought I needed to keep it, so the advice I heard was for me to tighten up the wording.

Setting concrete expectations for *Circling Picture Sentences*: I specify exactly the amount of revision I expect from students. I offer a standard expectation to students:1) Circling *4 to 6 sentences* in their *first drafts that make clear pictures return to* their *minds and 2)* expanding *2 of them into body paragraphs* earns them *a target* ($\odot$ = 85 points). I specify the length of each paragraph (4 to 6 sentences). As I observe students circling pictures in their drafts, I may see a need to adjust the expectation for some students in a short conference. Significant revision beyond these expectations earn students the + (+ = 100 points). Examples of significant additional revision include 1) expanding a third picture sentence into a full body paragraph or 2) jotting and blending significant details throughout the first draft.

In response to my model, students numbered two or three circles that they could write *the most more about* and set about doing just that. No talk of body paragraphs, suitable topic sentences, making new or adjusting existing paragraphs. All of that could come later. It was time to do revision.

The first time you use ***Circling Picture Sentences*** as a revision strategy, invite some students to share their additions aloud to the class. To make certain the shared revisions are model revisions, I circulate among the students in search of good examples of revision

REVISE

REFLECT

while students revise. When I find a good one like those below, I ask the student if his addition is an improvement. If he says yes, I agree with him and convince him to share his revision with the class.

Ms. O'Donnell of West Columbus Magnet Academy believes in writing as a major tool for empowering her Emotional-Behavioral Disability (EBD) students to work through issues of anger and other anti-social behavior. She focuses on writing journal entries first semester; she introduces the chance to revise entries periodically after Christmas break. Since the *Circling Picture Sentences* revision strategy readily adjusts to a wide variety of writers, I chose it on my recent visit to her class. From thumbing through Jack's journal, it was obvious that his writing voiced ripples of outburst and criticism, never very subtle. But look at what revision did for the bombastic presentation of his thoughts about teachers.

Teachers don't understand
by James

Teachers are crazy. They think the key to life is school. If I had a penny for every page of work they gave me, I could be a billionaire three times over. Everything they do has something to do with school. They like school so much that they go to it throughout their whole lifes. If you ask them where to get some candy, they go to the school and point you down the hall. I believe the food has something in it that makes you want to learn. If they are on a bus (1) and the bus driver says 50 cents they'll count up all their money. That's why teachers don't understand.

He circles the sentences that make clear pictures return to his mind and writes more about the last one.

If they are on a bus and the bus driver says 50 cents they'll count up all their money. **They will sit on the front row of the bus counting out their money. They start adding it, multiplying it and subtracting like a big deal word problem instead of just giving the driver 50 cents. They make a big deal out of counting money from a shiny red purse and watch it drop into the box.** That's why teachers don't understand.

He's on his way. In his addition to his first picture sentence, subtlety begins to emerge; beneath the veneer of abrupt impatience lies the roots of a more gently satirical mind. When his classmates broke out in applause upon hearing his revision, he showed obvious surprise. When I asked to share his writing as a model others throughout the day, he suppressed a grin and responded, "For real?" Two months later, I returned to East Columbus Magnet Academy, and James proudly hauled out a further revision of his critique of teachers that he had completed on his own.. The entry had grown half again in length and was more richly detailed with a increasing subtlety of voice. I pray that he finds a teacher like Ms. O'Donnell at his high school next year.

Another student, Andrew, more fluent than James, told about his thoughts with little evidence of the full pictures from his mind. His expansion of one sentence into a body paragraph has served well as a model for other middle school writers.

① On January 20, 2009 all things will change. Can you believe that we have the first African-American President of the United States? This is a great thing for not just our economy, but our country. I will always remember the moment Barrack Obama was elected. I think this situation will better us and all around our country. This was a miracle for a lot of people across the world. To me after his four-year term is over, I think he should run for president again. To some citizen this was disappointing and also surprising. Here's another little story I came up with. Barrack is going to be our president of the United States. He is going to be our president because he knows what's good for our economy. He wants to be our savior for the next four years. He wants to make sure that we are safe. He knows what is right for us. John McCain didn't stand a chance against Barrack Obama. Also, Obama will be our first African American president.

He shared this expansion of the opening sentence into an introductory paragraph aloud with his classmates.

Things will change in Washington, D.C. and many other cities and countries. Things will change because we will have a new president of the United States. This president's name is Barack Obama and he will make changes everywhere. There are supposed to be millions of people outside the Whitehouse when he becomes president. Imagine how packed it would be with stands and bleachers and platforms around. There will be people taking photos of people meeting other people. Imagine all the work to set it all up. Imagine all the food the people from the Whitehouse will have to buy. Imagine all of the commotion the planners will have to go through to get all these people in and out of Washington, D.C.

His new introduction transitioned nicely to the next sentence from his first draft, *Can you believe that we have the first African-American president of the United States?* This is the way **Circling Picture Sentences** works with all ages and abilities of students. Andrew expanded circles number 2 and 3 on his first draft in a similar fashion. With this kind of success, it was time to ask him what parts of his writing he could do without, he said, "Everything after 'Here's another little story I came up with.' I was just filling up the page." That was obvious to me and probably you, too, but more important, it became obvious to him. When students learn to fill out the details of their thoughts, they more readily pare away the filler.

An older student, tenth-grader Kelsey of Sequoyah High School of Canton, Georgia, found **Circling Picture Sentences** precisely the strategy her draft needed. Her teacher, Mrs. Chambers, complimented her on her expository strategies; she didn't resort to a plot summary. She pointed out that her examples of loneliness need much more detail. Enter **Circling Picture Sentences**.

> Loneliness is a common theme in the life of every human being, but although it is an emotion felt by everyone, it rarely manifests itself in the same way in any two people. One person may feel lonesome for one reason, someone else another. Just as diverse as the reasons for feeling lonely are the ways people cope with those feelings. Three examples of the diversity of loneliness appear in John Steinbeck's <u>Of Mice and Men</u>. The farmhand, Crooks, Candy and Curly's wife all suffer from loneliness, but the causes for their suffering and the way they cope with their loneliness are entirely different. These differences, of course, dictate the different outcomes in the story
>
> The third instance of loneliness focuses on Curly's wife. She is kept cooped up in her house by her foul husband. Whenever she does get to leave the house, none of the ranch hands associate with her because she is "trouble," and they call her a "tart." (1)

Kelsey added these details before and after the circled picture sentence.

> It is obvious that she gets no companionship from Curly since she reaches out in desperation to anyone who will pay her the least bit of attention. Whenever she does get to leave the house, none of the ranch hands associate with her because she is "trouble," and they call her a "tart." Actually, they are attracted to her, but shun her because she is the wife of the rancher's son. They fear if they get involved with her, they will get fired and have to leave the ranch. This isolation leaves her only

simple-minded Lennie as a possible solution for her lonliness, and that ill-fated relationship begins. What begins as a solution for loneliness results in the ultimate loneliness, death without experiencing a satisfying human relationship.

Student Self-Assessment

Students complete their reflection of the ***Circling Picture Sentences*** strategy by assessing the degree to which they met your stated expectation for their revision. When they expand 2 picture sentences into full body paragraphs, they assess themselves a target ⊙ (⊙ = 85 points). If they revise less, they self-assess a bar ⊟ (⊟ = 70 points). When they revise more (a third expansion or jotting and blending vivid details throughout the draft), they self-assess a plus + (+ = 100 points).

The first thing to learn from this chapter is to model this strategy with any mode of your writing whatsoever. Yes, I used the model of my ice-fishing narrative in an industrial arts class as well as English class to demonstrate ***Circling Picture Sentences***. I used the writing I had. The students knew I wasn't a skilled engineer or carpenter. They expected me to write about personal experience, not how to miter the corners of a box or drawer. They also saw how my revision brought life to my narrative. It inspired them to enliven the presentation of their *Explain a Process* essays required of them before they moved into the shop to start a project operating expensive equipment for the first time.

Once students have experienced ***Circling Picture Sentences***, I let them articulate the benefits of the strategy. The lists vary from class to class, so I have learned to listen carefully and summarize exactly what I hear each class of students say. One group concluded the following:

♦ You can add more in revision than you wrote the first time.

♦ Circled sentences become topic sentences in a new paragraph.

♦ A picture is worth a thousand words, but you only need 4 to 6 sentences.

♦ Not every addition improves your first draft.

♦ This strategy made me write some details I didn't know I knew.

Conclusion: See if a student can make a concluding statement about revising body paragraphs. One student quite clearly state, "The body paragraphs of your writing provide the substance of your thoughts. When you focus on the pictures in your mind, you find ways to make the substance more interesting." I would add, *Circling picture sentences helps you emphasize on paper what is most important in your mind.*

The next time you use this revision strategy, students can work in stations, small groups, triads or collaborative pairs. ***Circling Picture Sentences*** once completed is easy to remember. The smaller the group, the more efficient is the use of class time.

LEARN

Circling Picture Sentences with Marginal Writers

In the introduction to chapters 7–14, I mentioned that effective revision strategies automatically adjust to writers of different learning styles and abilities. *Circling Picture Sentences* adjusts especially well. Instead of saying, *Circle four sentences that make a picture come back to your mind,* replace the word "sentence" with "parts of your writing" for less fluent writers.

Look at this writing of a special education student in middle grades. He didn't write much in his first draft since he was writing just for himself. It helped him remember what he was thinking about peacocks and pigs. Notice how readily he circled parts of his three sentences without questioning my directions.

Picocks and Pigs

Picocks is real Big. They have Different colors on they fethers. A Picock is just a bird. Some people does not like birds but I Don't know why. Some people think pigs are Dirty but they not. They play in mud But that how pigs bath.   ①

Here's what he added to the circle he could write the most more about.

Pigs are kinda Dirty because they bath in mud. But they really be cleaning their self because the rocks scape against their skin. That how they clean their self every day.

Later I received an e-mail from his teacher stating that the experience gave him confidence that he could write much more substantially than ever before. Since this revision experience, he has never written a first draft shorter than ten sentences, and the drafts are gaining in fluency and clarity.

❮ Looking Back

In your response journal, describe two features of the *Circling Picture Sentences* that held value for you as a teacher in courses that you presently teach.

❯ Looking Ahead

Where in the future of courses you teach do you see opportunities to use *Circling Picture Sentences*?

9

Revise Whole Drafts with Me

*My aim is to put down on paper what I see and what I feel
in the best and simplest way.*
Ernest Hemingway

Many secondary teachers who appreciate my approach to revision feel the need to prompt students to revise their entire first drafts the first time they ask them to revise. I understand their point. At the same time, I have seen that with writers of all ages and abilities, revision starts best in small pieces until students accept and become confident, authentic and self-propelled revisers. Remember Andrew's revision in chapter 8. He expanded two *picture sentences* into full body paragraphs in the first half of his draft. When he saw that these improvements created a draft longer than he had ever written, he readily admitted that the second half of his first draft was filler and deleted it. Students who do not see the need for revision learn better by taking small steps before they lengthen their strides. Marginal writers are empowered by focusing on only parts of their first drafts. Better student writers seldom take suggestions to revise parts of their first drafts as criticism of their writing. Still, I empathize with the points I have heard teachers make:

♦ At some point, we have to quit this pussy-footing around revising parts of a draft and work on the whole paper.

♦ I can't help it if students are overwhelmed by revising complete drafts, we have to make up for lost time.

♦ Sorry, but my students' entire first drafts need serious help; I'm talking nothing short of a total overhaul.

♦ Focusing on the revision of sentences or paragraphs makes sense for younger students, but not secondary students.

♦ Maybe English teachers can follow a stair-step approach to revision; I teach science and cannot see that as an option for me.

So when your administrators, your curriculum standards or your own intuitions pressure you to start with the revision of entire first drafts, use this chapter to help your students revise whole drafts successfully. ***Framing Pictures in a Draft***, follows the same fundamentals for authentic revision as ***Jot and Blend*** (chapter 7) and ***Circling Picture Sentences*** (chapter 8) strategies. It is simple, concrete and easy to understand. It applies to all modes of writing and ability levels of student writing. It requires students to consider possibilities and make a clear decision based on those possibilities.

_____ Lesson for Framing Pictures in a Draft _____

Frame pictures in your first drafts with me. *Your teacher and I agree that it is time for us all to revise our complete drafts. Some of our drafts have too many parts and need to go. I cannot tell you which parts in your drafts they are, but I can help you identify which ones your drafts can do without. Some of your drafts contain parts that are fairly well developed, but they need to become robust and powerful with pictures. Some of your drafts do not emphasize one part over another, and readers rely on -emphasis for understanding. I assure you* ***Framing Pictures in a Draft*** *will help us all.*

I start with a model from an eighth-grade teacher, Ms. Crooks of East Columbus Magnet Academy, Georgia. She enjoys writing with her students and claims to be learning to write along with them. In this first draft, she analyzes a main character of *A Raisin in the Sun*, a play by Lorraine Hansberry from the 1950s. She reads the play with her students every year, remarking that the issues of fifty years ago continue to resonate with every group of students. She models how to identify the pictures or ideas that lie beneath the surface of her first draft. She chooses this revision strategy because it helps her students stand back from their drafts and see each of the components of their drafts clearly all at once. Then, and only then, can they decide what to do with each of the parts. Here are Ms. Crooks' first two paragraphs of a character sketch of a main character, Walter Lee Youngers.

> In *A Raisin in the Sun*, Lorraine Hansberry narrates the story of the Youngers, a lower-class black family who struggles to gain middle class acceptance./As the play opens, a sixty-year-old character, Mama, waits on an insurance check that was left by her recently departed husband. The drama focuses on how the $10,000 will be spent by the surviving family./Her son,
>
> **A-1**   Walter Lee, wants to be a better provider for the family by using the money to invest in a liquor store./Mama disagrees with his plan, and the conflict begins. She prefers spending part of the money on a down payment for a house in an all-white neighborhood which Walter rejects out of hand. Mama also wants some of the money for her daughter, Beneatha's, medical schooling./

INVITE

MODEL

Walter Lee, sometimes referred to as "brother," is full of energy and ideas about his dream that he is certain will end all of his economic and social problems. His social background, habits and gestures all point to him as a strong character. Yet throughout the play he displays his lack of business sense. When he meets George Murchinson, an educated college student, he is frustrated by the interaction. He accuses George of talking over his head. When George quips "Good night, Prometheus," he has no idea what he means, nor how accurately the comment applies to him. George speaks of Prometheus, the god punished for giving fire to mortals. He was chained to Mt. Caucasus where eagles tore out his liver that grew back every night.

On a separate sheet of paper titled REVISION in red ink (bolded here), Ms. Crooks expanded her Frame A-1 to clarify her introduction of Walter Lee. Since these details about Walter Lee did not appear later in her draft, they fit in the introduction and serve to engage the reader immediately by intensifying the conflict. A majority of her students agreed that she had to have this addition in her opening paragraph. I did, too. Ms. Crook also deleted two frames from later in her draft because her writing could do with out them.

REVISION

A-1 *He just knows that opening a liquor store will be fast money because he and all of the people he knows drink a lot in their free time. He ignores the fact that he has no experience running a business. He pushes his idea with no holds barred. After all, he's the only son, and the Youngers need the new man of the house to step up to the challenge.*

Setting Concrete Expectations for Framing Pictures in a Draft

I specify exactly what amount of revision I expect from students in ***Framing Pictures in a Draft***. I offer a standard expectation to students: 1) expanding two of their picture frames to body paragraphs, 2) moving one frame to a different place and 3) deleting 1 to 3 frames earns them a target (⊙ = 85 points). I specify the length of each paragraph (4 to 6 sentences). As I observe students framing their drafts, a student and I may see a need to adjust the expectation in a short conference. Significant revision beyond these expectations earn students the + (+ = 100 points). Examples of significant additional revision include 1) expanding a third frame into a full body paragraph, 2) rewriting a second frame or 3) jotting and blending details throughout the first draft.

REVISE

Read through your selected draft completely, noting where the pictures that lie behind the words begin and end. Then return to the beginning of the draft and focus your mind on the first picture that appears in your mind. When you see that the first picture ends and a second one begins, draw a forward slash (/). Draw a line from the top of the slash to the right-hand edge of the paper. From the bottom, draw a line to the left-hand edge of the paper. Then count picture frames and write the total at the top of the page. Complete the following steps.

1. *Read over your draft yet again and place the letter **A** (for add) by the frames that you can write the most more about (target of two additions).*

2. *Check your draft again for the frames that your drafts can do without (target of 1 to 3). Place the letter **D** by each and delete them in your revised or final draft.*

   Note: As I move about the room observing students identify frames for deletion, I conference with students who have marked more off than 6 to 8 frames in their drafts. I prompt them to consider combining closely related frames into a single paragraph. Students with a dozen or more frames often decide to delete the majority of their frames and spend time elaborating fully on the most important ones.

3. *Place an **M** (for move) by the frame(s) that fits better in another part of the draft (minimum 1), then draw an arrow to the better location.*

4. *Place an **R** (for rewrite) by the frames that are better written another way (minimum 1).*

5. *A peer (or two peers) tell you if your planned revisions will help them understand and enjoy the draft better as readers. Peers mark the choices that they approve with a (+).*

6. *On a separate, clean sheet of paper, students write everything that comes to their minds about the **A** frames and the rewriting of the **R** frame(s).*

7. *Students create a final draft that includes the additions, deletions, moves and rewrites appropriately.*

I have yet to meet students with insurmountable problems marking off the pictures in their drafts. Some appear to hold out just because I'm asking them to do something new. Once a capable writer said, "I can't tell where one picture begins and where one ends." He agreed that the first sentence created a picture, so I told him I'd start reading his sentences aloud and he should tell me when the picture changed. On the fourth sentence of silence, his buddy next him said. "Aw, man. You know the picture changed right then. I saw it over here." The buddy continued with more directness that I ever could: "Just make yourself try harder to see them. Then you're good to go. Trust me, you got pictures in there." I had to concur and shook my head in agreement. The questioning student began to frame his draft accurately.

Middle School. To solicit revision on a topic that addressed a standard from the state health curriculum, Ms. Myers helped her eighth-grade students at East Columbus Magnet Academy frame the pictures in their first drafts. The topic prompt required students to write a paper to a friend in class who is having difficulty staying awake. Several students used the writing task to summarize what they had learned in class. Tiffany, however, became authentically engaged in the hypothetical issue as she pre-wrote her thoughts for the task. In the lead to her first draft, she starts by putting her audience of one at ease.

First Draft

Are you aware that over 85% of all students have fallen asleep in class more than once? I wasn't. I knew I had fallen asleep. If you think about it, ever since you started school, you have seen many students fall asleep. So what are the causes? We'll look at some of them and see the same effect./Sleeping in class.

A student might fall asleep in class because they didn't get enough sleep outside of school. When they sleep in class, they miss the information they need to pass a test./For example, John stays up until 1:00 a.m. playing a new video game he got for his birthday. He goes to school and falls asleep in math class. He doesn't get the information he needs, so he fails his math test./

Unfortunately, there are other more serious reasons why a student might fall asleep in class. If a student is depressed or stressed, they might stay up and think about things that they shouldn't have to worry about. When they go to school, that might be the only time they don't stress, so they relax and fall asleep./For example, Baley overhead her mother and father talking about the bills. She started to worry and think that she wouldn't get to stay in her house and they were going to be poor./When she goes to school she is tired and falls asleep. Her teacher gives her detention every time she falls asleep and she sleeps in detention.

A-1

Note that in her revision, Tiffany does what she needs to do to show the audience the picture in her mind for frame A-1. She does more than add sentences to the frame; she rewrites it completely. When I see teachers and students place their focus on the pictures in their writing, they decide between rewriting a frame completely or simply adding to it. The choice occurs to them naturally.

REVISION

A-1   For example, late one night Baley tiptoed down the stairs and peeked around the corner to hear what her parents were talking about. Her dad mentioned that he didn't get the raise he needed so they wouldn't be able to pay the bills on time. Baley thought, *What if we lose our house? We will be on the streets? Will we be poor?* She started staying awake at night thinking about the things that she could do to help her parents.

Her revision of Frame A-1 leads seamlessly to the sentence that follows, *When she goes to school she is tired and falls to sleep.* As part of her audience, we picture clearly why Baley sleeps away her time in school. When students see their drafts as a sequence of picture frames and feel empowered to add (A), delete (D) and move (M) the frames, their sense of control is obvious. On the same topic, *Causes of Falling Asleep in School,* Cedric adds to one frame (A-2) and deletes (D) two others in order to combine some of the content from all three into a single, improved frame.

First Draft—Causes of Falling Asleep in Class

A-1   Students fall asleep in class for many reasons. They sleep because of boredom, fatigue or even stress. It is not hard to figure out when sleeping is affecting a student in class. Some features you could see would be: slouching,

D   falling behind in class, not paying attention, getting bad grades and acting lost in class. On the other hand, features you wouldn't physically see would be:

D   depression, household problems, staying up late, not getting enough sleep and emotional problems.

A student falling asleep cannot always be controlled by the students. As stated in the last paragraph household problems may actually be the reason. Because of problems at the house, this could cause the student to become depressed. The effect could be lack of sleep. This could cause the student to sleep in class.

As I read through Cedric's plan for adding and deleting, I thought, *You don't want to delete all of this content, now do you?* When I saw his revision, I was relieved. He had deleted two frames so that we could blend the content of each into Frame A-1.

REVISION

A-1

Some obvious features would be: slouching, falling behind in class work, not paying attention to discussions and getting bad grades on tests. Other features are more mental than physical: depression, household problems and different kinds of emotional problems. These symptoms are not all ones the students are responsible for, but they all cause the student not to get enough sleep. As students progress through school, their bodies feel the need to make up for lost sleep time.

Cedric's revision is a classic reminder that we write first drafts for ourselves. He didn't need to conference about what to do. When he framed the pictures behind the ideas in his first draft, he knew exactly what to do. All writers return to their first drafts to revise them so that others understand them clearly.

High School. To be sure, when I presented students with the option to add, delete and move parts of their writing simultaneously, most chose only one of the three options to revise. That was until I happened upon an additional directive. In a typical class, students marked off any where from 4 to 20 frames. So I asked the students to add up the number of frames that they marked off in their first drafts and place the number at the top of the first page. As I moved around the room, I reported the numbers as they appeared on each paper: *I see an 8, a 17, a 12; here's a 23, a 6, a 13 and a 19. Hmm,* I mused aloud, *How many separate frames (or ideas) does an essay of 300 to 500 words need?* I waited for a response; obviously, the question is not pressing on students' minds, but they humored me and responded. One said "Sixteen" because she had 16 frames in her draft; others say "Five" thinking I am fishing for the formula of the 5-paragraph essay. Still others say, "As many as you want." None are viable answers. Finally, someone, usually a soft voice, pipes up, "The number that makes your audience see what you are trying to write the best."

Of course, I take the lead, continuing, *I know you like your topic or you wouldn't be writing about it; but how about me, your unsuspecting reader?; how many pictures do I want you to drag me through on a topic I didn't choose to write about?* They usually catch my point, and I set the target expectation for the revision task.

> *Place **A**'s by two or three frames that you could write the most more about.*

> *Place **D**'s by a minimum of two frames (or write me a note explaining why your paper cannot do without any of the frames).*

> *Place an **M** by one part that is better located somewhere else in your paper.*

Recently, I presented **Framing Pictures in a Draft** to Mr. Turner's tenth-grade World Literature class in McDowell County High School, North Carolina. I moved about the room, encouraging wide use of A's, D's and M's. I noted that Ally chose only to add to three frames of her first draft. She did like so many first-time users of **Framing Pictures in a Draft**.

Revised Draft of *Music and Your Brain*

A-1   In the book <u>The Secret Power of Music</u> by David Tame, he writes, "music is more than a language; it is the language of languages. It can be said that of all the arts, there is none other that more powerfully moves and changes the consciousness." **Music can move people physically and mentally. When music moves people physically, they start to dance. The movement affects change in their consciousness and the people around them. When music moves people mentally, their mood changes, sometimes for the better, sometimes for the worse. We have all learned what kind of music points our minds in these two directions. People say things more clearly when they say them through music. The language is so clear it causes us to change.**

What a simple and clarifying addition to the quote that Ally found in one of the sources for her research essay. Following a quick read of her draft, I was convinced that she, indeed, did not need to delete or move any of the frames in her draft.

In the same class, Kaitlin's revision shows how she used all three options in the first four frames of her draft. Note how all three working together made a first draft that she had written only for herself open up to an audience.

First Draft of *The Hanoverian*

A-1   Show-jumping is one of the most well-known equestrian sports available. It is a popular sport for competing riders. Many different breeds of horse can be found competing in the many events offered for this sport. /One of the most

A-2   successful breeds of horses for the sport is the Hanoverian. /

D   Hanoverians have the build and movement needed for successful competing show-jumpers. /According to Horse Show Central, "The horse must have powerful muscles, especially in the hindquarters to provide the spring for high jumps. A long, extended stride in the gallop allows more speed rather than a

M   shorter stride that makes for scratchy leaps." These are the requirement for show-jumpers if they are to succeed, /and Hanoverians have these. "The back is medium length with adequate loins giving the power a jumper needs," says Horse Show Central of the Hanoverian.

Although Kaitlin created the additions on a separate sheet of paper, the results of the adds, deletes and moves produce this more informative draft.

Revised Draft of *The Hanoverian*

Show-jumping is one of the most well-known equestrian sports available. It requires riders to get their horses to jump over a series of obstacles without knocking any part of them down. Each pole knocked down is a fault and it adds time to the final time taken by horse and rider to complete the obstacle course. At the end, of course, the rider and horse with the lowest time wins. It has become a popular sport for competing riders. Many different breeds of horses compete in the many events offered for this sport.

One of the most successful breeds of horses for the sport is the Hanoverian. Hanoverians are a warmblood horse that come from Germany and are seen in the Olympic Games and other English riding competitions. They are one of the oldest, most numerous, and most successful of the warmbloods. They were first used by royalty as carriage horse. When they were bred with Thoroughbred blood, they became more agile and useful for competition. The Hanoverian is known for a good temperament, athleticism, beauty, and grace.

According to Horse Show Central, "The horse must have powerful muscles, especially in the hindquarters to provide the spring for high jumps. A long, extended stride in the gallop will allows more speed rather than a shorter stride that makes for scratchy leaps." These are the requirement for show-jumpers if they are to succeed, and Hanoverians have these. "The back is medium length with adequate loins giving the power a jumper needs," says Horse Show Central of the Hanoverian.

I remind you that all of the above changes appeared in the writing of students with little help from me or their teacher, Mr. Turner. *Framing Pictures in a Draft* helped them mark off the parts of their draft for possible revision and choose which parts to expand, delete or move. Our job was to keep them engaged in reaching the expectations we set for revision.

Student Self-Assessment: Students complete their reflection of the *Framing Pictures in a Draft* strategy by assessing the degree to which they meet your stated expectation for their revision. When they expand 2 frames, rewrite 1 frame and delete 1 to 3 frames, they

REFLECT

assess themselves a target ⊙ (⊙ = 85 points). If they revise less, they self-assess a bar ⊟ (⊟ = 70 points). When they revise more (a third expansion, a second rewrite or jotting and blending throughout the draft), they self-assess a plus + (+ = 100 points).

If you have already practiced letting students read their first drafts and revisions aloud to the whole class for responses such as *What is strong?* and *What questions do you have?*, shift to smaller response groups. I have been especially impressed with teachers who call pairs of students *revision consultants* and let each person read his paper aloud to his partner. When the students have finished revising, prompt them to

1. *Join your revision consultant and take turns reading your first drafts aloud to one another, showing how you framed pictures in your draft.*

2. *Read the additions you made to the "A-1" frame and write down your partner's response to the following two questions in the margin.*

The question	Possible notes in the margin		
Does the addition fit?	*The addition fits.*	*The addition does not fit.*	
About the length?	*Too much*	*Add more*	*About right*

3. *Show the frames marked for deletion and write down your partner's response in the margin: agree or disagree.*

4. *Show the frames marked for relocation and write down your partner's response in the margin: agree or disagree.*

Some teachers make the time to review these revisions before they allow students to move on to creating a final draft. Interestingly, reviewing the revision of writers and their partners takes considerably less time than if the teachers responded to all of the revisions themselves. Teachers who review students' revision and response find the authenticity of student interaction quite remarkable. I could not agree with them more. When students are empowered with a specific routine for responding to revision, they show no hesitance and a great deal of engagement in the process.

A group of eighth-graders drew several conclusions about the revision strategy, *Framing Pictures in a Draft*:

LEARN

♦ Framing really helped me see what I need to do.

♦ Since I'm good at revising words and sentences, changing the whole draft today was easy.

♦ Framing helped me understand revision for the first time.

♦ Framing made me feel in control.

♦ I never thought about moving parts of my writing around. That really felt different, kind of neat.

♦ I liked having a consultant. She helped me see I needed to write even more.

Conclusion: Not all of these comments actually present a lesson learned, but they do reflect how well the strategy validated revision in the minds of the students. It reaffirms the importance of presenting possibilities to students for revision and giving them choices. The resulting student engagement leads to authentic revision.

On subsequent uses of this revision strategy, allow students to partner with different revision consultants to ensure that they present their writing to a variety of people in their classroom audience.

Framing Pictures in a Draft with Marginal Writers

For some reason, a number of students stall on their first experience with *Framing Pictures in a Draft*. While there is value in revising your own writing along with your students, it is equally important to spot and conference with students who stall out on the first attempt at a new revision strategy. This is especially true for *Framing Pictures in a Draft*. Interestingly, these stalled revisers are often at both ends of the spectrum of writers.

For marginal writers, I take a moment to walk them through the procedure, employing a series of questions and comments.

♦ *What's the picture in your mind as you read your first sentence?*

♦ *Where does this picture stop and the second one appear?* When they tell me, I ask them to take their red pen and place where the picture ended. I may draw the line from the slash to the right margin, then let the student draw the line from the bottom of the slash to the left margin.

♦ *Now it's your turn to mark a slash at the end of the second picture and connect the top of the slash to the right and the bottom to the left.*

I stick around to see that they mark off at least two more frames in a way that makes sense. Rarely have any students required me to continue prompting them through their entire first draft. For certain, once they have framed a draft successfully, they are prepared to frame the next draft with little or no help. In Ms. O'Donnell's eighth-grade Emotional-Behavioral Disability (EBD) class of 14 boys at East Columbus Magnet Academy, Elijah caught on to framing and moved decisively through his first draft.

First Draft of *Thoughts on Music*

A-1	Music is a major part of my life. I couldn't live without music for even one day./Imagine you are at a football game and you need something to help hype
D	you up. That's what music is like./I was playing football for Fort Middle School.
A-2	Coach told us to make a song./You hit your pants two times, then clap one time, then pat your pants two more times. Then clap to times./Music is the life./

REVISION

A-1   Music is a major part of my life. I couldn't live without music for even one day. It hypes you up. Music can make you sing. You can dance to music. You can make music with anything—pots, balls, hands. Music helps you calm down too. Music is good to listen to. Music keeps you out of bad decisions. Music is a way to make money. A lot of people love music. Imagine you are at a football game and you need something to help hype you up. That's what music is like.

I was playing football for Fort Middle School. Coach told us to make a song. So we did

I don't know about how you read Elijah's first addition and deletion, but they fill in my understanding of music's major role in his life better than the original. It also leads nicely up to a second paragraph about his connection with music while playing for a coach at another Columbus middle school. You can go to this book's page on www.eyeoneducation.com for an additional example from Ms. O'Donnell's EBD students.

I didn't have to look far to understand why all of the boys in Ms. O'Donnell's EBD class moved confidently with a new strategy for revision. They wrote in their journals daily from Day 1 of school; they saw Ms. O'Donnell and her security paraprofessional write everything that she asked the students to write. The day I introduced **Framing Pictures in a Draft,** she wrote.

First Draft of **The Laundry Monster and Me**

A-2   The laundry monster is a huge pile of clothes that lives in my house. It shrinks and then it grows./Every time I walk into the living area near the laundry room some of the monster's edges are creeping out the door./Sometimes,

A-1   I close the door so I don't have to see the laundry monster, but the next thing I know, it's oozing out of the door again. sometimes I could almost swear that the laundry monster is actually alive./Once in a while, I get so tired of the

A-3   monster, I push every bit of its gushy mess into my van and take it to the laundry-monster-mat./There I attack it bit by bit until it becomes a nice tame folded pile of sparkling clean clothes. When I return home, it gets placed all over the house in drawers and closets. It doesn't matter, though. It eventually creeps out of those places and crawls back into my laundry room to scare me once again. /

She rewrites frame A-1 and shares it before she directs her students in steps of revision.

R E V I S I O N

Seeing the laundry monster upsets me so that I want to hide away from it. So I close the door to the sad laundry room. Before I know it, however, that vicious monster starts oozing shirt sleeves and pant legs out of the door, under the door and around its edges until finally the door pops open and the whole nasty mess of laundry spills out of the room. It may sound crazy, but I could almost swear that the monster is actually alive.

As she makes pictures from her mind clear for her audience of students, they see how to improve the clarity of the pictures behind their writing.

At the other end of the spectrum of student writers, some students stall because their first drafts are actually quite well written. and they do not see the need to revise. In fact, the best writers I've met in my travels often admit that few teachers they meet ever require them to revise. I usually smile and quip, *Is that so? Well, You'll be excited you met me. I help everybody revise. Everybody I work with gets to revise…that is if their first draft is good enough to qualify for revision.* This light touch usually works. I know they need help understanding that a revision strategy is not an indictment of their first draft. It is a compliment: this draft is worth revising. Further, ***Framing Pictures in a Draft*** is a way of considering most of the possibilities for revision at one time. I continue, *Who knows, once you revise parts of your draft, you may decide to keep it the way it was.* This reasoning often sells the student on moving with the revision strategy. It's absolutely amazing—I have yet to meet the student who marked his draft for revision and then decided to keep the draft exactly the way it was originally. Here's a case in point. In an advanced placement American history class, Joseph writes as a mayor of a thriving middle Georgia farming community, Dublin. He said he liked his letter the way he drafted it; it said what it needed to; there's power in simplicity and conciseness. Yet, he agreed to submit his draft to the ***Framing Pictures in a Draft*** out of deference to me as an invited guest speaker. As a result, he added

Dear President Lincoln,

My name is Joseph McAfee, and I would like to express how my community and I feel about the subject of slavery. We live in a small town and are a slave community. **The average number of slaves we have around here is very high as each family has an average of five slaves. We all work with a large plantation that grows cotton, and our system works very well.** As mayor of Dublin, Georgia, I would like to express why I agree with slavery.

The main reason that I agree with slavery is for the reason that our community needs its slaves. 80% of the workers in this town are slaves. Without them our community's economy would go downhill fast. **We have tried white workers before on many occasions, and they always perform unsatisfactorily. Blacks work longer and more productively in the fields during the long, hot middle Georgia summers.**

Another reason why I agree with slavery is, unlike the cheap labor slaves that people have in the North, we keep our slaves well fed and well sheltered. **Although I cannot speak for other southern towns, I can speak for Dublin. We give our slaves a new pair of slacks and a shirt every two months. We provide them with decent size homes and let them harvest all that they want to eat out of our gardens.** I hear that in the North, the workers live crammed up and barely have enough to feed their families. If the condition of our slaves is not justified, how can you claim that their condition is?

The last reason our community supports slavery is that although it may seem wrong, it has been around for thousands of years. We do not see why it has become such a big issue here in America. It feels better to enslave those whom you do not know than to enslave your own American brothers and sisters.

Though this letter may mean little to you, I would just like to inform you of how a little community in our growing country feels on the issue of slavery. I wish you will consider our thoughts when deciding how to handle the issue of slavery.

Sincerely,
Joseph McAfee

Joseph chose to include his additions in his final draft and mentioned two valuable lessons he had learned: "Up to now I thought good writing meant impressive vocabulary; now I know the words have to paint a picture for the reader. Mine didn't; now they do." He continued, "And everybody needs to revise; why hasn't anybody told me that before?" I wasn't sure of the answer, but said, *Maybe you weren't ready to hear it until today.* He nodded his head in a thoughtful response. Of course, I wasn't the one what told him he needed to revise at all; he figured that out himself as he was framing the pictures in his draft.

❮ Looking Back

In your response journal, describe two features of the ***Framing Pictures in a Draft*** revision strategy that were valuable for you as a teacher in courses that you presently teach.

❯ Looking Ahead

What is coming up in your curriculum that invites you to use ***Framing Pictures in a Draft*** with your students?

Empowering Students to Write and RE-write
Session Guide #3 for Professional Learning Teams

Responding to

Chapter 7: Revise words and phrases with me—*Jot and Blend, Slotting for Specific Nouns*

Chapter 8: Expand body paragraphs with me—*Circling Pictures Sentences*

Chapter 9: Revise whole drafts with me—*Framing Pictures in a Draft*

Before joining *Professional Learning Team (PLT) Session #3*

Make sure you have written your response to these topics in your journal.

1. Describe the classroom experience in which you helped your students understand the derivation of the term *revision* and what "picturing again" invites them to do to their writing.

2. In two or three sentences, explain how rereading first drafts leads writers naturally and seamlessly to explanations of what they mean.

Exemplars

As you read through student revision that used the strategies of chapters 7-9, select the ones that best illustrated their use. Bring the example of your own personal revision that you used as an effective model for your students to follow.

Discussion questions for *PLT Session #3*

1. What advantage or disadvantage is there to jotting additional details to a first draft on a separate sheet of paper before blending it into the text (chapter 7)?

2. How do you explain the immediate carry-over from *Slotting for Specific Nouns* to students' independent writing (chapter 7)?

3. Explain the advantage of asking students to *Circle Picture Sentences* in a first draft instead of circling *possible topic sentences* to expand into body paragraphs (chapter 8).

4. Describe a situation in which it is more important for students to revise parts of their first drafts instead of tackling the entire draft (chapter 9).

5. Should there be clear pictures behind the words of all writing (chapter 9)?

Compiling *Professional Learning Portfolios*

Bring artifacts of your plans and students' revision that you have gathered to include in your *Professional Learning Portfolio*. Share your ideas for adding to your portfolio and listen to the additions of other teachers.

10

Work on Style of Writing with Me

The difference between the right word and the almost right word is the difference between lightning and the lightning bug.
Mark Twain

A house in the country is not the same as a country house.
Gertrude Stein

In composing, as a general rule, run a pen through every other word you have written; you have no idea what vigor it will give your style.
Sydney Smith

On tests of written expression, students' scores of writing style remain the hardest to boost. In one state I work, scores of ideas, organization and conventions inch upward over the years, but not scores of writing style. Scores on the National Assessment of Educational Progress (NAEP) corroborate this trend. This puzzling plateau of scores of writing style just should not be, especially not scores on tests that define style so clearly. Look at the descriptors of style on any acceptable state or national rubric. The national writing test (NAEP) defines a proficient writer as follows

---

Assessment Content at Grade 8
THE NATION'S REPORT CARD

Proficient: Eighth-grade students performing at the *Proficient* level should be able to produce an effective and fully developed response within the time allowed that shows an understanding of both the writing task that they have been assigned and the audience they are expected to address. The writing should be organized, making use of techniques such as sequencing or a clearly marked beginning and ending, and it should make use of details and some elaboration to support and develop the main idea of the piece. **Their writing should include precise language and some variety in sentence structure, and it may show analytical, evaluative and creative thinking.** The grammar, spelling, punctuation and capitalization in the work should be accurate enough to communicate with the reader; there may be some errors, but they should not get in the way of meaning.

I prefer the description of style from Colorado's *"Kid-Friendly" 4-Point Rubric for Students* that defines what style is without ornamentation.

Colorado Department of Education Student Assessment Unit

4 Points (exceeds the standard): My writing is clear and does what the prompt asked me. My errors in spelling and punctuation are so few they wouldn't bother you.

Style

- My word choice is awesome. The words fit the prompt well.
- I tried to use interesting words or descriptions to make pictures in the reader's mind.
- My sentences are not all the same. I used different sentences.
- My writing is neat and almost perfect.

(http://www.cde.state.co.us/cdeassess/documents/csap/ rubrics/Kid-Friendly4-PtRubricStudents_Eng.pdf)

The Colorado rubric expects extensive variety of sentence lengths, structures and beginnings; the NAEP expects some variety in sentence structure. Yet they both present the essence of writing style—precise word choice and sentence variety. In any state in the United States, all we have to do to beef up students' scores of style is condition them to a rich vocabulary and a variety of sentences like the ones they enjoy when they listen or read. Most strategies that teach style just don't register on students' scores of writing style, that is, except one.

This vehicle for boosting scores of writing style has been around since the 1960s: sentence-combining practice. Psycholinguist John Mellon of Harvard University presented the notion of teaching students to combine sentences and to name the combinations they created based on Noam Chomsky's transformational-generative grammar. Mellon found that with sentence-combining practice, students' writing grew significantly in syntactic maturity, showing two years growth in a single year. From the sentence-combining research of the next ten years, we learned that, indeed, sentence-combining practice transferred mature sentence patterns immediately to the writing of students, especially **without** the teaching of the grammatical terminology. I have heard a number of experienced master teachers of writing say, "Give me a good literature text and a solid collection of sentence-combining lessons, and class after class of confident and mature writers will leave my room." And so they did. By 2009, most of these teachers are retired.

As is too often the plight of educational trends, sentence-combining grew rapidly as a part of the language arts curriculum in the 1970s only to disappear just as rapidly in a predictable 15- to 18-year cycle. Transformational grammar as viable instruction in grammar textbooks disappeared. Action research studies of sentence-combining declined. Sentence-combining, and its use in the classrooms, faded almost completely away. Fortunately, there are indications of resurgence in interest and use of sentence-combining practice.

Increased presence of sentence-combining practice rings positive for 21st-century student writers. A few years back, a middle Georgia administrator asked me to present the concept of sentence- combining to his middle school English Language Arts (ELA) teachers. In one 3-hour professional learning session, teachers received a full collection of sentence-combining lessons. They reported full use of the lessons. On the trait of writing style of Georgia's Grade 8 Writing Assessment, students from the middle schools of Houston County scored 12 percent higher than the eighth-graders the year before. This was especially interesting since the mean score on writing style of Georgia's ᵉ eighth-graders showed no significant change.

So what do students need to know about sentence-combining for it to impact scores of written expression significantly? They need to **know how** to combine two or more sentences into one that means the same using two signaled strategies. They need to practice creating these combinations until they achieve automaticity. The first strategy packs rich descriptive words into combined sentences. The second provides students with a wide variety of sentence patterns. When their minds are conditioned to these two combining strategies at a subconscious level, they start using them both automatically as they write.

The first sentence-combining strategy inserts descriptive vocabulary words from one sentence into another. Mellon started with a simple sentence called a ***base sentence*** and then taught students to move descriptive terms from closely related ***signal sentences*** into the base sentence. Without Mellon's references to the terminology of transformational grammar, an exercise for secondary students looks like this.

Base sentence:	The student does not like to be late.
Signal sentences:	The student is <u>new</u>.
	The student is in <u>ninth grade</u>.
	The student is <u>from Los Angeles</u>.
	Los Angeles is <u>south central</u>.
	The lateness is <u>for math class</u>.
	The math class is <u>second period</u>.
Combined sentence:	The ***new ninth grade*** student ***from south central Los Angeles*** does not like to be late ***for second period math class.***

(Combs 2005)

Students need to know two things about Mellon's underlining strategy. First, it signals students to retain only the underlined portions of sentences 2–7. They simply decide to place the underlined words in front of or behind the repeated words in the previous or base sentence.

Sentence 2:	Place <u>new</u> in front of the repeated word *student.*
3:	Place <u>ninth grade</u> in front of the repeated word *student.* (after *new*)
4:	Place <u>from Los Angeles</u> behind the repeated word *student.* (since it is a phrase)
5:	Place <u>south central</u> in front of the repeated word *Los Angeles.*
6:	Place <u>for math class</u> behind the repeated word *late.*
7:	Place <u>second period</u> in front of the repeated word *math.*

Let students voice the rules for placing adjective modifiers in a sentence: 1) single-word adjectives (like *new, ninth grade* and *second period*) are placed in front of the nouns they modify, 2) phrasal adjectives (like *from Los Angeles* and *for math class*) are placed behind the nouns they modify. The combinations are clearly signaled with the underlining for second language learners, although student's internalized understanding of spoken English helps them know **where** to place each underlined word or phrase.

Once students understand the workings of the underlining signal, frequent practice establishes *automaticity* in placing descriptive terms in a base sentence. Student demonstrate automaticity by reading a seven-sentence exercise like the one above and combining the seven sentences meaningfully without assistance or hesitation. For most students, three or four lessons of 10 to 15 oral and written exercizes are needed. Here's an example:

Sentence Building   (Oral, then Written Practice)

1. **Later the siren sounded.**
   Later was <u>at night</u>.
   The siren was <u>community</u>.
   The siren sounded <u>off in the distance</u>.

2. **A line entered the race.**
   The line was <u>lengthy</u>.
   The line was <u>of contestants</u>.
   The race was <u>on Independence Day</u>.

3. **The water splashed over the edge.**
   The water was <u>nearly boiling</u>.
   The edge was <u>jagged</u>.
   The edge was <u>of the iron cauldron</u>.

4. **My aunt squinted to see the movie.**
   The aunt was <u>aging</u>.
   The aunt was <u>decrepit</u>. (,)
   The movie was <u>at the private showing</u>.

See the complete lesson on www.eyeoneducation.com. Go to this book's page and follow the links. Students complete the lesson orally with students speaking the combined sentences aloud in small groups or with the whole class to establish automaticity. Then they write out the combined sentences in a notebook or journal page. Note the lesson started with students' performing the combinations. Once the combinations are completed orally and in writing, the teacher helps the students learn the terminology, in this case *adjectives* and *adjective phrases*.

The second sentence-combining strategy includes signals placed in parentheses at the end of each signal sentence that they affect. The signals are covered in seven distinct rules. Rule 1 results in the creation of both complex and compound sentences.

Rule 1: Move single words in parentheses to the front of the sentences that they follow. Then add the Signal sentence to the Base sentence.

Base sentence	**Jessie flopped back into bed.**
Signal sentence	The announcer predicted rain all day. (after)

Combined sentence	Jessie flopped back into bed **after** the announcer predicted rain all day.

Base sentence	**The girls went to lunch early.**
Signal sentence	The boys waited until almost 1:00 p.m. to eat. (, and)

Combined sentence	The girls went to lunch early**, and** the boys waited until almost 1:00 p.m. to eat.

If there are repeated words in the signal sentence, Rule 2 suggests that the students leave the second occurrence of the repeated word out. In Rule 2, the first example creates a complex sentence, and the second creates a simple sentence with a compound direct objective.

Rule 2: If there are repeated words in the signal sentence, leave them out of the combined sentence.

Base sentence	**The hawk swooped down on the rabbits.**
Signal sentence	The rabbits scrambled for cover. (that)

Combined sentence	The hawk swooped down on the rabbits that scrambled for cover.

Base sentence	**The four of us carried our equipment on our backs.**
Signal sentence	The four of us carried our food on our backs. (and)

Combined sentence	The four of us carried our equipment and food on our backs.

When the repeated words in the combined sentence cannot be deleted, students replace the second occurrence of the repeated word with an appropriate pronoun.

Rule 3: Replace repeated words with a pronoun (*he, she, it, they* or *him, her* or *them*).

Base sentence	**Aaron tried on the shirt.**
Signal sentence	Aaron made the shirt in Family Studies II. (that)

Combined sentence	Aaron tried on the shirt that he made in Family Studies II.

Although four rules remain, these three provide a clear idea of how sentence-combining exercises prompt students to increased sentence variety.

Describing different sentence-combining strategies requires serious effort, but performing the combinations for students does not. Once they understand how a signal works, they combine with alertness and speed. They see each new exercise as a puzzle and fall prey to its allure.

Sentence Building   (Oral, then Written Practice)

1. **The immigrants had no money to their names. (Although)**
   The immigrants were soon self-supporting. (,)

2. **Le Won was visiting a dozen college campuses. (While)**
   Le Won received three scholarships in the mail. (,)

3. **Our teacher takes a go-cart from the parking lot.**
   Our teacher could use the exercise. (even though)

4. **The lake behind the school is stocked with fish. (Since)**
   Trolling and bobbing for fish is a P. E. elective. (,)

. . . the complete lesson is available at www.eyeoneducation.com.
Go to this book's page and follow the links.

Grammatical Pattern Practiced: The puzzles present adverb clauses. The Signal sentence joins a previous sentence with a *subordinate conjunction* (such as **because, if, even though** or **although**), making it a *dependent clause* (unable to stand alone). Since the clause *modifies* (describes) the *verb* in the Base sentence, it is an *adverb clause*.

_____ Lesson for Combining Sentences _____

INVITE

Work on our styles of writing with me. I see from reviewing your first drafts that many of you have a couple of habits like mine. You write so quickly that you leave out vivid words and write sentences that would be better combined with another sentence nearby, and that's normal. When we draft our thoughts the first time, we are writing for ourselves. We see the pictures in our minds that go with the words of our drafts. We hear the voice of our minds dictating our thoughts on our topic, but we don't write down all of the words our audience needs for a full and enjoyable reading experience. We see clear pictures, but our repetitious sentence patterns blur the focus. Our first drafts lack our own personal writing style.

Look at the writing of a sixth-grader Lucy of Monticello, Georgia, summarize an article for her science class on the prospects of robots in the lives of U. S. Americans in the future. Her first draft is nearly devoid of her personal style that she uses in writing stories. Her first draft here misses the energy of an exciting possibility, falters and even confuses us at times. Notice what a difference **Combining Sentences** *makes.*

Soon Robots Will be at your Service

These days robots are not very strong. They can't do very much for us. In the future we want them to be able to do more things. It would be nice if they got our breakfast for us. How about cleaning the car? Doing the dishes would be nice. I hope that they will do a lot for us but not so much that it makes us lazy. We could get real clumsy.

Joseph Bosworth, president of Robot Sciences of Golden, Colorado, thinks that robots can change our lives. It will take fifteen to twenty years. He is sure it will come. Research in medicine will play a big part. So will the technology in Disney World called animatronics. Robots will have artificial limbs, too. They are made for people now. They will be on the robots of the future. I think movie producers might be able to make a show of just robots. Only some of this is for sure.

Lucy combined the sentences that she marked for that purpose. Notice how differently the summary reads.

REVISION, Soon Robots Will be at your Service

These days robots are not very strong. They can't do very much for us. In the future we want them to be able to do more things. It would be nice if they got our breakfast for us, **cleaned the family car and even washed the dishes**. I hope that they will do a lot for us but not so much that it makes us lazy. We could get real clumsy.

Joseph Bosworth, president of Robot Sciences of Golden, Colorado, thinks that robots can change our lives **in** fifteen to twenty years **for** sure. Research in medicine **and** the technology in Disney World called animatronics will play a big part. Robots will have artificial limbs **like the ones** made for people now. I think movie producers might be able to make a show of just robots.

I needed the **Combining Sentences** revision strategy when I summarized what I had learned about life in medieval England as a visitor in a social studies class. I circled groups of two and three sentences that would be better off combined.

Medieval England

Peasants made up the largest social class in medieval England. The serfs were a much smaller group, but we know much more about them. Many peasants lived the lives of vagabonds. They lived at the mercy of the weather. They joined wars even if just to survive. They felt the brunt of the economic evils of the times. Serfs actually had a nice go of it. They lived in the care of a Lord. The Lord may control a castle, huge farm or a small village. Their lives were well defined. They resembled the lives of employee in 21st century US America.

Serfs' assets were assigned to them, and they showed appreciation for them. The Lord separated his manor into large fields. The fields contained strips. Some strips produced goods for him. Some produced goods for the church. The remaining goods went to the serfs. Of course, the serfs agreed to do all of the work for the entire field.

Then I applied what I had learned in sentence-combining practice.

REVISION, Medieval England

Peasants made up the largest social class in medieval England. **Although** the serfs were a much smaller group, **they are the group about which we know the most.** Many peasants lived the lives of vagabonds, **thrown to** the mercy of the weather **or many regional** wars **which they use to** survive. They **were the group that always** felt the brunt of the economic evils of the times.

By comparison, the serfs actually had a nice go of it, **living** in the care of a Lord **who controlled** a castle, a huge farm **called a manor, even a** small village **or all three. As a result** their lives were well defined **much like the hard-working** employee in 21st century US America.

Actually, it is possible to combine most sentences next to one another in a way that states the same information more efficiently. See Lucy's and my complete drafts at www.eyeoneducation.com. *Go to this book's page and follow the links.*

Setting concrete expectations for *Combining Sentences* in a draft: Specify expectations for the two types of sentence-combining practice: 1) insert descriptive vocabulary words and 2) combine two or more sentences into one. Set an expectation of inserting descriptive words to 6 to 8 sentences and combining 2 to 3 pairs of sentences into one. When students reach these expectations, they can assess themselves a target ⊙ (⊙ = 85 points). They may insert descriptive words in more sentences, combine more pairs of sentences or perform an earlier revision strategy to assess themselves a plus + (+ = 100 points). When students fail to reach the expectations, they assess themselves a bar ⊟ (⊟ = 70 points).

Read through your selected first draft completely, then, as you saw in the model,

1. *Circle all of the vague or unspecific nouns in your draft. Then return to each circled noun and insert richly descriptive words before and prepositional phrases after 6 to 8 nouns. Picture the sentence-combining exercises that we practiced with words and phrases underlined in the signal sentences. Add the descriptive words and phrases using a contrasting color to make the additions easy to locate and assess.*

2. *Circle at least three pairs of closely related sentences in your first draft that would be better when combined. See if you find a sequence of three sentences to combine. Recall the sentence-combining exercises in which we moved the signals to the front of the sentences they followed.*

A high school English teacher focused on circling vague or unspecific nouns in students' drafts. Ninth-grader Erica from western South Dakota circled the nouns in her first draft. She circled 19 nouns that she knew needed details like she had practiced in sentence-combining lessons.

> My getaway place is riding my horse in the pasture. This place is not very specific, but it is my favorite place to be. I ask myself, "Why do I enjoy this place?" or "What would I do there?" I never gave any thought to it until now.
>
> Riding my horse in the pasture is my favorite getaway place. I enjoy it because I love the smell of grass and fresh air. I like to talk to Grandpa Lawrence along because I feel embarrassed when somebody else is around. Thinking about happy thoughts helps me get over the hard day that I have had. Sometimes my happy thoughts are about the past, for the most of my good and happy years happened in the past...

(See her complete draft at www.eyeonedeucation.com)

Since her draft was written without space between the lines, she listed the nouns on a separate sheet of paper and committed to add details both in front of and behind 12 of the words. She kept her first draft in clear view.

mixed-breed Chestnut [horse] named Red

large old [pasture] north of our barn

new-mown green [grass]

[air] from out of the west

[happy thoughts]

[day] at school or cleaning stalls in the barn

[years] with my family

Erica became so engaged adding descriptive details to circled nouns that she added details in front **or** back of 15 nouns and in front **and** in back of six, well beyond expectation. As she rewrote her draft, she asked if she could add more details to help her writing improve. Of course, the answer was *yes*. Notice how improved her first two paragraphs read.

My getaway place is riding my **mixed-breed, Chestnut** [horse] **named Red** in the **large old rundown** [pasture] **out behind our barn.** This place is not very specific, but it is my favorite place to be. I ask myself, "Why do I enjoy this place?" or "What would I do there?" I never gave any thought to **questions like these** until now.

Riding my horse in the pasture is my favorite getaway place. I enjoy it because I love the smell of **new-mown green** [grass] **and fresh** [air] **from off the prairie.** I like to talk to Grandpa Lawrence along because I feel embarrassed **talking about what I really want to** when somebody else is around. Thinking about [happy thoughts] helps me get over the hard **long** [day] that I have had **at school or cleaning stalls in the barn.** Sometimes my happy thoughts are about the past, for most of my good and happy [years] **with my family** happened in the past.

A Marginal Writer

Brandy describes a trip on a day of remarkable importance to her. Since she relied largely on short sentences, her teacher and I prompted her to revise by *Combining Sentences*. Since she was so pleased with the result, she continued revising for descriptive words and phrases on another pass through the paper.

My Specil Day

My best day. My best day was when I was going to Arizona. It was awesome except waiting at the Denver airport. We had to wait four hours until the next plan came. Then once the plan came, we took off. When we arrived to Arizona, I could already see how hot it was. It was like a hot bath with a little lava in it. Then we arrived to my grandma's house. It was Thanksgiving. I could already smell my grandma's cooking. We got in the house. It was already time to eat. We had turkey, mash potatoes and a roll and some strawberry short cake. It was delicious. After that me and my brother got our swimsuits on and sent swimming. My grandma has a built-in swimming pool in her back yard. I was just about to jump in. I saw a lizard in the pool. It was cute. My grandmas said we could have it. But we couldn't take it on the plane. After that we got to go to the zoo. It was awesome. We saw all the animals.

Although there is much more than **Combining Sentences** that needs to be revised, Brandy does a solid job of combining sentences as she had them circled in her first draft. For sure, most of the combinations include *When,* but the draft reads smoother; there are other days and other drafts to work on other revision strategies.

My Specil Day

My best day **My best day** was when I was going to Arizona. It was awesome except waiting at the Denver airport. **When we** had waited four hours, the plan came, and we took off. **Then When** we arrived to Arizona, I could already see **that** it was like a hot bath with a little lava in it. **W**hen we arrived to my grandma's house, it was Thanksgiving. I could already smell my grandma's cooking **when we** got in the house **and got** ready to eat. We had turkey, mash potatoes and a roll and some strawberry short cake. It was delicious. After that me and my brother got our swimsuits on and sent swimming **in the** built-in swimming pool in her back yard. I was just about to jump in **when** I saw a lizard in the pool. It was cute. My grandmas said we could have it. But we couldn't take it on the plane. After that we got to go to the zoo. It was awesome. We saw all the animals.

When we were there we got to see a baby gorilla be born. They named it Sasha. It was so cool. I wanted to keep it. Well, that's all I have. Thanks for listening.

REFLECT

When the students have finished the prompted revision activity, ask them to

1. *Join your revision consultant and take turns reading your first drafts aloud to one another, showing how you inserted descriptive terms before and after the circled nouns. For each noun that you have modified, ask*

The question	Possible notes in the margin		
Does the addition fit?	The addition fits.		The addition does not fit.
About the length?	Too much	Add more	About right

Write "too much," "add more" or "about right" in the margin by each addition.

2. *Now show the combined sentences to your assigned consultant for a response. Write "too much," "add more" or "about right" in the margins next to the combined sentences.*

Student Self-Assessment: Students complete their reflection of the **Combining Sentences** strategy by assessing the degree to which they met the stated expectations for their revision. When they insert descriptive vocabulary of 6 to 8 nouns, combine 2 to 3 sentences into one, they may self-assess a target ⊙ (⊙ = 85 points). If they revise less than expected, they self-assess a bar ⊟ (⊟ = 70 points). When they revise more (more than 6 to 8 insertions, 4 or more combined sentences or perform an earlier revision strategy), they self-assess a plus + (+ = 100 points).

Students in a ninth-grade ELA classroom observed the following about **Combining Sentences** as a revision strategy:

♦ Add more details than you think you need to add.

♦ It's hard to add too many details in your writing.

♦ Some short sentences need to stay short.

♦ Combining two sentences together makes them easier to understand.

♦ A complex sentence is really two simple sentences combined.

♦ Rearranging the words in a sentence helps you say things better.

Conclusion: Ask students to respond to the statement, *Longer sentences are not always better sentences.* The **Combining Sentences** revision strategy makes it possible for students to consider rewriting sentences to clarify meaning. In this revision strategy, more than in earlier ones, students learn that attempted revisions do not always improve a draft. **Combining Sentences** empowers them to consider several possibilities in wording sentences as they search to be better understood.

LEARN

Reaching All Styles of Learning in Combining Sentences

In **Sentence Building**, the teachers who helped me design the lessons emphasized the importance of providing aural, visual and kinesthetic styles of participation. The first two styles of learning are simple enough to provide. Students combine the sentences orally, then in writing. Curiously, many students who combine sentences orally with ease stumble at writing out the combined sentences for the same puzzles. It is obvious that oral and written practice provide different challenges for secondary students. Since they do offer two distinct challenges, written and oral practice must appear in a sentence-combining regimen in the ELA classroom.

The addition of kinesthetic learning enhances the oral sentence-combining practice. From observations of students attempting to master a new sentence-combining signal, I see students work quite hard to coordinate a gesture with the changes required in a specific combination. For example, in

The immigrants had no money to their names. (Although)
The immigrants were soon self-supporting. (,)

students had to

1. move (Although) and (,) to the front of the sentences they follow

2. change the second appearance of the repeated word *immigrants* to *they.*

To set up the kinesthetic feature of the exercise, students bent their right arm at the elbow, holding their upper arms in an upright position. As emphasis to these three essential changes, they let their arms drop down 90 degrees in front of them and back up in a chopping movement. The combined sentence was spoken and emphasized as follows.

Capital A [chop-up] Although [chop-up] the immigrants had no money to their names **Comma [chop-up], they [chop-up]** were soon self-supporting.

Students said the word *comma* to emphasize its placement in the Combined sentence. In classes of beginning sentence-combining, I instruct the students to *chop* and say *Capital A* at the first of the sentence and *chop* and say *period* at the end. Time after time, I receive reports of students whose transfer of punctuation and word placement are enhanced through the kinesthetic feature. In one long-time *Writing to Win* district that has consistently required sentence-combining practice of all their students for more than the last decade, 17 to 32 percent of their students exceed the standard on the state's 5th, 8th and 11th-grade writing assessment. Statewide, fewer than 9 percent of all students exceed the standard expectation. The administrators continue to require frequent and extended use of sentence-combining, and the students' performance is maintained. For sure, it is a remarkably curious correlation.

Spotting Weasel Words

On occasion, I read a student's first draft and the weasel words jump off the page at me. Enter the strategy, *Spotting Weasel Words*. These are words that add little substance to the draft and when used repeatedly sap the writing of its energy or special character. Any word used repetitiously could then become a *weasel word*. The draft I found one day was in Mr. Van Leur's industrial arts shop in Emery, South Dakota. Carl read his first draft aloud as his classmates and I listened. Carl's directions were quite complete, and Mr. Van Leur declared that his writing qualified him to move the next day into the shop to try his hand at using the miter box himself. I could not agree more, but what about those repetitious weasel words. You will see what I mean.

> We use miter boxes to guide our saws and make angle cuts in the shop. **You would** always do this before joining two pieces of wood. Miter boxers **would** make sure the two pieces fit right. Mr. Van Leur's miter boxes have slots to make cuts at 90-degree angles and 45-degree angles. A miter box without the slots **would** make the cut harder.
>
> It **would** be easy for you to use the miter box if you **would** only follow these steps. First, **you would** measure the wood carefully and mark the angle with a good pencil. Next, **you would** put a piece of scrap wood on the bottom of the miter box. If **you** ever **would** saw through the wood, the scrap **would** keep you from cutting up the miter box.
>
> Next, **you would** lay the boards you want to miter in the box. You have to be sure to push them up against the wall which **would** be on the far wall of the box. Hold the wood firmly. Next **you would** set the guide in the miter box for your right cut. If you don't have a 90-degree or 45-degree angle, **you would** create them by marking the miter box and sawing across the sides. For the last step, **you would** pick the right size backsaw and set it in the groove. Then **you would** cut the material for a fit that would be perfect every time.

When Carl finished reading aloud, his classmates responded with what was strong about his writing and asked a few questions. One was precisely what I was set to asked, *Did you need all of the "you woulds?"* Carl was stumped and grinned to camouflage his confusion. He simply said sharply, "Well, I bet you would too now, wouldn't you?" Then I stepped in and lightened the air. I just asked him to read his first two paragraphs again without the *you woulds*. After he read this way, he readily sighed and quipped, "It's better, isn't it?" So

I had a little fun saying, *As the doctor on call in this class to analyze first drafts, I diagnose Carl's draft with a serious case of the you woulds and order that he surgically remove all that he possibly can.* The class chuckled. Actually, Carl used 16 *woulds* in his 240-word draft, half of them *you woulds*. When he excised all of these weasel words, his directions were much more direct and helpful to the reader.

> **We use miter boxes to guide our saws when we make angle cuts in the shop before joining two pieces of wood.** Miter boxers make sure the two pieces fit right. Mr. Van Leur's miter boxes contain slots to make cuts at 90-degree angles and 45-degree angles. A miter box without the slots make the cut harder.
>
> It would be easy for you to use the miter box if you only follow these steps. First, measure the wood carefully and mark the angle with a good pencil. Next, put a piece of scrap wood on the bottom of the miter box. If **you** ever saw through the wood, the scrap keep**s** you from cutting up the miter box.
>
> **Next, lay the boards you want to miter in the box. You have to be sure to push them up against the far wall of the box.** Hold the wood firmly. Next set the guide in the miter box for your right cut. If you don't have a standard 90-degree or 45-degree angle, create them by marking the miter box and sawing across the sides. For the last step, pick the right size backsaw and set it in the groove. Then cut the material for a fit that **is** perfect every time.

It is interesting that he combined two pairs of sentences when he pared away the weasel *woulds*. That entitled him to a (+) for his revision of the day. He was a happy camper, and he had a better final draft.

I also warn of the dulling impact of passive voice used by beginning writers to affect a dignified, formal prose. In a sense, *a great time was had by us all* and *the final solution was finally decided upon by the whole group* contain weasel words that are better left out. *We all had a great time* and *The whole group decided upon a final solution* reads more directly and effectively. Shaving off the two or three weasel words in these two phrases enliven the style.

Weasel words bleed into persuasive writing, too. Since persuasive writing explains opinions or positions that the writers hold, it is a collection of ideas writers *think, believe* or *feel*. Therefore, there is no need to state *I feel, I believe* or *I think*. Just cut to the chase and state what it is that you feel, believe or think. Read the first two paragraphs of Wesley, a tenth-grader at Sequoyah High School, who found it easy to dot his sentences with weasel words.

The high school dropout rate increases yearly. **I believe** this is because many students find school too stressful to handle. **I think** they see this time of their life as a time for them to enjoy their talents and gifts instead of taking tested so often. **I'm convinced that** standardized tests are an unnecessary process that does more harm than good. **I believe** since these tests do not adjust to the different minds, and **I know** this puts too much stress on students.

    I honestly believe that standardized tests are not an effective way to observe what students have learned. **I know for a fact that** in some cases, the whole structure of standard tests stresses students and confuses them. **I have no doubt that** having one big test that decides whether a student passes a class is a big pressure on that student. Albert Einstein, one of the most brilliant scientists of all time, flunked out of school. **I believe** he could not handle the pressure that tests bring. Maybe standardized tests are not the best way to measure students' achievement after all.

In conference, I asked Wesley about the effect of all of his *I think, I believe* and *I know* phrases. At first, he said, the phrases added conviction to his opinion, then he changed his mind. He next said, "I don't need them at all." I agreed. The weasel words distracted from the meaning of the draft and focused on **the fact that Wesley was feeling, thinking and believing** instead of on **what he felt, thought and believed**.

In matters of writing style then, students need practice deleting or modifying words that rob writing of its energy and effect. They need to delete weasel words that contribute little meaning (*would, could, should, will* or *I think, I believe, I know*) and modify unspecified nouns with vivid details placed before or after them. Effective instruction in writing style also requires students to consider matters of sentence variety and whether their sentences are consistently

♦ short and need to be combined.

♦ long and need to be de-combined and/or re-combined.

When students understand these four matters of revising for writing style, they have the power to boost their scores on the trait of style on tests of writing. Even more important however, they have four reliable ways to bring the features of their own personal writing style into full bloom any time that they write.

〈 Looking Back

In your response journal, describe the value of ***Combining Sentences*** and ***Spotting Weasel Words*** for you as a teacher in courses that you presently teach.

〉 Looking Ahead

How can lessons, chapters or units coming up in your curriculum invite you to prompt your students to combine sentences and excise weasel words?

11

Nail Down Effective Word Choice with Me

"I do not choose the right word. I get rid of the wrong one."
A. E. Housman

Let me guess. Several of your students jot and blend many red words into their first drafts; they even expand picture sentences and frames into full paragraphs, but their word choices fall short of precise, crisp or vivid. Housman has a point; students may need to replace words, not simply modify them. This chapter presents such an occasion for these writers. Effective as the preceding strategies have been, some students succeed in holding out on their specific thoughts, dotting their drafts with vague or general words. Their writing continues to **tell** us what they are thinking instead of **show** us what they mean. They write quickly, sticking with a few trusted sentence patterns on which they rely. On command, they follow all of the revision strategies; they have yet to use any of the revision strategies unprompted.

This chapter approaches revision from a different angle. The first strategy, ***Framed Drafts***, doesn't act upon students' first drafts. It helps them create first drafts with a sharpening eye for vivid detail. These drafts require students only to insert words into blanks within sentences. It imprints students' minds with the idea that voids occur in their sentences as others read them. Although this strategy occurs separate from students' writing, it carries over to their independent writing. In some cases, student writing from framed drafts are arguably the most vivid writing that they have created to date. The second strategy, the ***Sentence Check Chart***, more than any other strategy I use, moves students to the realization of just how much their first drafts need the power of precise word choice and sentence variety. Many students complete the charts with an *ah-hah* realization of what needs to change in their writing habits.

Both strategies provide the perfect opportunity for students to learn to operate outside of the *restrictive language register* discussed earlier (Chapter 3). In *The Five Clocks*, Martin Joos describes five language styles—intimate, casual, consultative, formal and frozen. I greet and converse with my wife, children and grandchildren in the intimate style. People the world over exchange vows during a wedding ceremony in Joos' frozen style.

U. S. American students have experience with both of these extremes in language styles. A task of classroom teachers is to prompt students into writing experiences with casual, consultative and formal writing styles.

The first strategy for such help, ***Framed Drafts***, provides the general framework of paragraphs: sentence patterns with punctuation and structured paragraphs. All that is left for students to do is provide the additional, specific details needed to flesh out the frame. ***Framed Drafts*** extend the concept of framed paragraph of Individualized Language Arts (ILA), a federally funded program disseminated nationally over 30 years ago.

_____ Lesson for Framed Drafts _____

Nail down effective word choice with me. *Let's try something different today—a way to write that begins in a curious way. We'll practice creating a first draft from a framed draft. All you need to do is sit back and relax, realizing that you will be doing something you've never done before. This first time, you need not perform the task well, just give it your best try.*

The introductory framed draft requires you to write what you are thinking that fits the frame and creates a clear picture of your thoughts. Your fictional narrative must be realistic fiction, fiction that could actually occur.

Possible Characters		Function Words
scientist	One day _____ to the jungle. _____ wanted to find _____ for _____. All of _____ came running to _____. They were _____.	*in*
photographer		*on*
lion		*over*
missionary	The chief _____ was standing _____. She was _____. She knew _____ and decided to _____. She was _____.	*but*
hunter		*for*
native		*who*
cartographer		*that*
explorer	At last the _____ developed a _____. With _____ they _____. As they winged their way _____, they said, "_____." _____ was very _____.	*which*
archaeologist		*because*
tourist		*against*
		although
		of
		from
		at

First I'll read all three paragraphs of the narrative. Follow along and let me know what you think of its potential.

> "One day *(blank)* to the jungle. *(blank)* wanted to find *(blank)* for *(blank)*. All of the *(blank)* came running to . . .

> . . . As they winged their way *(blank)*, they said '*(blank)*.' *(blank)* was very *(blank)*."

There you have it? What did you think of the narrative? You're right, it was rather (blank).
But what do you know for sure about from the frame. One class I met recently concluded:

> The setting is in a jungle.

> A group visited the jungle with a specific purpose.

> A crowd and a chief observed the arrival of visitors.

So it sounds like you could improve on this narrative? Let's get off to a solid start then.
First we brainstorm possible main characters as illustrated in the model. Then we jot list small
*function words that will help us reach the minimum of five **per blank** in the frame. See the list*
in the right margin of the model. Here's what Ms. Maher of Timber Lake High School, South
Dakota, added to the frame. The function words that she used to reach the minimum for each
blank appear in bold font.

> One day the once famous and well loved actor Neddy Peabody
> scrambled breathlessly into the jungle. His journey had been long, arduous,
> and financially costly, but he was banking on this venture to restart
> a battery-dead career. Saddened and despairing over his lost youth
> and good looks, he desperately wanted, no needed to find the fountain of
> youth for the purpose of regaining the glory of his former self—the days
> of screaming female fans, non-stop paparazzi hounding him for just a
> shot and movie after movie offer from the most respected producers in
> Hollywood. Everyone wanted him—in those days—and now he wanted them
> too, needed them more than anything, this trek to find the fountain of
> youth wasn't just a hopeful adventure. It was a journey into who he was
> and who he wanted to be again. And now it was more.
> But it wouldn't be easy. All of the warriors of the local Shibaba
> tribe came running to the front of our area of excessive vegetation. Bones
> and bramblesator thorns blocked the way to the passageway, along
> with around seventy spear-armored, able-bodied, determined shibaba
> warriors. These men were the gate keepers, the keepers of all that is holy
> and scarce in order to protect and provide as they wished. They stood
> before Peabody.

Where did she these ideas to add to the frame? Obviously from knowledge of the world
around her and her own imagination. The students are usually amazed at how much Ms.
Maher added to the frame, how fluently her version read for them to understand and enjoy,

and most of all, a 58-word sentence. She added 201 words (28 words/blank) to the first paragraph of seven blanks and expanded it into two separate paragraphs. The dramatic additions made it literally impossible to identify a frame as the original source.

My model retained more evidence of the frame even though my main characters never made it to the jungle.

> One day *a group of young missionaries from Schenectady filed into the international concourse of La Guardia Airport to board Delta flight 1457* to the jungle. *These newly graduated seminary students* wanted to find *the site of the discovery of the Gnostics scrolls for souvenirs for a mission convention on their return to the United States.* All *of the group of 31* came running to *the gate in anticipation of a quick departure.* They were *eager to complete the purpose of their short journey.*
>
> The chief *attendant of the overnight flight* was standing *at the entrance to the jet way that was supposedly attached to a waiting aircraft.* She was *unusually pensive, causing a minor stir among the excited group; the talkative cluster grew silent.* She knew *that they had sensed something was wrong* and decided to *break the news of an undetermined delay to them gently.* She was *tactful, but it was easy to see the pronounced disappointment in a group that held no feelings back.*

I added 235 words to the frame; 45 function words helped me create the additions fluently in the 21 blanks, 11 words per blank. I can assess myself a (+) for adding more than the expected five words per blank.

Some students mused that I didn't even get my characters out of La Guardia International Airport! That's not surprising for a guy whose never been to the jungle. You can do better; your visitors can make it to the jungle and return with precisely what they were seeking, right? Once a couple of you complete the first two blanks for the whole class, you have 15 minutes to complete the rest of your draft.

Teacher: *Who can add at least five words to the first blank for us all to hear?*

Stephen: *One day an archaeologist and photographer went to the jungle.*

Teacher: *Stephan met the bare minimum. Who can help him complete the first blank with more words?*

Allie:	*One day <u>an archaeologist and photographer met at O'Hare International Airport to catch a flight</u> to the jungle.*
Teacher:	*That puts us up to 11 words. Now, who can add at least five words to the second blank?*
Stephen:	*<u>The two men</u> wanted to find <u>a prehistoric site</u> for <u>a magazine article</u>.*
Teacher:	*Your additions make sense, but they don't meet the minimum. Who can help him out?*
Pedro:	*<u>The two men who never met before that day</u> wanted to find <u>a prehistoric site to excavate down to a new level</u> for <u>a feature article in an archaeology magazine</u>.*
Teacher:	*Now, we've got the idea. You all have 15 minutes to complete the additions to your own blanks.*

Remember to choose one or two main characters for your narrative like Stephen did, then read through the frame of the jungle story again. Final tips:

1. *If you think of words to add outside of the blanks, use them.*

2. *You can add more than one sentence to a blank.*

3. *Try to stick with the frame. If your narrative takes a different direction than the frame, I still expect the high level of details that you achieved in your additions to the blanks.*

Recently, I met a class of 10th-grade students from McDowell County High School, North Carolina, to help them begin their study of persuasive writing. As I talked with them of *voice, pictures* and *flow* in writing, I heard them use terms and phrases that served as red flags for me: *five paragraphs, the last sentence is the thesis statement, three reasons for your opinion* and *restate your reasons in the conclusion.* I heard no one mention the words I had just talked them through, so I asked, *Where does voice* and *pictures fit into persuasive writing*? Complete silence, some looking around from person to person. One timid soul asked what others were thinking, "Aren't they only for writing narratives?" I remained calm even though my serious presentation of *voice* as style, *pictures* as ideas and *flow* as organization just evaporated at the mention of persuasive writing. All I heard was the formula of the five-paragraph theme.

So I cut to the chase. *Let's start again,* I heard my voice say, *the reason we just completed that wonderful discussion of voice, pictures and flow is that all writing has voice, pictures and flow. Good writing includes a strong voice, clear pictures and clarifying flow. That means that good persuasive writing has a strong voice, clear pictures and clarifying flow. Everybody understand?*

I had their attention, and continued.

Good persuasive writing **might** include . . .	Persuasive writing **must** contain
◆ *five paragraphs, but not necessarily.*	*clear voice*
◆ *a thesis statement as the last sentence in the first paragraph, but not necessarily.*	*pictures*
◆ *three reasons in three body paragraphs, but not necessarily.*	*and flow*
◆ *a summary of the reasons in the concluding paragraph, but not necessarily.*	

I distributed a persuasive framed draft, one that claimed people have fun in cities. The class brainstormed possible function words. I set an expectation that the writing be realistic and contain a minimum of seven words per blank. Two students took the frame to a level that brought applause from their classmates. Jessica wrote

Support an Opinion

People Have Fun in Cities

Function Words

People live and work in cities, but they also find time for fun. Cities have large parks to run with dogs or to ride skateboards, skates or bikes. Companies provide places to socialize with friends or meet new people with similar interests. Some places are overrun with people who enjoy beauty and art because they have so many beautiful art museums and street vendors to see.

City parks sprawl over acres of land covered in trees, flowers and benches for walkers who may need to rest or want to sit outside on a sunny day. They have slides and toys that young children brought by care-givers or parents for an afternoon of playing and rough-housing away from mom's priceless vase on the living room sideboard. Some have gardens that consist of flowers blooming endlessly, bringing people form all around to look and enjoy. Others provide beaches for young couples to visit and explore while picnicking near the water. Many provide lakes with ducks and geese that bird watchers observe from a distance and families feed bread crumbs up close. City parks help people who feel stressed on the job or who just want to go something selfish away from work.

and
while
on
for
from
at
in
beside
with
of
between
during
but
without
mean-while
that
which
who
under
while
when

Jessica added 138 words to 12 blanks, an average of 11.5 words/blank, easily exceeding my expectation of seven words/blank. Tiffany elaborates on the blanks in the draft even more extensively as shown in her second paragraph.

Support an Opinion

People Have Fun in Cities

	Function Words
City parks sprawl over acres of <u>vast land, stretching farther than the eye can see. It is absolutely</u> amazing how <u>such exhibits of nature's beauty can lie amidst so many man-made wonders.</u> They have slides and <u>jungle gyms,</u> picnic areas and several features especially designed for <u>families with young children</u> for <u>get-togethers, friendly and safe hang outs or solitude watching the enjoyment of others.</u> Some have gardens that <u>astound the most meticulous of prize-winning planters.</u> Others provide beaches for <u>a fun day out in the sun to relax or expend all of the extra energy that one wants.</u> Many provide lakes with <u>boats and canoes for rowing or blinds for watching waterfowl in their native habitat up close.</u> City parks help people <u>make a quick and enjoyable escape while spending time</u> away from work.	and while on for from at in beside with of between during but without mean-while that which who under while when

Tiffany inserted 213 words in 17 blanks or 12.5 words per blank. When the applause trailed off, I asked, *Why the applause?* Several students responded with a variation of "They were good." I continued with a follow-up question, *What was so good about them?* I listened and enjoyed the response.

♦ "They both painted convincing pictures of fun in big cities. Jessica painted specific pictures of people having fun. Tiffany's picture was like a huge mural."

♦ "Their voices were very different. Jessica's version was very personal and detailed. Tiffany's sounded like an advertisement, like there's so much to do in cities."

♦ "Their writing flowed very naturally. It was hard to tell that they were filling in blanks in a frame. It sounded like their writing."

I concurred; indeed, it was their writing. I also couldn't resist having a little fun at the expense of the class whose students claimed just half an hour previously that persuasion was all about five paragraphs, thesis statements, three reasons and a concluding summary.

What about five paragraphs, three reasons and a summary? The class became completely silent until a student, apparently never at a loss for words, quipped "What about them?" We all enjoyed a hearty laugh, and I trust that they remember the power of persuasive writing lies in the *voice,* the *pictures* and the *flow* just like all other modes of writing.

When the students have finished the prompted revision activity, continue by saying

1. *Join your revision consultant and take turns reading your first drafts aloud to one another, showing how you inserted descriptive terms in each blank. For each blank that you have completed, ask*

The question	Possible notes in the margin		
Does the addition fit?	*The addition fits.*		*The addition does not fit.*
About the length?	*Too much*	*Add more*	*About right*

   Write "doesn't fit," "too much," "add more" or "about right" in the margin by each addition as appropriate.

2. *Rejoin the whole class and be ready to volunteer your partner to read his/her first draft if it exceeds the expectations set by your teacher.*

Student Self-Assessment: Students complete their reflection of the *Framed Drafts* strategy by assessing the degree to which they met your stated expectation for their revision. They need to add a minimum of 7 words per blank, and the additions should paint clear pictures of their thoughts for the readers. When students add more than an average of 7 words per blank, they assess themselves a target ⊙ (⊙ = 85 points). If they add fewer or their writing does not flow, they self-assess a bar ▭ (▭ = 70 points). When they add more than 7, they self-assess a plus + (+ = 100 points).

A group of social studies students in a 7th grade classroom commented on the use of the framed draft.

- ◆ "Too much structure for me at first, but then I got used to it."
- ◆ "This was fun and easy; I just added the details; the sentences were already created for me."
- ◆ "Adding 10 to 15 words to a blank is not too many.'"
- ◆ "This taught me how to add really good details to my sentences."
- ◆ "We started from the same frame, but our narratives were very different."

Conclusion: Help students conclude that adding more details to a draft than usual makes for writing that readers understand. They all need to realize that in revising a draft for an audience, they will have to add more words than they think they should, not fewer. Even students who exaggerate their additions made a game out of the exercise and benefited from it. They may even find that a more elaborated style of writing fits them to a "T."

REFLECT

LEARN

Other Framed Drafts Based on a Social Studies Curriculum

Here are six additional framed drafts that introduce six modes of writing in the expository genre. One is printed here; see the others at www.eyeoneducation.com. Visit this book's page on the website and follow the links.

Character Sketch

The Trail Boss

Read through the following draft expressively, saying "blank" at every blank. Words that fit in the blanks will come to your mind as you read. You will see it is a frame for a first draft. On a clean sheet of lined paper, begin copying the frame up to the point of the first blank. Then add at least the minimum of seven words for each blank. Use small function words such as *on, beside, that, at, from,* or *with* to help you reach the minimum. The more words you add, the more the frame will become your own, and the prouder you will be.

Trail bosses are usually found _____. They serve people who _____. Some bosses work _____ and _____. Trail rides often occur _____. The need for _____ bosses is growing _____.

In the saddle, trail bosses _____ and _____. They wear _____ and _____. They would never be seen _____ or _____. They may lead _____. With _____, they lead _____ with pride.

All trail bosses show _____ and _____ on the trail. In danger they _____. They also _____ people in good _____. They know when _____ and when _____. They even know _____ about _____. There is no _____ like a _____.

Sentence Check Chart

The second strategy for nailing down effective word choice is the **Sentence Check Chart**. The chart never fails to make indelible points about revision to students even though they are points often heard before. The chart applies to the first thirteen sentences, not the entire first draft. Thirteen sentences readily exposes students' habits of writing, and they see instantly how to address them.

Before filling out the chart

Provide these two procedures for students prior to using the chart:

1. *Place a slash (/) after each of the first 13 sentences, whether the sentences are punctuated correctly or not. Number them from 1-13.*

   Walk-by conferences—As students mark off sentences, confer with those who need help with adjusting stray or omitted slashes.

2. *Circle the first verb included in each of the 13 sentences. Be sure to circle at least the main verb in a verb phrase (could have been **running**).*

   Walk-by conferences—As students work on circling verbs, help some of them quickly adjust any stray or omitted circles.

Once students have completed these two tasks in their first drafts, ask them to transfer the information from each sentence to the **Sentence Check Chart**. The chart highlights needless or excessive repetition, contrived sentence length and vague or empty word choices. Allow students to discuss conclusions about their writing from the columns of words and numbers on the chart.

After filling out the chart

Follow up the completion of the chart with prompts like these.

1. *Replace half of the first words with more interesting words or phrases.*

2. *Replace half of the subjects listed with more descriptive synonyms.*

3. *Replace half of the verbs with more descriptive ones.*

4. *After you add the replacement words into the sentences of your first drafts, check the lengths of the sentences. Add to, combine and compact sentences to ensure sentence variety and ease of reading for anyone who reads your paper.*

Ms. McCarthy, an 8th-grade English teacher from West Hall Middle School, Georgia, immediately saw the need for the **Sentence Check Chart** when her class drafted their thoughts about "A significant adult who is a hero to me." She saw that although all students went through the rigor of prewriting as described in chapter 6, they presented honest emotions in vague generalities and repeated sentence patterns.

Mason completed the **Sentence Check Chart** on a character sketch of his mother. Previously in Ms. McCarthy's class, Mason exhibited full sentence variety in essays and short stories, but for the character sketch of his parent, he shifted into a conversational language style that blunted his style and its subsequent impact. In fact, throughout the class, whether students chose to sketch a person they knew intimately or not, their normal style of writing lost its personal voice.

Mason followed the guide of the **Sentence Check Chart** for 25 sentences and concluded that he repeated far too many nouns—*he, she, mom, dad,* and *we*. He relied on vague verbs—*do, like, have, go, want, get, ask, love* and several forms of the verb *to be*— that could communicate with only those audiences who already knew his mom well. His revision required the rewording of more than the verb, in some cases rewording entire sentences.

Sentence Check Chart

Student's Name: ___Mason G.___

Grade/Teacher's Name: ___Mrs. McCarthy___

Before filling out the chart, number the first thirteen sentences in your draft and circle the first verb in each.

No.	1st Word	Subject	Verb	More Vivid Verb	# Of Words
1	My	Mom	is	has turned out to be	5 → 18
2	She	She	will be	earned the right to	8 → 14
3	If	you	see	follow her closely	12 → 22
4	My	mom	is	continues	9
5	At church	mom	is	serves	11
6	Sometimes	she	is	remains	9
7	She	she	goes	regularly attends	7 → 16
8	On Sunday	pastor Stan	asks	chooses	9 → 11
9	My	mom	is	stands ready to	8 → 13
10	Right	there	is		9
11	My	mom	loves	studies and appreciates	7 → 23
12	She	she	spends		8
13	Sometimes	my brother	goes	accompanies her and helps	9 → 19

Sentence Check Chart

Student's Name: ___Diana M.___

Grade/Teacher's Name: ___Mr. Turner___

Before filling out the chart, number the first thirteen sentences in your draft and circle the first verb in each.

No.	1st Word	Subject	Verb	More Vivid Verb	# of Words
1	Have	you	heard	has turned out to be	17
2	Well	quinceanera	is	describes	9
3	This	party	is	includes an elaborate	8 → 16
4	All	girls	look	anticipate	51 → 14, 28, 8
5	This	party	is	resembles	17 → 21
6	What	quinceanera	is	know the derivation of	4 → 9
7	The	word	is	consists of	15 → 19
8	It	it	is	chooses	16
9	A	quince	is	exists primarily	9 → 14
10	The	ceremony	embraces		13
11	The	custom	is	celebrates the coming of...	21 → 24
12	The	celebration	highlights		10
13	At	girl	is	transitions into	27 → 34

Sentence Check Chart

Student's Name: _Chelsia M._

Grade/Teacher's Name: _Mr. Turner_

Before filling out the chart, number the first thirteen sentences in your draft and circle the first verb in each.

No.	1st Word	Subject	Verb	More Vivid Verb	# of Words
1	What	it	does take	is required	8
2	The	pharmacist	has	must satisfy	22
3	They	they	have	acquire extensive...	16
4	A	pharmacist	should be informed	memorize	20
5	There	there	are	requirements abound	10 → 6
6	To	you	have	must earn	16
7	The	courses	include	consists of	37 → 11, 29
8	The	degree	require		15
9	Some	programs	admit		29
10	Most	schools	require		10
11	A	pharmacist	should be	must perform	11
12	The	things	make	standards acquired	15
13	A	pharmacist	must know	demonstrate	24 → 31

The tenth-grade students checked the sentences in their expository research projects. Interestingly, their subjects and verbs shook out much like the seventh-graders, which remains a continual puzzle to me. Their sentences, however, turned out to be remarkably varied in length, ranging from as few as 7 words to over 50. As they recast their subjects and verbs, they readily rearranged whole sentences to an even greater extent than their seventh-grade counterparts.

In order to use the *Sentence Check Charts* effectively, simply let students complete the assignment, and then ask them what they learned about themselves as a writer from the experience. Most students say things like

- "I started way too many of my sentences with the same word."

- "Weak subjects and verbs used too many times."

- "I used the same verbs over and over, and they don't give readers much information."

- "All of my sentences were between 8 and 11 words long. And I thought I was varying the length of my sentences."

- "Why didn't you tell me my writing had so many repeated words?"

This last comment reminds me that

> *When the student is ready, the teacher will appear.*
> a Buddhist proverb

❰ Looking Back

In two journal entries, explain fully the benefits of *Framed Drafts* and *Sentence Check Charts* for you as a teacher in courses that you presently teach.

❱ Looking Ahead

In the next month or two, what lessons or units invite you to use *Framed Drafts* drawn from texts in your course content to aid student comprehension of what they study? Where will the *Sentence Check Chart* enhance students' complete and accurate explanations of what they are learning in the coming curriculum?

12

Fine-Tune Beginnings and Endings with Me

Great is the art of beginning, but greater is the art of ending.
Henry Wadsworth Longfellow

At first, the beginnings and endings of all human undertakings are untidy.
John Galsworthy

All beginnings are somewhat strange; but we must have patience, and little by little, we shall find things, which at first were obscure, becoming clearer.
Vincent De Paul

Chapter 12 considers two parallel strategies for revising first drafts: **Writing Leads** and **Writing Closes**. These strategies move writers closer to their intended audience than any of the previous chapters, but they stop short of letting the audience initiate the revision process. First, it presents the challenge of hooking and engaging the readers from the beginning (**Writing Leads**). Then it moves to leaving those readers with good memories of reading the students' drafts (**Writing Closes**). It answers questions like, *What choices do I have to catch readers' attention and make them want to read on? What can I do to make sure that readers think and speak well of my writing once they have finished reading it?*

_____ Lesson for Introducing a Draft – Writing Leads _____

Fine-tune the beginning with me. I have a draft here that I like a lot. In fact, I am sure that the words in the body of my draft make the pictures in my mind show up clearly on the page. The beginning makes me wonder, though. Will my first words catch my readers' interest right away? Will they keep them reading? Will they ever get to the word pictures in the second and third paragraphs that I have worked hard to create?

As in earlier lessons, a simple invitation for your students to write with you suffices. Since students have written drafts on several topics before you invite them to revise, they may choose a draft that they like the best. Choosing the best draft re-engages their minds securely in their written thoughts, and they are ready to follow your invitation to *fine-tune the beginning* of their drafts.

I always follow my invitation to write leads with a model of three leads that I wrote for an expository essay, a character sketch of a person who influenced me positively. I simply read each lead aloud and ask them to vote on which lead they recommend me to use in my sketch of an influential uncle.

Model Lead #1 (from the first draft)

I met my Uncle Don Guinn after my family moved from Toppenish, Washington to Bradenton, Florida when I was nine. All three uncles I met in my Florida years were memorable in their own way, but none had the impact on my personal growth like my Uncle Don.

Model Lead #2

The impact of the speeding sports car on the rail of the bridge forced Uncle Don's head squarely into the silver plated knob mounted on the steering wheel. It bent his dangling cigarette in multiple folds and singed the hair of his full-grown mustache. It opened his nose at one corner and his temple enough to start a stream of blood flowing. I was petrified, frozen in a stare that felt the blow of the accident fully in my gut. I felt my stomach contract and push up through my esophagus. I knew it was my fault; I just knew it was.

Lead #3

"What you staring at, bug eyes! Get a rag out of the jockey box. . .," he paused long enough for me to fumble with the shiny latch and then the contents of the over-stuffed glove compartment. He held the cloth firmly against his bleeding temple punctured by the silver-plated knob mounted on his steering wheel. Surveying the scene: his new sports car bored fully into the bridge railing, no traffic in sight and a telephone booth just beyond the railing in a parking lot, as I squeaked, "Yes, sir." He gestured and spoke more calmly, "Run dial 'O' on that phone." I had never before seen my favorite uncle angry before. I knew not to hesitate.

When I ask students which of my three leads catches their attention and makes them want to read the character sketch that follows, a lop-sided majority always selects Lead #3. They explain that the first lead is plain, the second is graphic in its description, but the third one made them wonder how I was going to explain that an angry uncle was my favorite.

REVISE

As the teacher of your students, it is best for you to read your model of three leads for your students, not mine; however, feel free to use mine until you have created your own. Your model sets the mood for serious revision, but the model is not enough. The following steps are essential for helping students make the most of following your model. Take time to show students each step in your own writing as you ask them to follow your lead. They will accept your invitation to write with you, and the revision of their leads emerges naturally.

Steps for Revising a Lead

1. *Read through a selected draft carefully from the beginning. Mark off the first two or three mental pictures that return to your minds as you read. Remember **Framing Pictures in a Draft** (chapter 9)?*

2. *Place a large #1 by the first frame. It is your **Lead #1**.*
   Note: At step 2, let students confer with a collaborative partner to choose the part of their drafts that serve as Lead #1. The partners may determine that a draft lacks a lead. If so, a student's Lead #1 is null, and they move on to writing Lead #2. The partners may also discover that the lead contains several mental pictures. It may include one or more paragraphs. Often, Lead #1 is part or all of a first paragraph.

3. *Brainstorm with me techniques for writing an effective lead for your first draft.* Since many students have met different techniques for beginning their first drafts, help them create a list of possibilities. Prompt them with an obvious question like, *Do you think it is possible that you could have started your first draft a different way?* The answer "yes" signals buy-in, and the **Writing Leads** strategy has begun in earnest.
   Admit to them that, *There are literally dozens of ways to start a draft. Tell me some you know. As I list them on the board; write your version of the list on your paper.* Here's a list of techniques for leads from one group of students:

   ◆ A series of related questions

   ◆ A quotation (like *to be or not to be* or *life is like a box of chocolates)*

   ◆ A vivid little story (*anecdote*)

   ◆ A joke (clearly related to the main idea)

   ◆ A surprising or shocking opinion

   ◆ The story of how I came up with my topic or thesis

   ◆ Exciting, amazing, startling fact(s) or statistic(s)

   ◆ A vivid little mental picture (*vignette*).

Make sure that the list comes exclusively from students. At most, prompt them to include techniques they should have met. Students write their version of the list on notebook paper intended for revision or on page 18 of their *Working Portfolio for Students* (Combs 2007b).

4. Students may choose any of the techniques from the list as long as their writing 1) relates naturally to their draft and 2) truly introduces their selected first draft. Some students choose a fine technique for a lead that was not even on the list.

5. *Just beneath the list of techniques for writing leads, write a #2, then write the beginning of your first draft an entirely different way, any way that you choose, just so that it is different from Lead #1. You have four to six minutes to write five to seven sentences.*

   Note. If some students sit without writing, help them circle a technique from the list and remind them with, *Get your pencils moving; the best way to think is to move your pencil and leave words on the page.* Allow a bit longer than 6 minutes if you see most students using the time productively. Write your lead along with students.

6. Once you have brought the writing of Lead #2 to a close, move on without hesitation. Instruct the students to *move your pens/cursor down the page/screen a few lines below **Lead #2** and write the words **Lead #3**. Now begin writing the introduction to your draft again, any way you want as long as it is different from the first two leads. Go back to our class list and circle a technique you have yet to use, or come up with one on your own. It matters not. Just begin your draft an entirely different way. You have five minutes. You may begin.*

Let them continue writing beyond 5 minutes if most of the class remains engaged in writing. Write along with your students, but you may need to prompt students to trust their minds and get their pens moving. Remind them: *Moving your pens/cursor and leaving words on the page/screen is the best way to think.*

Setting concrete expectations for *Writing Leads*: Specify expectations for writing two additional leads: both leads #2 and #3 must 1) be a clear example of one of the techniques we have brainstormed and 2) contain 4 to 6 sentences. When students reach these expectations, they can assess themselves a target ⊙ (⊙ = 85 points). When they write fuller examples of Leads #2 and #3, they can assess themselves a plus + (+ = 100 points). Exceed requires them to use an additional revision strategy introduced in an earlier chapter such as ***Circling Picture Sentences*** or ***Jot and Blend***. When students fail to write two full leads, they assess themselves a bar ⊟ (⊟ = 70 points).

The first time that you use the ***Writing Leads*** strategy, ask some students to read their three leads aloud to the class.

♦ *In a sentence or two, mention the topic of your draft.*

♦ *Say Lead #1 and read it exactly as written.*

♦ *When you finish Lead #1, pause a moment. Say Lead #2 and read exactly what you have written for Lead #2.*

♦ *When you finish Lead #2, pause a moment. Say Lead #3 and read it.*

♦ *Got it? No comments about your leads, just read them. Ready?*

REFLECT

On the board, tally the votes of the whole class as you ask, *How many of you think Alexis should use Lead #1? Lead #2? Lead #3?* Make certain all students participate and vote only once.

Student's Name	Lead #1	Lead #2	Lead #3
Alexis	0	2	23
Carlos	1	15	9
Toneka	0	4	21
Totals	1	21	50

Eighth-grader, Erica of Dublin Middle School, Dublin, Georgia, chose to fine-tune the beginning of a babysitting experience that she claims made her "grow up" overnight. Before this experience she tried without much success to enjoy the only work available to young girls in her small hometown.

Lead #1 (from first draft—thesis)   Babysitting can be an exciting experience for anyone. I enjoy babysitting and have become quite good at it. This is thanks to an important night when I went babysitting for a child in a body cast. After that night I developed a few rules I go by each time. These rules can help even the worst babysitter begin to find enjoyment.

Lead #2 (preview)   I have experienced a long life of babysitting. But never before had I babysat a child in a body cast! I actually looked at it as a challenge. It became the experience that helped me learn how to enjoy babysitting no matter what. That first job with Kenly Duffy made me see now babysitting can be nothing but pure joy.

Lead #3 (scenario)   It's seven-thirty and my alarm clock is ringing. I shut it off and think to myself, "Why did I say I would take this job?" I finally pull myself out of bed one leg at a time and make my body enter the shower. Back in my room, I still think to myself, "Why?" But I keep moving. I decide what to wear and put on my make-up. As I head out the door, I think to myself, "Remember my trusty rules for enjoying babysitting no matter what." And once again they worked for me in an unusual way.

Erica's classmates voted 0-3-22 for Leads #1, #2 and #3 respectively, a decisive group, and they knew why. One classmate quipped, "Writing that shows instead of tells is always better." Another concurred, "Yes, Lead #3 shows us the experience was important. We didn't have to be told." They had learned well.

Katie, a tenth-grader at Sequoyah High School of Canton, Georgia, wrote these leads for an essay that explained a quotation from among a list provided by her teacher, Mrs. Dryden.

Lead #1
(from
first
draft)

Edmund burke once wrote, "Nobody made a greater mistake than he who did nothing because he could only do a little." In this quote, Burke is stating that the biggest mistakes are made when one is able to do something, but chooses not to do anything. This is because the little that one person could do seems not to make a difference. If one does not even try to solve a problem, the problem will only get worse.

Lead #2
(questions)

If nothing is done, is that a mistake? Is it better to do little even though it may not have great significance? Edmund Burke wrote, "Nobody made a greater mistake than he who did nothing because he could only do a little."

Lead #3
(Series of
"ifs" and
scenario)

If one has a few cents in change, it seems not to make a difference if he gives it away. If one neglects to donate that money to an organization, imagine how much money is lost. If everyone donated one dollar a year to the American Red Cross, millions would be made. The organization would never have to campaign for funds again. That little amount from many does make a difference. Million dollar mistakes are made when people neglect to do the little things. Edmund Burke wrote it this way, "Nobody made a greater mistake than he who did nothing because he could only do a little."

Her small group recommended Lead #3, citing the passion and personal engagement in her topic. The group agreed that, "Lead #1 is too cut and dried and Lead #2 doesn't seem finished."

After requiring her students to use the **Writing Leads** revision strategies several times, Ms. Heckenlaible (Vermillion High School, South Dakota) reduced the required leads to two. She saw that Lead #1 of most students was strong and a second lead gave them ample choice. One of her ninth-graders, Beth, wrote two leads.

Lead #1
(from
the first
draft)

More and more teenagers these days have computers in their own bedrooms, The idea appealed to me, and the more I thought about it, the more I liked it. There may be controversy between some people, but I am a strong believer in the idea. As long as the child respects his or her privilege a computer in the bedroom is a great way to stay ahead.

Lead #2
(questions)

You slump down in you chair and empty your lungs. This huge essay is due and none of the library computers are open. Your time is running out just as fast as your patience is. First thing tomorrow morning you will have to turn in a hand-written paper as a result of not having an available computer, which means a ton of docked points. Teachers aren't sympathetic with students, even if their excuses are true. Who knew not having a computer could cause all this stress? Here's a simple solution: your own computer to use whenever you need to work. As long as your child respects his or her privileges, a computer in the bedroom is a great way to stay ahead.

Beth's partner felt #2 was far better, much more engaging with a crisp clear introductory picture. See additional samples of students writing leads and closes at www.eyeoneducation.com. Go to this book's page and follow the links.

Student Self-Assessment: Students complete their reflection of the ***Writing Leads*** strategy by assessing the degree to which they met your stated expectation for their revision. They need to complete three robust leads, leads of quality. Each lead needs to be a clear example of a technique their class brainstormed. When each lead shows definite potential for reaching readers as an introduction to their draft, they assess themselves a target ⊙ (⊙ = 85 points). If they revise less, they self-assess a bar ▱ (▱ = 70 points). When they revise more (include another revision strategy like ***Jot and Blend***), they self-assess a plus + (+ = 100 points).

Every group of students who meets ***Writing Leads*** with me draws conclusions before I ask for them. Get positioned to chart their summary statements about writing leads. Be sure to write specifically what you hear them say. Some students have concluded that

♦ We always preferred leads #2 or #3 to #1. Is that the way it always is?

♦ *Almost nobody chooses the first lead.* This conclusion may spark the reading of a Lead #1 from a student who thinks her Lead #1 is her best. The class usually does not agree.

♦ The more times you write the beginning, the better it gets.

♦ You need several runs at getting your readers' attention.

Conclusion: Allow students to reach their own conclusions, but wrap up the session with a consensus statement like, ***All writers need to revise their leads. Sometimes they stay with Lead #1, changing it only slightly. Most of the time, however, they find a better way to engage their readers by starting their draft an entirely different way.*** For students choosing Lead #1, clarify that they knew #1 was best only after they made an honest attempt at writing leads #2 and #3.

On subsequent uses of this revision strategy, allow students to share their leads and receive responses in small groups as opposed to collaborative partners.

The serendipitous side effect of inviting students to write leads with you is obvious: you receive authentic help in fine-tuning leads in your own personal writing. Most of my drafts get shared with several classes. My sketch of Uncle Don has met over a dozen audiences. Without hesitation, the last group of 27 eighth-graders registered their preference, 1-10-16. I saw immediately that Lead #3 foreshadowed the major theme of the draft.

Combinations of Revision Strategies

Writing Leads is best combined with another revision strategy to assist in revising a student's complete draft. The possible combinations include the revision strategies covered in chapters 7–11. Two combinations I have seen work especially well.

+ ***Writing Leads—Framing Pictures in a Draft*** for a draft that contains specific word choices, but has too many components, too few components or components that are unevenly developed.

+ ***Writing Leads—Jot and Blend*** in a draft that is well organized, but needs help in establishing a consistent voice or adding crisp details throughout a draft.

A short conference with a student or a written teacher commentary (see ***First Draft Response Form,*** chapter 14) leads students to choose effective combinations of revision strategies themselves.

____ Lesson for Concluding a Draft – Writing Closes ____

At first glance, ***Writing Closes*** seems to mirror ***Writing Leads***. They are indeed quite similar. They both ask students to

+ *Identify key pictures in their drafts.*

+ *Write two additional versions of part of their drafts.*

+ *Receive immediate help from peers in choosing their best version.*

+ *Combine their lead/close with another revision strategy to revise the draft completely.*

+ *Write three quality leads/closes to receive full credit for revision.*

The sequences for using the two strategies are parallel, but the purposes for writing a lead and a close in writing a draft dramatically differ.

Leads engage readers. If students do not get their leads to engage readers, the readers never read the close. When a lead does its work effectively and the body of a draft presents effective *voice, pictures* and *flow,* the close must be ready. At the close of the sale of an automobile, a house or a life insurance policy, sales people help the buyer leave the sale with the feeling that a good thing has happened. In fact, it is such a good thing that buyers stride out and brag to friends and neighbors about the good deal that they just negotiated.

Likewise, the close of a draft carries the same charge. In an effective close, the student makes sure that readers leave the final draft satisfied, perhaps prompted to take specific action. Like the buyer of a new car, the readers of a good final draft leave the draft and tell their friends, "You have to read Alexis' essay on pollution that I read today. It's in the class binder on Mr. Shefler's desk. You won't believe what mercury in our food is doing to us, dude." And thus the life of an effective piece of student writing goes on from reader to potential reader.

Fine-tune the ending with me. *Here's a draft that I wrote recently. I have tried out the beginning and middle on readers. They like them well enough, but I need help with the ending. Writers call endings* **closes,** *and my writing needs an effective one. Will my readers leave my writing satisfied? Will they say something positive about it to others? Will my writing provoke healthy thought, a change of mind, or maybe even specific action?*

I have shared these three closes of the character sketch of an uncle with students in many schools with identical results. Every class so far prefers Lead #2. See if you agree.

Model Close #1 (from the first draft)

That was my Uncle Don. There's nothing much else to say. He was neither intellectual nor athletic, just a friend several times my age.

Model Close #2 (summary)

Meeting Uncle Don taught me not to rush to judgment about a person. I don't know if other people around me rushed, but they all judged. Don Guinn harshly. I know he smoked and drank and drove too fast, but my Aunt Annie Merle loved him. I now know that I was one of the few people who really got to know and appreciate him as the affable and likable person he was.

Model Close #3 (warning)

My relatives continued to ignore Uncle Don, but it definitely was at their own peril, not to mention his. They were miserable going out of their way to avoid him at weddings, reunions, sports events or chance meetings at church or a neighborhood store. And Uncle Don? Left to interpret the social snubs that barraged him day in and day out, he compensated by living the party life. He smoked Camel cigarettes and drank mixed drinks heavily to an early death, an obvious attempt to pretend that his isolation didn't bother him.

The students all say that Close #1 is too short, and some think it abrupt. They all agree that Close #3 is too long; worse, it spins off into another direction about my view of my Uncle Don. One student said Close #3 was more about me than my Uncle Don. They thought I was proud of myself for being a friend to a man with few friends. My attempt to show the audience the folly of judging others obviously missed the mark.

As I suggested in **Writing Leads**, it is important for you to follow specific steps to fine-tune the ending (close) of a draft that you are writing. Show students each step of this strategy in your own writing as you ask them to follow your model.

Steps for Revising a Close

1. *Read through a selected draft carefully from the beginning. Mark off the last two or three mental pictures that return to your minds as you read. Recall the lesson in chapter 9,* **Framing Pictures in a Draft***.*

2. *Mark the last frame in your draft with a large* **#1***. It represents the first conclusion to your draft,* **Close #1***.*

   Note: At step 2, students confer with a collaborative partner in choosing the part of their draft that serves as Close #1. The partners may determine that a draft lacks a close. If so, a student's Close #1 is null and they move on to writing Close #2. The partners may also discover that the close contains several mental pictures. It may include one or more paragraphs, although that is rare in student writing.

3. Since students have met alternative techniques for concluding drafts, ask an obvious question like, *Do you think it is possible that you could have ended your first draft a different way?* Once again the answer "Yes" represents buy-in; **Writing Closes** has begun.

   Remind them, *As I make the list on the board, write your version of the list on your paper.* For example,

   ♦ *A prediction*

   ♦ *A warning*

   ♦ *A call to action*

   ♦ *A little story (anecdote)*

   ♦ *A recap of the main idea or ideas*

   ♦ *A little mental picture (vignette).*

4. *Choose any of the techniques from the list that 1) relate naturally to your draft and 2) conclude your selected first draft or use one of your own.*

5. *A couple of lines below the list of possible closes, write* **#2***. Then write the ending of your first draft a different way, any way that you choose. You have five minutes to write five to seven sentences. Remember that writing words with a pen or on the word processor is the best way to think.*

6. Move seamlessly to the next step, *Move your pens/cursor down the page a few lines below **Close #2** and write the words: **Close #3**. Now begin writing the ending to your draft again, any way you want as long as it is different from your first two closes. Pick another technique from our list or use one on your own. Begin your draft a new way. You have five minutes. You may begin.*

As long as most students remain engaged in their revision, let them continue writing a bit beyond the announced five minutes.

Setting concrete expectations for *Writing Closes*: Specify expectations for writing two additional closes: both Closes #2 and #3 must 1) be a clear example of one of the techniques we have brainstormed and 2) contain 4 to 6 sentences. When students reach these expectations, they can assess themselves a target ⊙ (⊙ = 85 points). When they employ an additional revision strategy from an earlier chapter, they can assess themselves a plus + (+ = 100 points). When students fail to write two full closes, they assess themselves a bar ▭ (▭ = 70 points).

Ask some students to read their closes aloud to the class for its response as follows:

♦ In a sentence or two, mention the topic of your draft.

♦ Then say Close #1 and read Close #1 in your draft.

♦ When you finish Close #1, pause a moment. Say Close #2 and read it.

♦ When you finish Close #2, pause a moment. Say Close #3 and read it.

Got it? Just say the number of the close and read the close word-for-word. No comments about the closes, just read them. Ready?

On the board, tally the votes of the whole class as you ask, *How many of you think Juanita should use Close #1? Close #2? Close #3?* Make certain all students participate and vote only once.

Student's Name	Close #1	Close #2	Close #3
Tameka	5	2	21
Michael	9	10	9
Juanita	0	0	28
Totals	14	12	58

Here Taylor, a junior at Clarke Central High School, Athens, Georgia, responds to the prompt that "technology has advanced to the point of time travel. Assume that your history class was chosen to be the first group of students to travel in a time machine. Write a speech to present to your classmates that convinces them to choose the time period that you prefer."

Close #1
(from
the first
draft—
summary)

Society's willingness to accept changes in music and lifestyle made the 1970's exciting. People were able to expand their areas of interest and advance their cultural knowledge. The 1970's was the first decade to make everything possible, and I think you'll like it.

Close #2
(prediction)

Many great time periods have passed through history, and they have all left their marks on the future and present. While some were very long ago, there are also periods like the 1970's which our parents had the joy of experiencing. We could all learn so much by experiencing the 1970's, and we would enjoy ourselves as well. We could unleash the rebellion in us, yet use it productively much like the hippies did. Our ears would be freed by the music of Led Zeppelin, and our souls would be unchained from their chairs. The 1970's was a great set of years that I hope all of you will join me in visiting.

Lead #3
(warning/
prediction)

Excitement is what empowers us to get through the duties of our daily lives. Beware of the Romans and the Egyptians because their lives revolved around work, religion and no play. If you really want to dissatisfy yourself, then, by all means, choose one of those time periods to visit. But if you want to learn more about yourself and the society you live in, then you should come and experience the joy of the 1970's with me.

Taylor's class liked his essay on time travel, but their vote of 0-13-12 told him to abandon his original close, leaving the choice of #2 or #3 up to him. The call of freedom and enjoyment attracted those who preferred Close #2. The warning "beware of the Romans" convinced those who chose Close #3. Interestingly, when I asked the class if they would choose to travel back to the 1970's, most said no. Most thought his paper was better written than theirs. So there you have it. Oh, the plight of being an author!

Seventh-graders enjoy **Writing Closes** once they have experienced the strategy. Kelsi from West Hall Middle School in Oakwood, Georgia, thought her first close was exactly what she needed to bring closure to her persuasive essay on autism. In the introduction and body of her first draft, she noted that her older autistic brother gave her valuable insight into how to appreciate every person she met, not just those with diagnosed health disorders. She explained that autism has become increasingly widespread. Autistic people find it hard to adapt to change, and while they are very sensitive themselves in social situations, they seem insensitive in relating to others. She concluded her call for learning to appreciate people with autism like this.

Close #1 (from the first draft— warning/ prediction))	I don't know if anyone would disagree with my points, but I do know this: you will never know what is going on in someone else's life. The next person you meet could have a disorder such as autism. If you go off and make fun of them, you are not benefitting anyone. Not only would this prevent hurting the feelings of the person with the disorder, it would help make the world a better place.

She reluctantly agreed to follow the **Writing Closes** strategy, writing these two optional closes in four or five minutes each.

Close #2 (challenge)	Anyone you meet could have Autism, especially Asperger's Syndrome. We don't know what's going on in their life, so why be rude? Why be hurtful? Everybody's living in their own situation. What will you do?
Close #3 (prediction/ challenge)	We will never know if someone we encounter has autism. Here's an idea. Show respect to anyone you encounter. That way, no one ever gets hurt. Since people with autism tend to have more delicate feelings, it could prevent them from having a meltdown. I challenge you to go and be friendly and respect everyone, especially someone you know with Autism.

In Close #2, Kelsi shifted to asking a series of questions which six of her classmates thought made it the close of choice. Twelve classmates chose Close #3; they thought it added real power to a draft that seemed to be a call to action from its beginning.

Student Self-Assessment: Students complete their reflection of the **Writing Closes** strategy by assessing the degree to which they met your stated expectations. They need to complete 3 robust closes, closes of quality. Each close needs to be a clear example of a technique their class brainstormed. When each close shows definite potential for reaching potential readers as an ending of the student's draft, they assess themselves a target ☉ (☉ = 85 points). If they revise less, they self-assess a bar ☰ (☰ = 70 points). When they revise more (combining sentences or jot and blending vivid details throughout their drafts), they self-assess a plus + (+ = 100 points).

Once again, students are eager to draw conclusions about **Writing Closes**. Some students I have met concluded that

♦ "We preferred Closes #2 or #3 over #1."

♦ "Almost nobody chooses their first close." *When a student claims his Close #1 is his best, let him read his three closes for a quick response from the class. It's always an interesting judgment.*

♦ "I learned that conclusions were supposed to leave others feeling good about you."

♦ "Closes can lead you to writing something different. It's like a new beginning of something you write later."

♦ "Good closes get readers to talk to others about your writing."

Conclusion: It is important to bring consensus into a single statement if at all possible. *All writers revise closes to their writing. Sometimes they stay with a version of Close #1, but most of the time they find a better way to help their readers feel good about reading their drafts. A good close can inspire readers to tell others that they need to read what they just read.* When students choose Close #1, they are confident of their choice because they tried two other versions of their close—and still preferred Close #1.

On subsequent uses of this revision strategy, allow students to share their closes and to receive responses in small groups of their peers. Like responses to **Writing Leads**, small groups seem to respond more productively to **Writing Closes** than do pairs.

Combinations of Revision Strategies

Writing Closes is best combined with another revision strategy to assist in improving other traits of students' drafts. Possible combinations include the revision strategies covered in chapters 7–11. Guide students to experience several combinations that you have seen work well.

♦ *Writing Closes—Combining Sentences* for a draft that contains specific word choices, but has too many short or compound sentences.

♦ *Writing Closes—Jot and Blend* for a draft that is well organized, but needs help in establishing a consistent or engaging voice.

A short conference with a student or a written teacher commentary (see **First Draft Response Forms,** chapter 14) can lead students to choose effective combinations of revision strategies themselves.

Extending Student Understanding of Effective Closes

After using this sequence for introducing *Writing Closes*, help students draw further conclusions about the purpose of closes. Let them help you list the different purposes of closes in different *genres* and *modes* of writing.

A conventional mode of writing may serve the purpose of different genres.

Mode	*Genre*	Purpose of a Close
Contrast-Compare	*Expository*	Help readers **understand** clearly that two or more ideas are 1) decidedly different 2) indeed quite similar 3) more alike than different 4) more different than alike.
	Persuasive	**Convince** readers that two or more ideas are 1) decidedly different 2) indeed quite similar 3) more alike than different 4) more different than alike.
Explain a Process	*Expository*	Help readers **understand** clearly how 1) a procedure works 2) to perform a procedure themselves 3) to explain a procedure to others.
	Persuasive	**Convince** readers 1) that a procedure works a specific way 2) to perform a procedure a specific way 3) to explain a procedure to others a specific way.

Mode	*Genre*	Purpose of a Close
Character Sketch	*Expository*	Help readers <u>**understand**</u> clearly 1) a character's appearance, qualities, preferences and behaviors 2) how to describe a character to others 3) how a character fits a class of characters.
	Persuasive	<u>**Convince**</u> readers 1) that a character has specific qualities 2) that a character fits a class of characters 3) of the writer's personal opinion of the character 4) to pass the writer's sketch on to others.
Cause-Effect	*Expository*	Help readers <u>**understand**</u> 1) that a cause and effect are related 2) how cause(s) may have had certain effect(s).
	Persuasive	<u>**Convince**</u> readers 1) that a cause resulted in a specific effect 2) that an effect is the result of specific cause(s). 3) to share a cause-effect relationship with others.

Other modes of writing—classification, extended definition, editorial or feature story—fit in the expository or persuasive genre when the purpose of the writing is to clarify for or convince an audience respectively. In theory, a genre of writing can appear in most any mode of writing. While the terms *genre* and *mode* for classifying writing vary from text to text, they do help students control their writing for effective communication.

❮ Looking Back

In your response journal, describe two ideas about *Writing Leads* and *Writing Closes* that were valuable for you as a teacher in a course that you presently teach.

❯ Looking Ahead

In what aspects of your future curriculum will *Writing Leads* or *Writing Closes* increase effective student learning?

Empowering Students to Write and RE-write
Session Guide #4 for Professional Learning Teams

Responding to

Chapter 10: Work on writing style with me—*Sentence Building, Spotting Weasel Words*

Chapter 11: Nail down word choice with me—*Framed Drafts, Sentence Check Chart*

Chapter 12: Fine-tune beginnings and endings with me—*Writing Leads, Writing Closes*

Before joining *Professional Learning Team (PLT) Session #4*

Make sure you have written your response to these topics in your journal.

1. Explain why all teachers across the curriculum need to work on writing style.

2. Explain how getting rid of the wrong words is the key to effective word choice.

3. Explain how writing effective leads and closes illustrates mastery of a course standard.

Exemplars

As you read through student revision that used the strategies of chapters 10-12, select the student samples that best illustrated their use. Bring your own personal revision that you used as an effective model for your students to follow.

Discussion questions for *PLT Session #4*

1. Describe the features in your students' writing that show their need for sentence-combining practice (chapter 10).

2. In two or three sentences, explain the evidence in your students' writing of their use of weasel words (chapter 10).

3. What advantage or disadvantage is there in presenting a *Framed Draft* of a passage in a textbook that students find difficult to understand (chapter 11)?

4. Explain how you succeeded in helping students move from completing a *Sentence Check Chart* to revising their first drafts significantly (chapter 11).

5. How important is it that others help writers decide which lead out of three is the best (chapter 12)?

Compiling *Professional Learning Portfolios*

Bring the artifacts that you have gathered since PLT #3 to include in your *Professional Learning Portfolio*. Share your ideas for expanding your portfolio and listen to the portfolio plans of other teachers.

13

Call on Your Audience with Me

In chapters 7–12, you invited students to follow well-tested strategies for improving the *voice* (style), *pictures* (ideas) and *flow* (organization) of their first drafts themselves, sometimes following your model, always returning to the picture they had in their minds when they wrote their first drafts. They tried their revisions out on an audience **after** they had completed a revision strategy.

It is time, now, to help them bring all of the tools and strategies into play on writing and RE-writing their drafts. Beginning with chapter 8, you and I encouraged students to combine a previous strategy with the current one to exceed their teachers' expectations. Once students have succeeded in using two or three of these strategies, they develop confidence in knowing when to use which one. They

- ♦ know which advance organizers fit which topic prompts (chapter 6)

- ♦ jot and blend details into patches of spare sentences (chapter 7)

- ♦ circle sentences to expand into paragraphs for readers to visualize (chapter 8)

- ♦ recognize which frames in their drafts they can

  - ◇ write the most more about

  - ◇ do without

  - ◇ move to a better location (chapter 9)

- ♦ spot sentences that would be better when combined (chapter 10).

So why not list the revision strategies on a permanent wall chart or collect the instructional tools and revision strategies in file folders for easy student access. Use samples from www.eyeoneducation.com, order them from www.writingtowin.com, or better yet, use the samples to create your own

- Assignment pages
- Advance organizers
- *Jot and Blend* script
- *Circling Picture Sentences* script
- *Framing Pictures in a Draft* script
- *Framed Drafts*
- *Sentence Check Charts*
- *Writing Leads*
- *Writing Closes*

It is best to use sentence-combining exercises in print like *Sentence Building*, levels 4–9, www.writingtowin.com.

In meeting a writing prompt or revising a first draft, students pull out a copy of the strategy they think will help, take it to their desks, use it and return it to the file for others to use. When students show the confidence to browse and select these strategies as needed, they have attained a strong sense of revision. They show evidence of an independent mindset for revision.

Chapter 13 changes the focus from writers revising their drafts alone to readers initiating the revision. This shift requires students to have some confidence in their own ability to revise. It is one thing for students to revise and then check out their efforts on an audience. It is quite another to let the audience participate in the revision from the start. It requires writers who are practiced revisers like your students whom you have invited to revise with you through chapters 7–12.

In this chapter you invite the students to interact with readers in pairs or small groups. They read their first drafts aloud to peers and listen to real people in an audience respond, restate and voice ideas for revising their drafts. This chapter is a way for students to test out their writing on an audience and listen carefully to its reaction. They read their drafts to peers and take notes as they listen to these interested responders. Your students may be surprised that when they present an elaborated first draft that a real audience demands even more detail and explanation. They may discover that they need to proceed a completely different way. Chapters 13–14 open all aspects of the writing to analysis and response from others.

Lesson for Introducing a Peer Response Form

Use a peer response form with me. I have a first draft here that came to me in reader-ready details. Has writing every come to you that way? My thoughts engaged me so fully that the specific details just poured onto the page. You see, the story marks a turning point in my life. The narrative is quite full. When I read it, no ideas for revision come to mind; it seems complete to me; it is the kind of draft that needs an audience up front. I need to test it out on readers who don't know me all that well—like you guys. When you hear me read this full narrative aloud, will you experience it as I did? Will you see the importance of what happened? Or will you be distracted from the meaning by something I've included? These are a few of the questions that made me enlist your help first. Listen for what the experience meant to the narrator.

Whether students are writing personal narratives or not, this invitation asks them to select a draft that they think is complete and see if it gets the desired effect that they want. They are ready to *call on the audience with you.*

Model First Draft

This past April as a celebration of a wedding anniversary, I motored with my wife, Arnelle, through the Yakima Valley of Washington where I spent most of the first thirteen years of my life. Mt. Adams' prominence imposed itself from the West. Arnelle's response was immediate, "Now, that's a mountain." We focused on that majestic, dormant, snow-capped volcano at each stop on our tour of the lower valley of fruit orchards, vineyards, hop lots and struggling farm towns.

I was shocked by the size of the house in Toppenish that I called home up through the third grade. I remembered a large front lawn for endless games of softball. However, now the diminutive patches of grass on either side of a short path from sidewalk to porch appeared too small for one of our famed lemonade stands, much less rambunctious innings of ball. The boulevard with a tree-lined wide strip of grass between two paved ribbons of the avenue still impressed me, and I visualized long afternoons of hide-and-go-seek and permutations of freeze-tag.

As I sat in the front seat of a rental Prius that cool morning, I reentered the drama of neighborhood softball on the tiny front lawn with home plate and three bases as points on the sidewalk that outlined one half of the front lawn. Somehow, my wife knew to sit in silence and let me gaze. My revelry of soft-pitch competition among fun-loving elementary school children evaporated when a stronger memory intruded from the theater of the front porch, a bright yellow addition on a tiny white frame house with pull-down shades, shear curtains and no shutters.

It was a Sunday afternoon, and my older brother, Larry, and I were playing on the porch out front. We took a board off of the crate our new refrigerator was delivered in. Larry laid the board down flat so that about two feet of it hung over the edge of the porch, just above mom's favorite Iris bed.

Larry stood firmly on the porch end and double-dog dared me to walk out to the diving end. Since he said "double-dog," I was honor bound to walk. With each step I took, the board bent closer and closer to the flowers. At the end, I put my full weight on it, and it responded with a "thwang-a-thwang-a-crack." Oh, how my left hip hurt. I felt a throbbing and saw a red spot on my gym shorts begin to spread. The cotton began sticking to my skin.

I sat hard on my tailbone, silent at first, in the middle of mom's prize flowers, staring through blurry eyes at the jagged end of the board. It took a few seconds for my open mouth to project a sound. When it did, my screams brought my mom out of the house on the run. In a second she figured out what had happened. . . .

"You visiting anyplace interesting?" Arnelle' voice broke my gaze.

I shook my head. "Just remembering what happened on that porch that made me start standing up for myself," I replied.

"Want to talk about it?" she inquired.

"Sure, that porch used to be yellow," I quipped with a grin and pressed the accelerator of the silent hybrid back to the real and present celebration.

I read my first draft to students about your age. They responded with a form like the one distributed for your use today, **Response Form #1**. I'll show you how one person responded to my draft, but only after I field responses from you all. You respond to the "Phrases or parts that stuck in my mind," then I'll let you see the earlier student's response.

Response Form #1 (Narrative)

Author: _Dr. Combs_   Consultant: _Stacy F_

Phrases or parts that stuck in my mind:
Mt. Adams' prominence, thwang-a-thwang-a-crack, quiet Prius

What I want (or need) to know more about:
More about Larry, more about the slat—what does one look like? More about double-dog dare

1. *What is the setting and what meaning does it contribute to the story?*
   Front of a childhood home with a life-changing childhood experience. It's the for a "coming of age" event.

2. *Who are the main characters and how do they relate?*

   In the present, you and your wife are on an important trip that you like; in a flashback you, your mom and brother have a run-in on a Sunday afternoon.

3. *What's the problem and how is it brought to a climax?*
   You poke a gash in your hip after Larry dared you to dive off of a pretend diving board. The climax happened when your mom appeared on the porch

4. *Is there a resolution? A lesson learned? A realization? Explain.*
   The resolution happened when Arnelle interrupted your memory. You remember that what happened helped you start standing up to your brother.

5. *What is the point of view? What other point(s) of view would work?*
   First person with a flashback. You could have just told the story, but the flashback made for a surprising story that was more interesting than the first one. You could start with the flashback and end with the valley tour.

REVISE

Stacy captured the details of the story rather well, although he missed the problem of big-brother domination that I wanted the story to transmit; the accident may need to be less graphic. When you model a personal narrative for your students, you will be surprised by their insight into memories important to you—the more important and vivid the memory in your draft, the more detailed and insightful their responses. Be prepared to take copious notes about their comments. Students need for you to model serious note-taking of the audience response.

When students have helped you complete their response to your draft, ask them to follow these steps in setting up the response to their first drafts.

1. *Sign your name as the author on* **Response Form #1**. *Then move to the partner that I've assigned to share your draft and receive a peer response. Let your partner sign in as the consultant. Consultants are more than buddies or partners; they carry the responsibility of serious and full written responses and suggestions.*

2. *Read through the draft of your partner and write a full response to the first two items on the response form. Write detailed responses in compact handwriting. You receive full credit when you fill out every line of the form.*

3. *Continue responding to each of the next five items by filling up each of the two lines supplied for each item. Your responses will be assessed for their perception and insight.*
   Note: As you observe students completing the forms, help them be complete and informative in their responses.

4. *When you have completed the requested information, write additional responses in the margins or on back of the response form. Your partner is counting on you.*
   Note: Written peer responses should always be positive, constructive recommendations for improving the quantity or quality of the first drafts.

Once the response is completed, the revision begins. Students return the response forms and first drafts to the writers. The authors read the written responses for each item carefully and place a symbol by each observation to show the degree to which the reader has understood the narrative accurately and completely.

+ Perceptive and insightful understanding

◎ Moderate understanding

⊟ Misunderstood

For each response that the authors mark with a ◎ or a ⊟, they return to their draft and revise it to assure a + response from the peer consultant. They consider

♦ adding to the parts that are incompletely understood

♦ changing parts that are misunderstood

♦ deleting or downplaying parts that are distracting or misleading.

At this point of the peer response strategy, encourage partners to consult with one another. Authors share their additions, changes or deletions with their consultant and ask them to respond to the feature as revised.

As you try out this revision strategy, return to the model ***Response Form*** related to your model that you have projected on the board. Assess each of the student responses to your draft with a **+,** ◎, or 🖿. Show how the student responses on the ***Response Form*** helped you revise your draft; however, show that you may not follow every suggestion they make. For example, although several students in the audience wanted to know what our mother did when she arrived, I avoided adding in the punishment. It was more important to the draft that my student-audience focus what the experience taught, not on the punishment my brother and I endured. Good luck.

On a page from a flip chart that can be affixed to the wall, lead the students in reflecting on the process of revising their writing using an appropriate *Response Form*. They may come up with reflections like the following from a class of ninth graders.

"We need to write full drafts before we use a response form."

"As consultants, we need to write as much as we can."

"We use the consultant's response to assess how well we wrote."

"Our revised drafts are easier for our consultant to understand."

"We might want to revise our writing even further."

Since this activity is so engaging for the audience, students enjoy drawing conclusions about the value of peer response forms in helping them revise. Listen carefully and summarize exactly what you hear them say. Use another sheet from the flip chart to document what students have learned. Here are some student conclusions:

"We can work on painting a word picture in our writing, and it still isn't enough for some readers."

"It's very easy for readers to miss what we mean to say."

"Writing is work between an author and a consultant."

"Response forms make it easy for consultants to be helpful."

"Writing is like a mirror of reading."

"Writing a simple draft so readers understand takes work."

Of course, the list of conclusions from your classes will vary from this list, but the lessons learned should overlap.

REFLECT

LEARN

Credit for Expectations of Students as Consultants and Authors

Students receive full credit for the **Response Form** strategy when they complete three tasks.

♦ As consultants, they complete a response form on the first draft of an author.

♦ As authors, they assess if their consultant's understanding of their draft matched their intended meaning.

♦ As authors, they revise their first drafts to improve the accuracy of their consultant's understanding.

♦ As authors, they confer with their consultant to assess the effectiveness of their revision.

Extending Student Understanding of Peer Response Forms

After using this sequence for introducing peer response forms, consider using response forms for other modes of writing that you assign. See this book's page on www.eyeoneducation.com for samples of **Response Forms** for other modes of writing—Character Sketch, Cause & Effect, Compare & Contrast, Explain a Process and Support an Opinion. Let these response forms guide you in creating a response form in the mode that you have assigned. Just remember that response forms poll the audience—in the role of consultants—for their understanding of the writer's ideas. While these serve to make improvements, they are not direct suggestions for improvements that turn the reins of writing over to the consultant.

Caveat. As teacher-facilitators of growing writers, we have the task of discerning when the consultant's understanding of a first draft is more of an issue than the first draft itself. When a consultant's understanding of a draft is markedly different from that of the writer, the issue may be the consultant's skills of reading comprehension rather than the writer's skills of presentation. We need to realize these instances are possible, spot them readily and decide with which student to conference.

Say It Back and *Author's Chair*

For decades, *Say It Back* and *Author's Chair* have helped students work through the writing process to a final draft. Whether students present science projects, a report on the care of their musical instruments in band, a summary of a current event in social studies or a draft of a person narrative, the process is the same. If you know that the students have little to no experience sharing their writing aloud with others, start with *Say It Back*. Go ahead and set up a circle of chairs with one sporting the label, *Author's Chair*. A director's chair serves this purpose well. Move through the following procedures for helping students speak and listen productively.

1. Students read their selected drafts aloud to their peers, then they use one or more of the following that you have requested they use:

   a. **"Say it back."** Students make certain that the major points of a draft are restated or summarized by peers who listened to their reading. If no one can recall a point that was important to the draft, the writers circle it for later elaboration or clarification.

   b. **"What part of my writing can you picture in your mind?"** As peers respond, the writers note which parts of their drafts reached their audience.

   c. **"What questions do you have about my writing?"** As peers pose questions, the writers jot them down in the margins.

   Note: *Say It Back* is at first a whole-class activity, then a small-group activity. Eventually, *Say It Back* is completed in pairs who reciprocate.

2. Once the students have completed making notes from their peers' suggestions, they can be assigned a partner to judge how well the notes fit into the first draft (an option teachers may find important to require).

3. Students make last minute revision to their final drafts.

   Note: For the first use of *Say It Back*, teachers read their own writing aloud, modeling the procedures for eliciting student responses. Teachers set the expectation for writers to use 2–3 responses to improve their first drafts.

The *Author's Chair* routine occurs after *Say It Back* has conditioned students to

♦ reading their final drafts aloud for all to hear.

♦ listening to the final drafts of others well enough to respond to specific parts of it.

Students sit in a circle much as they did for *Say It Back*. For sure, the students introduce themselves loud and clear with the following statement:

My name is (first name)*, and I am a writer!*

Encourage them to mention what they want the audience to help them with, like *I want to know if you see the pictures of my science experiment that surprised the whole class.* Not all students comply, but most of them present a version of the standard statement. This autumn, I launched an **Author's Chair** publishing routine with the *Asheville Writing Club* of homeschool students. Each of 16 students published their final drafts by reading them aloud, projecting their voices for all to hear. They showed pictures or sketches to support the publication of the final draft. Since there were five parents present, a parent shared, followed by three students, then a parent, and so on. Parents and students alike began with the standard statement. Some students divulged interesting information about themselves as writers.

Evan   "My name is Evan and I have a problem. You'll see." [Actually, his writing presented a problem for the main character, not for the writer.]

Daniel   "My name is Daniel. Hi!" [waving sheepishly] "Here's what I wrote."

Nathan   "Hello. I'm Nathan and I write."

Nicholas "My name is Nicholas, and I'm. . .I'm not that good of a writer, but I still am one."

These statements veered the farthest from, "My name is _____, and I am a writer" among the sixteen and let the parents know which students were comfortable stating that they were, indeed, writers; most students stuck with the script. For those like Evan and Daniel, it was important to give them a pass and talk with them in private before the next **Author's Chair** experience. They do need to confess publicly that they are writers. That day will come.

Hi, My name is _Warren_ , and I am a writer. I recorded this memory in the summer after my first experience ice fishing. I'm interested in what you can picture about the setting in my writing because I know most people do not have accurate pictures of ice fishing in their minds. Be ready to tell me.

Bud helped each of his two sons and me set up our fish houses for spearing North Pike on Upper Red Lake of northern Minnesota in 5 degree weather. Fortunately, there was little wind. Bundled up in long underwear, snowmobile suits and leather choppers, we warmed ourselves in the bright sun by clearing 18 inches of snow from the surface so Bud could chainsaw a rectangle in the ice the size of large televisions for four ice houses.

The 4 feet x 4 feet portable houses folded out of the homemade ply board boxes and sat atop the rectangle of dark water. I positioned my house so the hole in the floor sat directly over the hole in the ice. I lit the lunchbox-size stove filled with kindling and newsprint and felt the fire instantly draft up the four-inch chimney through the roof. I stepped inside in a crouch and sat on the bench and prepared the minnow bait and pole. I cinched the four-inch minnow in a harness on the end of a line that hung from a stick that served as a rafter in the tiny house. The length was perfect. The minnow dangled two feet beneath the surface of the water in the center of the dark hole.

I took out a white potato and did as I had been shown. I sliced it into paper thin circles and watched each circle sink to the bottom of the shallow lake, probably no more than 10-12 feet. When a lethargic Pike swam slowly over the potato circles, I'd see its form and release the twenty-pound spear in my hand, trapping the unsuspecting fish in the tines. A thin rope secured the end of the spear to my right-hand wrist so I could retrieve my catch.

Then came the wait, a long one, at least long enough that the heat at the top of the house around my head must have reached 80-90 degrees while my feet in snowmobile books approached frostbite. I fought sleep. I felt my head nod.

"Thwong!!!" The 12-inch pole in the rafters of the canvas house alarmed my ears in the deafening silence and went straight to my heart. A stream of jerky thumps followed and I shook my head enough to see that the minnow was out of sight.

"What the deuce do I do now?" I tried remembering the instructions back at Bud's house. Indeed, the minnow was nowhere to be seen. Only an 8# test line tensed off to the left side of the hole.

I focused hard to recreate the thorough directions when it dawned on me that a big Pike was coming, ever so slowly since the water was so cold. I grabbed the spear and positioned it over the hole's center. I stared in the opposite direction that the minnow was headed. I thought I saw a dark shadow at the edge and counted to three and pushed the spear into the cold lake. It hit the bottom and stuck for a moment, then started moving like it was attached to an engine. Engine my foot. I had just angered a somnambulant Pike; it was time to get busy. I pulled up the slack rope until the spear's end slipped into my mittened hand. As I pulled on the spear, it flailed about in my hand, but I remembered to back out of the spring-loaded door to my left. I stepped one snowmobile boot out first and then the other. I stayed crouched on my pass through the door, bringing behind me the spear, the rope and a 14-pound Northern Pike wriggling in three of the tines.

"Hodie-Hodie-Ho," Bud gave his standard howl at the landing of a fish, and I stood tall, grinning and listening for the directions of what to do from here. Fishing with Bud, there were always directions, and I understood the value of following them.

Back inside, I sat on my bench staring at the minnow in the harness dangling in the center of the hole, almost motionless, as if no trauma had just occurred. All was back to normal for these parts: the cold and the deafening silence of a frozen mid-winter. Once again, I sat freezing cold at my feet, fighting sleep at my head in the 90 degree heat of a sub-zero day.

The students' applause was warm and seemed long. I felt gratified by their comments that taught me what my audience needed to know to picture the homemade fish house accurately in their minds. Their pictures were close, but they helped me see what work I needed yet to do.

"I could see the 90-degree heat of a sub-zero day. Ironic."

"I could really feel the cold."

"I never thought of silence being deafening. What did you mean?"

"Did the house have carpet in it? A TV?"

"How did you get to the lake?"

"Were the houses close together?"

"Do you have any more stories like this one?"

Their comments and questions told me exactly how to work on my draft. But my draft had met a real and diverse audience who all sat engaged in my narrative. Like others seated in the **Author's Chair** *before me, I felt published.*

❮ Looking Back

In your response journal, discuss the pros and cons of revising first drafts yourself and letting an audience initiate the revision with a tool like a **Response Form**. In a second entry, discuss the value of using an **Author's Chair** in a class you currently teach.

❯ Looking Ahead

What things coming up in your curriculum invite you to use **Response Forms, Say It Back** or **Author's Chair** strategies in this chapter?

14

Talk About Writing with Me

Do not bother just to be better than your contemporaries or predecessors.
Try to be better than yourself.
Willam Faulkner

People never improve unless they look to some standard or example
higher or better than themselves.
Tryon Edwards

If students are going to keep writing with us, we need to engage them in ongoing discussions about their writing. In the U. S. of America, teachers have typically read students' writing, written comments in the margins and returned it to their students. Teachers comment and students accept the comments as they are or dare to challenge them. The comments supposedly justify the grade that the teacher gave to the paper. That is the model my teachers followed; it is the model I see most often today. It does not lead to students' peak performances as writers. There is a better way that I happened onto quite by accident.

Early in my career as a writing consultant in schools, I saw that my approach to writing solved the problem of students unwilling or unable to write. A new problem emerged, one larger than the original, demanding immediate attention. In one large south Georgia high school, teachers glowed at their students' increased fluency and articulation in writing during the first months of our implementation. Their students wrote willingly, wrote more and better quality pieces. The problem? Teachers took stacks of fluent first drafts home on weekends and spent their weekend poring over the interesting thoughts of 70 to 100 students. When they returned students papers to them, the students either stood in line to challenge the grade they received or they put their papers away without reading their teacher's extensive comments. Some students complained that they scored a C for papers longer than they had ever written. Others said, "You wrote more on her paper and she still got a high grade."

I listened to teachers air their feelings and thought aloud. *Isn't that amazing? What a better problem than students who will not or cannot write!* Immediately, I knew that I had misspoken, blushed and smiled broadly. Not a teacher returned my smile; no head nodded in agreement. I knew I was in for a sober, problem-solving session of great intensity. We had to reclaim the sanctity of weekends for these teachers; until we achieved that, there was nothing more to discuss.

Fortunately, the department chair, Mrs. Davis, spoke up. "I noticed that I kept writing some comments in the margins over and over again; one comment I wrote on almost every paper. So I collected these repeated phrases and placed them on a half-sheet of paper and checked the comments that applied to each draft," she said. We had just witnessed a precursor of the scoring rubric. Her response form reminded me of the primary trait-scoring rubric that I had presented earlier to the members of the department. I suggested we combine her form and the primary trait scale. They liked the idea; two hours later the **First Draft Response Form** was born; we created one for each mode of writing assigned to students throughout their four years at Central High School, Thomasville, Georgia. I have promoted the use of **First Draft Response Forms** for decades.

Essentially, the **First Draft Response Form** filled the top half of an 8½ x 11 inch sheet of paper and literally cut to the chase; it told students precisely what their first draft would receive if it were submitted as a final draft unchanged. Since most first drafts garnered a C or lower, the teachers had their students' attention right away. The bottom half of the page was titled *Teacher Commentary*. In this space, the teachers explained in a sentence or two what was needed to earn the coveted *A*. That's it; no corrections made on the paper; no suggestions for what to add where, no repeated comments to *Be more specific!* or *Explain what you mean here!*

The teachers tried out the forms and reported immediate, positive impact on students and greatly reduced number of students questioning their grades. Here are the conclusions of one group of teachers who recently met the **First Draft Response Forms** and tried them out on their students' next first drafts. Since they did not mark up the students' drafts, they

♦ focused their comments on the main purpose of the paper: the sketch of a character, the comparing and contrasting of two ideas and so forth

♦ were not derailed by correcting obvious errors

♦ did not comment on interesting side points other than in the commentary

♦ read and responded to all the papers in a fraction of the time required for the traditional, write-comments-in-the-margins technique.

In addition, when students talked with them about their performance on the first drafts, **they** confined their questions to the main purpose of their papers. More important they talked about what they earned, not what the teachers gave them. They accepted that they wrote first drafts for themselves, that there was more work to do. The form dignified the response; the teachers' direct and constructive comments invited the students to talk with them about their writing, and important and productive conversations ensued.

So first of all, invite students to talk with you about your response to their writing using a **First Draft Response Form**. When you focus on the main purpose of students' writing, the students will, too. Here is how teachers at East Columbus Magnet Academy, Georgia, prompted their students with writing a persuasive topic in the manner of their state writing assessment.

> **Writing Situation**
>
> "In metropolitan Columbus, there are an estimated 2,350 homeless persons. The fastest growing segment of this population is women and children. Help the Metropolitan Columbus Taskforce for the Homeless by opening your home to a family today!" the radio announcer invited.
>
> Your parents heard this commercial and decided to take in a homeless family with children; one child is your age. The mother, father and two younger children sleep in the guest room; the one your age shares your room. Now there are 2,245 persons who need a place to stay.
>
> **Directions for Writing**
>
> Write a letter to your best friend's parents, persuading them to take in a family also. Convince them that it is important for them to have a part in doing away with this social problem in our community.

Seventh-grader Tiara wrote in a first draft,

Dear Mr. Sherman,

Metropolitan Columbus is a large population of homeless people. Please help the homeless, there are now 2,345 who are in need for help. If more people help more, homeless people will be more happy and less in need and less sadness. Women and children are mostly in this situation. "How can we help?" There are many ways to help poor. You can take them in your home or send supplies for them.

It is very important and you won't feel guilty because you didn't help the poor or homeless. I'm not blaming on you or anybody else, it makes everybody happy.

Your friend,
Tiara S.

Her ELA teacher provided a written commentary on a First Draft Response Form.

Support an Opinion

Writer _Tiera_

Title _Adopt a homeless family_

Evaluator _Ms. Mills_

_____	Little or no planning; reads like freewriting	1
_____	Limited explanation of opinion	(2)
_____	Limited explanation of opinion and supporting reasons	3
_____	Adequate explanation of opinion and supporting reasons	4
_____	Extensive explanation of opinion and adequate supporting reasons	5
_____	Engaging explanation of opinion and supporting reasons	6
		Unscorable

Teacher commentary:

Tiara,

   Your writing is improving. You stay on the topic. To meet expectations, explain your main point like it was assigned in the Writing Situation. Then add details to the two reasons that support your main point. Write more about each reason so we can **picture** what adopting a family has been for your family and what it can be like for your friend's family. Your proofreading partner can help you fix the many errors.

                                —Ms. Mills

The number that your teacher circles indicates the grade your 1st draft will receive with no revisions:
1=F, 2=D, 3=C, 4=C, 5=B, 6=A.

Joshua responded to the same topic prompt with this letter.

In the world today there are millions of homeless people. The city of Columbus, GA we have a couple thousand. We see them on the street, and sometimes we don't see them at all. They live in alleys, and on corners. Some live in abandoned buildings, or houses. We as people should realize that these people might be homeless, but we can do something about it. Almost everyone has a house to open up to the less fortunate.

One of the main reasons to let a poor family stay with you is to help them. The mother and the father of the homeless family might find inspiration from working parents. You can also try to help them money wise also, give them enough to get back on their feet. Your families can help them feel comfortable with people again. The point is that you can just help out a family less fortunate than yours.

We as people don't know that much about other people, but we know about ourselves. Taking in a family can help you learn more about people and yourself. If you take in a family with another race, you can learn another culture, or a religion. The other family can learn the same stuff from you also. Both families can learn about life from another perspective.

The final and main reason is to give back to your community. To let yourself be known as a generous person, and a good human being. When you see someone having a hard time to help them out. You show what type of person you are, and your amount of character. So next time you see a homeless person on the street think of this letter, and be generous.

Support an Opinion

Writer *Joshua*

Title *Adopt a homeless family*

Evaluator *Ms. Crooks*

_____	Little or no planning; reads like freewriting	1
_____	Limited explanation of opinion	2
_____	Limited explanation of opinion and supporting reasons	3
_____	Adequate explanation of opinion and supporting reasons	4
_____	Extensive explanation of opinion and adequate supporting reasons	5
_____	Engaging explanation of opinion and supporting reasons	6
		(Unscorable)

Teacher commentary:

Joshua,

Your writing is full, clear and keeps my attention, but it is unscorable. It is not a letter. It a good article for a newspaper. Read the Writing Situation and Directions for Writing carefully. Then write a personal letter. Pick a family you know and write out these same points to them. Mention family members by name.

—Ms. Crooks

The number that your teacher circles indicates the grade your 1st draft will receive with no revisions:
1=F, 2=D, 3=C, 4=C, 5=B, 6=A.

In the first commentary, Ms. Mills states directly that Tiara needs to add details and correct errors. She doesn't mark up the paper with suggestions that take over the paper, and Tiara's final draft is much improved. Joshua, a confident writer, was surprised that his paper could not be scored, and he knew exactly what to do to convert his essay into the form of a letter. It was much better that he turned in an unscorable paper to his teacher than to the raters of his state's Grade 8 Writing Assessment and bring his readiness for 9th grade into question.

See how Kayla, a 10th-grade Family and Consumer Science (FACS) student from Emery High School, South Dakota, revised her first draft in line with the ***First Draft Response Form*** completed by her teacher, Ms. Clarke. She received a 3 out of 6 points and saw that her paper was headed for a C if she didn't beef up the details. Ms. Clark wrote a single sentence *Remember to make me see your pictures of our little dying town.* That's it, and the revision came pouring out of Kayla.

Death of Businesses?

Are Emery's businesses dying from a lack of people? **Many small town businesses have died out because of a declining population. Our four downtown streets are lined with storefronts that are empty and ugly. About one in every four places of business remain open, and they aren't that busy. Only two gas stations are open, and the stores keep putting less and less on the shelves.** With a declining population in the Emery School and in the general community, our town is slowly becoming smaller. Businesses in Emery will have a hard time surviving as the population declines, gets older, and state and local services consolidate...

Many years ago, we had a bowling alley, a movie theater, three bars, and a couple of cafes. Now, we can't even support the buildings. **People aren't depending on these small town businesses anymore.** Those services are consolidated into large corporations like Wal★Mart and McDonald's to supply them with their needs. Few people go to the local Total Stop to buy a week's worth of groceries, but most people find themselves traveling to Mitchell or Sioux Falls for their needs. **State services are being consolidated to. We used to have an county extension office here. Now we go to Mitchell for that service. There is talk of consolidating our elementary school with Bridgewater. Families with small children will leave Emery and move to Bridgewater so their kids can walk to school.** I don't blame them, but without the need of these small town companies and services, more and more buildings will become vacant....

I believe Ms. Clarke is beginning to see the pictures in Kayla's words. See the full final draft at www.eyeoneducation.com. Visit this book's page on the website and follow the links.

_____ Lesson for Final Evaluation Forms (rubrics) _____

Talk about writing with me and your peers. *I know that most of you may not choose writing as a career. You will, however, need to write clearly no matter what career you attempt. I'm going to help you learn how to talk about your writing. You can talk with me. You don't have to be excited to talk with me. You don't even have to want to. You just need to get good at it. We are all proud when we get someone else to understand us. We are even prouder when we get someone to agree with us, especially when there has been disagreement before. So talk about writing with me and your peers.*

We'll use Final Evaluation Forms (rubrics) to get the conversations rolling, ones that are student-friendly, easy for you to understand and use. They are formative rubrics. As you use them, you will form a better idea of what makes up good writing. I will use the same rubrics, too. Thanks to the rubrics, I'll be part of the same conversation with you and your peer.

The first Final Evaluation Form focuses on a draft you have just written for your second nine-weeks benchmark in writing. Notice how different this form is from the First Draft Response Form that responded to one trait of writing, the main purpose of your writing. Final Evaluation Forms respond to several traits of writing. When you add up the value of the assessment of each trait, you arrive at a final grade that goes into the grade book. Notice the Final Evaluation Form on page 171.

INVITE

MODEL

Writer: _____

Evaluator: _____

Support an Opinion

Circle one comment and corresponding number in each row that best tells how you respond to that trait of writing in a draft of a fellow writer. Multiply the circled number by the number listed at the far right and place the product in the margin at the right. For the total raw score, add the numbers in the right-hand margin. Convert the total raw score, using page 176. Comments on this form are a guide. Modify any comments to represent your assessment more accurately.

Personal Voice—Vocabulary

1	2	3	4	5	x 3 pts =
You seem to use only words that you can spell. Use the best words that come to your mind.		Check for voice-killers (*sort of, would, could, awesome*) and watch for wordiness. You get tangled up in your words.		Your writing has a distinct voice. Word choice gives your writing power.	

The Beginning—Lead

1	2	3	4	5	x 2 pts =
Next time write several leads. Your first sentences move slowly.		Work harder on the lead. It can make/break persuasive writing.		Excellent lead. I felt drawn into the issue immediately!	

Main Idea and Supporting Ideas—Mental pictures

1	2	3	4	5	x 7 pts =
Too much "I think" and "I feel." Spend time explaining what you think and feel fully. Little development at all.		Main idea clear, but supporting reasons need support with examples, details, emotional appeal and/or evidence.		Fully explained main idea and supporting ideas. Convincingly developed reasons and support.	

Organization and Close—Flow

1	2	3	4	5	x 3 pts =
Parts ill-defined or too obviously presented in a formula. Few, awkward or obvious transitions. Weak or no close.		Ideas fairly well organized. Transition unnatural or rough at times. The close needs to be reworked.		Well organized. Smooth and natural transitions. A specific and compelling close.	

Quotations or references

1	2	3	4	5	x 2 pts =
Did not find any.		Need to use them more.		Well used. Correct form.	

Proofreading

1	2	3	4	5	x 3 pts =
Call each word out as you check for errors.		Just a few obvious errors, but they need attention.		It was tough to find any errors at all!	

Converted Score ☐   **Total Raw Score** ☐

Teacher: *Read through the Final Evaluation Form with me. Someone read the first line aloud. The rest of us will circle the key words in each of the three comments as we hear them read. [After the reading] Someone tell us what words you circled in the left comment.*

Student: Only words that you can spell.

Teacher: *Good, when we use only words we can spell, we muffle our writing voice or style. Someone tell us what you circled in the middle comment.*

Student: Good words.

Teacher: *Good words, not exceptional words; even more vivid words are needed. What words did someone circle in the right comment?*

Student: I circled 'show me exactly how you think'.

Teacher: *Nice, will someone remind us of the difference between words that show us and words that tell?*

Student: **Telling** words just give facts without details; **showing** words help us picture what the writer really means.

The discussion of the rubric continues in like manner until the dimensions of each trait have been explained by members of the class. When the rubric is fully explored, the students are ready to apply it to their own writing and the writing of their peers

Assessing Writing with a Final Evaluation Form

Read completely through the paper that you are assessing before you start marking the Final Evaluation Form. Then, without looking back at the paper, circle the comments on the first three traits (personal voice, the beginning and main and supporting ideas) *that describe your assessment of them. Once you have circled the comments, select a corresponding number from 1 to 5. If you circled the left comment, you must circle the number 1 or 2. If you circled the middle comment, you must circle a 2, 3 or 4. You may circle the number 5 only if you circled the right comment.*

Return to the beginning and ending of the paper to assess the effectiveness of each. Finally, check for errors to score the trait of proofreading. If you read through the paper easily even if there were a good many errors, you must circle the middle comment and at least the number 3. The paper was not difficult to read because of errors in proofreading.

When you have scored all six traits of the Support an Opinion draft, it's time to compute the raw score. Simply multiply the number you circled for each trait by the multiplier to the right and place the total in the right margin. Then add up the total for the traits and place the sum in the box labeled "raw score." Use the conversion chart on page 173 to convert the raw score to a score that can be entered into the grade book for a grade on a 70–100-point scale.

Conversion Chart—for converting a raw score to a 70-point scale

If the raw score is:	The converted score is:	If the raw score is:	The converted score is:
98	99	58	79
96	98	56	78
94	97	54	77
92	96	52	76
90	95	50	75
88	94	48	74
86	93	46	73
84	92	44	72
82	91	42	71
80	90	40	70
78	89	38	69
76	88	36	68
74	87	34	67
72	86	32	66
70	85	30	65
68	84	28	64
66	83	26	63
64	82	24	62
62	81	22	61
60	80	20	60

Now that you have a working knowledge of the formative rubric called the Final Evaluation Form, use it to assess a first draft of yours and see how it helps you improve your writing. Once you have completed the Final Evaluation Form in pencil, I will complete it in ink. Then we'll talk.

REVISE

Dear Mrs. Banks,

The Metropolitan Columbus Taskforce for the homeless has 2,349 families left that need a place to stay. My family took a family in, and I would like you to consider taking one family in also. You say that you would love to help the community, so this would be a great opportunity to help out.

It would mean so much to a family. Brittnee would love to share her room. I didn't like that I had to share my room either. Once I got to know Kenya, it was good and is still good up to this day. It would be a great idea for that room that you don't use, to let them stay in that room.

My family feels good that we opened our home up to the homeless. We are excited too. The Miles family loves our house and appreciates us. It feels good that would help somebody. The parents even went out to get a job to help with the bills. The Miles are so grateful, appreciative, and loving.

Think about everything that I have told you. Talk to your husband and children about it and see how they feel. Explain to them how good my family feels, and how the family feels about it. Explain to them that it would be a great opportunity and I would love to see us working together to help the community.

Sincerely,

Janay

Janay and her teacher scored her final draft with some variation in the final score.

Trait	Janay's Score	Weighted Score	Teacher's Score	Teachers' Weighted Score
Voice	4	12	3	9—a case of *woulds,* seven of them
Beginning	5	10	3	6—more engaging and less direct
Main idea-details	4	28	3	21—a vivid picture of your expanded family?
Organization-close	4	12	5	15—natural well-organized; full conclusion
References	1	2	3	6—one reference, 2349 homeless
Proofreading	3	9	5	15—had to hunt for errors
Raw score	21	73	22	62
Converted score		**86**		**81**—reaches the standard; could easily exceed the standard with elaboration of ideas

Fourteen-year-old Daniel responded to an expository prompt that asked him to explain the possible causes to a classmate who has begun sleeping in class. A confident homeschool writer who had just finished a *Writing Cycle* in the narrative genre, he wrote an opening paragraph. His complete first and revised drafts appear at www.eyeoneducation.com. Go this book's page and follow the links.

> Hello, my name is Osmosis McMan, and I'm a detective. My agent number is 23, like Michael Jordan. Some of my cases are on dolls getting stolen, wedgies, and toilet dunkings. I track down the bad guy and turn him in to Mr. P., Oh yea, the big man, Mr. Stinkouch, the principal of Mary Dale High. When I go to school my name is Frankie Tupali, but I usually have to go run into the bathroom whenever I get a call from my secretary about some nerd's sandwich getting poured on with milk. That's a messy job. So one day I walk into the classroom for Geometry and Billy is conked out! He's a fellow agent and a really big nerd. Why is he asleep on his desk? He rarely sleeps during class. Maybe his mom is a secret bad guy and poisoned his scrambled eggs for breakfast; that would knock him out. Then she would take her disguised corvette and drop him off at his desk so he would get in trouble. But wait that only happens in Florida. This was a really tough case.

A clever approach that is certainly written on the topic, but the draft cannot be scored as expository genre. When Daniel understood that the *Explain a Cause* rubric would present a score much too lower than he was used to, he decided to review the rubric and convert his thoughts into the *Explain a Cause* mode of the expository genre. He wrote.

> How to get sleepy!
>
> A long time ago, one of my friends fell asleep during class. I never thought about why he fell asleep before, but I now know a few causes of the problem.
>
> One reason could be too much exercise! A lot of people exercise a lot to stay in shape, lose weight, and look fashionable for some dance. But sometimes, too much exercise can make someone really sleepy. I play basketball and after a tough game, I am usually pretty tired. The funny thing is that to help keep you from being over-tired after exercising is to do more exercising. Well, it's actually called conditioning. Conditioning is running up and down neighborhood roads just running a couple of miles. It helps with stamina a lot, too.

Daniel scored his paper with the *Explain a Cause* rubric, then asked his mom and me to allow him to rewrite the introduction to his essay because it was too short. I agreed as long as he promised to reread the topic prompt with care before revising his lead. He held up his end of the bargain.

Hey, good buddy. You know we've been friends for a long time, and I never get negative on you, ever. I have to make an exception. Everyone is talking about how you fall asleep in class and try to cover it over like nothing's wrong. I never thought about why you are falling asleep before, but it's getting embarrassing with us being good friends. I did some reading and think, and I now know a few causes of the problem.

Daniel used the rubric with benefit; that's how it should be. We provide the tools; students use them to package what they are thinking. No questions about whether they are using the rubric the right way or if we like their writing, just a more effective presentation of their thoughts. You can see Daniel's complete first and revised drafts at www.eyeon-education.com. Go to this book's page and follow the links.

Writer: _____

Evaluator: _____

Explain a Cause

Circle one comment and corresponding number in each row that best tells how you respond to that trait of writing in a draft of a fellow writer. Multiply the circled number by the point value listed at the end of the row, and place the product in the margin at the right. For the total raw score, add the numbers in the right-hand margin. Convert the total raw score, using page 176. Comments on this form are a guide. Change any comments to represent your evaluation more accurately.

Personal Voice (Vocabulary)

1	2	3	4	5	x 4 pts =
You are using only words that you can spell. Use the best words in your mind.		Some good words, but read your writing aloud and add the words that come to your mind.	Your words let me know exactly how you really think.		

Word Pictures With Your Ideas

1	2	3	4	5	x 7 pts =
What exactly are you describing? I do not see pictures of a cause in my mind.		I can see some pictures of the cause(s) coming to my mind. I need to see more detail.	I see complete and clear pictures of the cause(s) you are describing. Nice job!		

The Beginning

1	2	3	4	5	x 3 pts =
The first sentences do not introduce what the cause or problem is.		Your first sentences introduce me to the cause or problem somewhat.	You introduce the cause or problem in a way that catches my attention.		

The Ending

1	2	3	4	5	x 3 pts =
No ending. Writing just stops.		Ending seems rushed.	A complete and strong ending!		

Proofreading

1	2	3	4	5	x 3 pts =
Your errors make your draft hard to read.		Just a few obvious errors. You know what to do.	It was tough finding your errors at all!		

Converted Score ☐　　**Total Raw Score** ☐

Kayla used her teacher's response with the **First Draft Response Form** to revise her first draft**,** and Daniel used a **Final Evaluation Form** to revise his first draft. Her teacher and his mother implemented best practices in teaching writing with fidelity even though they employed different instructional forms. **First Draft Response Forms** work best when the first draft is genre-appropriate; **Final Evaluation Forms** work well when a change in genre is needed.

Beyond knowing when to use the best form at the right time, Kayla's teacher Ms. Clarke writes with her students on each assigned writing task, and she trains other Career and Technical Education teachers in her state that writing with students is the top priority of any teacher who gives writing assignments to students. Daniel's teacher and mother, Ms. Torres, writes with Daniel and his four other siblings on many of their writing tasks. See for yourself how Ms. Torres' confidence as a writer bolsters that of her son.

A Hairy Experience

When I was growing up my family never had any dogs. It was not that we didn't like pets, but for some reason, we just never had a dog. We were not "dog" people. The only pet I ever remember having was a goldfish. As a result I was always a little uncomfortable around dogs at friends' homes. In fact, even my aunt's little yappy Chihuahua made me uncomfortable.

Our neighbors had a large purebred German Shepherd, though. He was nearly as tall as I was. His coloring was the typical black and brown. I don't remember the dog's name, but it was fitting for a ferocious beast – something like Rufus, or Rex, or Thor. His bark was deep and piercing, and his growl could scare away even the bravest of men.

Our neighbors also had a mean teenage daughter. Her name was Kristy. She was extremely large for her age. If you looked up the work "bully" in the dictionary, Kristy's picture would probably have been there. She was tough, and she was mean. The perfect example was the day she pushed me down and sat on my head. I thought I was going to die!

*(Ms. Torres' final draft is available online at www.eyeoneducation.com.
Go this book's page and follow the links.)*

It is time for us to talk about how you and I score your writing. Let's mark this chart first. Then let's each explain

♦ what you need to understand in order to move your assessment up or down to agree with mine.

♦ why we scored a trait the same. What was each of us considering in arriving at the same score?

> **Note:** Our talk can help me see that you understand the standards of writing that I am teaching. That is not to say that when you and I differ in our assessment, that I may not move my assessment up or down to agree with you. Talk about your writing with me!

The trait	Your assessment compared to mine		
Personal voice	*Lower*	*Same*	*Higher*
Word Pictures	*Lower*	*Same*	*Higher*
Beginning	*Lower*	*Same*	*Higher*
Ending	*Lower*	*Same*	*Higher*
Proofreading	*Lower*	*Same*	*Higher*

Once each student has participated in this instructional conference, move to a more efficient model for this "talk about writing with me." Let student pairs review the self-assessment that they each completed and compare and contrast it with the one that I completed. They can mark any changes in assessment that they want me to consider. In this way, they are talking with each other and me about their writing.

So what do students learn from reviewing the self-assessment and the assessment of a teacher responsible for teaching state or national standards for writing? Listen in on a classroom of eighth-graders who are feeling the appearance of the fast approaching Grade 8 Writing Assessment required by their state department of education.

"The teacher is not always right."

"Final Evaluation Forms make it easy to talk about writing."

"It teaches us what is important about writing, like an answer key."

"There's a lot of traits in writing to grade."

"Word pictures are the most important trait."

"It doesn't take much to make good writing excellent writing."

"Errors don't count as much as I thought."

Benefits of the rubric listed by teachers:

- ◆ saves time
- ◆ simplified procedure
- ◆ specific process for teachers
- ◆ structured

- ◆ teachable
- ◆ reliable
- ◆ as unbiased as grading can be

Conclusion: Final evaluation rubrics can effectively appear throughout the writing process. When students see one before they start to prewrite, they get a clear picture of their end goal in mind. When they apply one to their first draft, it leads them to consider all of the traits important in a final draft. When they apply one to their final draft, they receive clear instruction on what they should focus on for the next writing assignment.

Creating Usable Rubrics from State or National Standards

So many state writing rubrics are at best ponderous. The Georgia Grade 8 Analytic Scoring System is a typical example. It includes more descriptors for each feature of writing than a reader could possibly process while assessing a paper. To its credit, it lists only four features of writing—Ideas (pictures), Organization (flow), Style (voice) and Conventions, a real nod to simplicity. Then it describes the features so fully that they are rendered unwieldy. A copy of the Georgia *Analytic Scoring System* appears at www.eyeoneduction.com along with a usable, one-page version that teachers helped me create.

Scoring student writing with rubrics should be a huge time-saver. When appropriate procedures are followed, final drafts of 300 to 500 words can be scored by two separate teachers in half the time it takes one teacher to score it using the "mark and comment-in-the-margins" routine. In many schools that I serve, the entire faculty takes time at least twice a year to score the students' writing on a substantial draft. Teachers arrange themselves five to a table as shown in the following diagram. A stack of unscored student papers is placed on one end of the table. A rubric printed on both sides of a page is placed next to the student drafts. Once raters have scored a paper using the rubric on one side, they turn

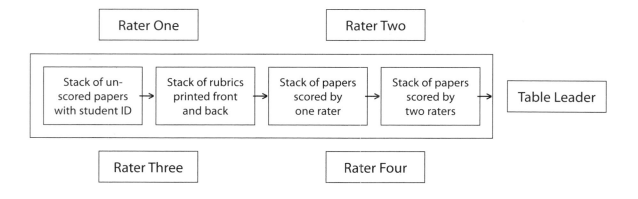

the rubric over and place it in a stack to be scored by another rater at the table. Once the draft has been scored twice, it moves to the table leader. Table leaders tally up the score of both raters and read the paper a third time if the two raters disagree by more than 15 out of 100 points. The last faculty I assisted in rating papers completed all students writing in 2 ½ hours, and the students received an objective assessment of their writing 72 hours after they had written their papers. The students were happy; the teachers, especially the ELA teachers who usually have the job of scoring papers, were happy. In fact, here are the conclusions that they drew from what I call the ***Reliable Scoring Session*** that will now become a recurring part of their school year:

1. Helped me be more objective overall, not just letting the mechanics and grammar affect me

2. Helped me understand the state standard

3. Less time-consuming

4. Gives students feedback quickly

5. Shows what help students need—guides RETEACHING

6. Confirming my assessment with the assessment of others

7. Lets us know if we need to tighten up or lighten up on our expectations of students

8. Students have the benefit of agreement of teachers

9. Teachers have benefit of knowing expectations are more consistent throughout the school.

10. Helps teachers see glaring shortcomings in their teaching

11. The quicker we graded, the more consistent we became

12. I got over my fear that others would find out I was insecure about the way I assessed writing.

It appears, then, that inviting students to talk with us about their writing benefits us as much as it benefits them.

❰ Looking Back

In your response journal, describe two ideas from *the **First Draft Response Form, Final Evaluation Form** and **Reliable Scoring Session*** in this chapter that were valuable for you as a teacher in courses that you presently teach.

❱ Looking Ahead

What things coming up in your curriculum invite you to use *the **First Draft Response Form, Final Evaluation Form** and/or **Reliable Scoring Session***?

Empowering Students to Write and RE-Write
Session Guide #5 for Professional Learning Teams

Responding to

Chapter 13: Reach an audience with me— *Response Forms, Say It Back* and *Author's Chair*

Chapter 14: Talk about writing with me—*First Draft Response Forms, Final Evaluation Forms*

Before joining *Professional Learning Team (PLT) Session #5*

Make sure you have written your response to these topics in your journal.

1. Explain the difference between revision completed by writers to share with readers and revision initiated by readers.

2. Describe the class experience in which you have used a four-to-six trait rubric to help students revise?

Exemplars

As you read through student revision that used the strategies of chapters 13-14, select the student samples that best illustrated their use. Bring your own personal revision that you used as an effective model for your students to follow.

Discussion questions for PLT Session #5

1. When is it time for writers to start letting the response of their audience initiate the revision of their first drafts (chapter 13).

2. Is the *Author's Chair* an example of the evaluation or publication of writing (chapter 13)? Explain.

3. Explain the role of the primary trait rubric in the *First Draft Response Form* (chapter 14).

4. Why is it so important that *First Draft Response Forms* include a written teacher commentary (chapter 14)? How long does the commentary need to be?

5. What are the differences between student-friendly rubrics and ones that adhere strictly to the language of state or national standards for writing (chapter 14)?

Compiling *Professional Learning Portfolios*

Bring the artifacts that you have gathered since PLT #4 to include in your *Professional Learning Portfolio*. Share your ideas for expanding your portfolio and listen to the portfolio plans of other teachers.

15

Implementing a Mindset for Revision

How do I know what I think until I see what I say?
E. M. Forster

I don't know what I know until I read what I write.
M. Flannery O'Connor

Some surprises about my approach to teaching and learning came out of writing this book. First, I realized that my most efficient mode of operation included teaching students and teachers simultaneously. I insist now, that in every classroom I enter where teachers are observing me demonstrate best practice in writing, every teacher in the room and I write with students. When all adults in a crowded room are writing, all students are, too.

Very likely, demonstrating your writing routines in your class for observing teachers finds you using writing at your best. Session III for Professional Learning Teams provided this experience for you. When your administrators recognize the power of teachers demonstrating for teachers throughout the school, teacher demonstrations will become part of the fabric of teaching and learning at your school.

The second surprise in this book is the discovery that revision is not just part of the writing process but at the heart of the teaching of writing, the learning of writing and the writing process itself. In this book on revision, you and I have covered writing from the topic prompt to publication. I have long accepted the central position of revision in the writing process and emphasized the recursive process of writing. Yet my colleagues who have read the manuscript of *Empowering Students to Write and RE-write* are surprised that revision is at the center of my understanding of each step of the writing process. Go figure. In the fourth decade of my career, this message is clear: a developed mindset for revision presents itself in two ways at each step of the process.

- ◆ Spotting possibilities available to writers at each step of the process

- ◆ Choosing one of the possibilities with confidence, knowing that it can make all the difference in the final draft

Like all of us, my first attempts at using writing to learn reflected how I was taught—and that had to change. With effort, I overcame the limitations of my secondary teachers who, well meaning as they were,

- ♦ talked about the ideas that they felt I needed to know . . . and talked . . . and talked . . . and talked.

- ♦ assigned writing and monitored the classroom to keep everyone on task, distracting an entire class with advice that only one person needed.

- ♦ followed a tradition of teaching and learning without tracking the quality of our performance in writing. Some students caught on, many did not; that was the way writing played out in school.

Change came to me in a hurry once I decided to leave the university scene and immersed myself in a life of classroom experiences; *the solutions to the problems of the classroom are to be found in the classroom,* I heard myself say, and somehow it justified my leaving the security of steady employment. I stopped being the professor who visited classrooms on occasions. I became a self-employed action research consultant in classrooms daily, keeping my ears and eyes open and my mind attuned to research in best practice of teaching and learning.

It took a wide variety of classroom circumstances and experience for me to develop strategies for writing that worked every time I called on them. I insisted on the scrutiny of classroom teachers and school administrators who observed my demonstration lessons with their students from the back of the classroom. That appeared to be my only choice. Fortunately, a viable model for *Learning to Write* and *Writing to Learn* materialized; the livelihood of my growing family depended upon it. Students, teachers and administrators all had the perception that *Writing to Win*© worked, not just as a lesson, but as a model for writing across the curriculum.

Students provided the most help for me in honing an effective model for writing in the classroom. Their expressions and reactions exuded signs of engagement or lack of it; I took mental notes. Observing teachers provided plenty of advice, too, especially the ones who said, You *don't know my kids*. Sometimes I met those *kids* and found I had more to learn. I have learned plenty from teachers who demonstrate their use of my framework for teaching writing and using writing to learn. I have also learned much from building and district administrators who have partnered with me. Specific practices from needs assessment, project launch, program monitoring, teacher self-assessment, student surveys to recognition of exemplary teachers and students have provided the substance of the *Writing to Win*© guide for administrators,

None of these experiences, however, brought my understanding of writing into focus better than writing it out for myself in this book. I had quoted and heard others quote Flannery O'Connor often—

I don't know what I know until I read what I write.

Unless we write, we cannot be sure what we know or believe. I have taken the length of my career to practice this fully. Ironically, secondary students, whom I have made a career of helping, recognize this almost immediately. After explaining what they have learned in class daily for a couple of weeks, they announce it in clear and simple terms, "Journaling helps me learn better. Writing helps me figure stuff out. Writing lets me tell my teachers what I know, not what I don't know. Writing helps me review and study for tests." When I succeed at helping teachers write along with their students, they report positive benefits. Too often, decisions about the use of time in classrooms cause teachers to revert back to less writing for themselves and their students. Maybe, just maybe, this presentation of a mindset for revision as the center of the writing process will keep your writing and the writing of your students remain alive and well in your classrooms.

Revision is a natural state of mind for young writers at every step of the writing process. In writing, students naturally ask, *What do I do now?* When they are prompted with the possibilities for writing at each step, they make a choice that moves them forward seamlessly. The following two tables attempt to graph what I intended to portray in this book. A version of the tables to duplicate for your students is at www.eyeoneducation.com. Go to this book's page and follow the links.

Step of the writing process	Possibilities for students to consider	Choice(s) for students to make
Meeting the topic prompt	Circle key words that may define the topic prompt.	**Choose** the words that precisely define the issue, purpose, task and audience for your writing.
Prewriting	Consider several modes of writing available to serve as advance organizers of responses to the topic prompt.	**Choose** the mode that best fits your thoughts about your topic prompt.
	Brainstorm a list of possible specific topics related to the topic prompt without judging their value.	**Choose** the topic from the brainstorm list that you can write the most about.
	Jot list possible vivid ideas/words that come to mind about a selected topic.	Group the ideas/words in your list(s) that are closely related. **Choose** the groups to use in your draft and arrange them logically.
Drafting	Analyze parts of prewriting to select for the beginning, middle and end of a first draft.	**Choose** to begin writing your first draft with the part on which your mind is focused.
Revision	Consider 1) revising own draft for an audience or 2) asking the audience to initiate the revision.	**Choose** a revision strategy that provides help at the level your first draft needs.

(continued)

Step of the writing process	Possibilities for students to consider	Choice(s) for students to make
Examples of each level of revision	Strategies for revising first drafts selected in concert with teachers/parents.	
	Word level: circle the first verb of every sentence in a first draft.	**Choose** half of the circled verbs and change them to create a clearer picture and/or voice in your writing.
	Parts-of-a-sentence level: circle 7-10 phrases/clauses throughout first draft that make a vivid picture return to your mind. Number the circled phrases/clauses. On a separate sheet of paper, jot additional vivid words/phrases.	**Choose** to include the additions that make clearer pictures and/or voice in your writing.
	Sentence level: circle 4-5 pairs or trios of sentences that might be better when combined. Number the circled sentences. On a separate sheet of paper combine the sentences in each circle.	**Choose** which combined sentences create clearer pictures and/or voice in your writing.
	Paragraph level: circle 4-5 individual sentences that make a picture return to mind.	**Choose** 2-3 circled sentences that you can write the most more about [minimum one paragraph each].
	Paragraph level: mark off the first picture frame [or introduction] of a first draft and number it as *Lead #1*. Write Lead #2 and #3.	With the help of peers, **choose** the most effective lead for your writing.
	Whole draft level: frame each picture in a first draft.	**Choose** which frames 1) you can write the most more about, 2) do without, 3) move to a better place and 4) rewrite to clarify.
	Project level: analyze each feature of a project: the collection, the analysis, the written and the graphic presentation.	**Choose** the parts of the written presentation to change so that they more fully represent the corresponding features of the project.

Step of the writing process	Possibilities for students to consider	Choice(s) for students to make
Proofreading	Observe two peers read through your final draft, one calling out each word/feature. Allow and help peer(s) make corrections on an attached proofing strip.	**Choose** the corrections on the proofing strip that will improve your final draft and transfer them to the draft. Make minor improvements of voice and pictures that come to mind.
Evaluation	Read the three comments for each trait of the rubric for self or peer-evaluation.	**Choose** the comment in each trait of the rubric that best fits the final draft you are evaluating. Be prepared to justify your selections.
Publication	Brainstorm strategies and places for publishing final draft appropriate to the topic.	**Choose** the publication strategy and location that best suits your writing and audience.

When you have to teach students the standards of expository, persuasive or narrative *genres*, marry the above chart to a realistic timeline. In most state curricula, a window of time in a framework for writing in a specific *genre* varies from 4 to 8 weeks. The following timeline for teaching the standards of the writing process for a specific *genre* project a 6-week cycle.

Timeline	Step of the writing process	Possibilities for students to consider	Choice(s) for students to make
Week One	Topic prompt for 1st Draft #1	Circle possible key words that may define the topic prompt.	**Choose** the words that precisely define the issue, purpose, task and audience for your writing.
	Prewriting	Consider all modes of writing available to serve as an advance organizer of your response to the topic prompt.	**Choose** the mode that best fits your thoughts about your topic prompt.
		Brainstorm possible specific topics related to the topic prompt without judging their value.	**Choose** the topic from the brainstorm list that you can write the most about.

(continued)

Timeline	Step of the writing process	Possibilities for students to consider	Choice(s) for students to make
Week One	Prewriting *(continued)*	Jot list vivid ideas/words that come to your mind about your topic. Use as many lists as needed.	Group the ideas/words in your list(s) that are closely related. **Choose** the groups to use in your draft and arrange them logically.
	Drafting	Consider the parts of your prewriting that work best as beginning, middle and end of your draft.	**Choose** to begin writing your first draft with the part on which your mind is focused.
Week Two	Read the topic prompt, prewrite and create 1st Draft #2.		
Week Three	Read the topic prompt, prewrite and create 1st Draft #3.		
Week Four	Revision	Consider 1) whether to revise your own draft for an audience or or 2) ask the audience to initiate the revision.	**Choose** a revision strategy that provides help at the level your first draft needs.
	Examples of each level of revision	Strategies for revising first drafts selected in concert with teachers/parents.	
		Word level: circle the first verb of every sentence in your first draft.	**Choose** half of the circled verbs and change them to create a clearer picture and/or voice in your writing.
	Examples of each level of revision	Parts-of-a-sentence level: circle 7 to 10 phrases/clauses in your first draft that make a vivid picture return to your mind. Number the circled phrases/clauses. On a separate sheet of paper, jot additional vivid words/phrases.	**Choose** to include the additions that make clearer pictures and/or voice in your writing.
		Sentence level: circle 4 to 5 pairs or trios of sentences that might be better when combined. Number the circled sentences. On a separate sheet of paper combine the sentences in each circle.	**Choose** which combined sentences create clearer pictures and/or voice in your writing.

Timeline	Step of the writing process	Possibilities for students to consider	Choice(s) for students to make
Week Four	Examples of each level of revision *(continued)*	Paragraph level: circle 4 to 5 sentences that make a picture return to your mind.	**Choose** 2 to 3 circled sentences that you can write the most more about [minimum one paragraph each].
		Paragraph level: mark off the first picture frame [or introduction] of your first draft and number it as *Lead #1*. Write Leads #2 and #3.	With the help of peers, **choose** the most effective lead for your writing.
		Whole draft level: frame each picture in your first draft.	**Choose** which frames 1) you can write the most more about, 2) do without, 3) move to a better place and 4) rewrite to clarify.
		Project level: analyze each feature of your project: the collection, the analysis, the written presentation and the graphic presentation.	**Choose** the parts of written presentation to change so that they more fully represent the corresponding features of the project.
Week Five	Proofreading	Observe one or two peers read through your final draft, calling out each feature as one reads. Help your peer(s) make corrections on an attached proofing strip.	**Choose** the corrections on the proofing strip that will improve your final draft and transfer them to the draft. Make minor improvements of voice and pictures that come to mind.
Week Six	Evaluation	Read the three comments for each trait of the rubric you use for self- or peer-evaluation.	**Choose** the comment in each trait of the rubric that best fits the final draft you are evaluating. Be prepared to justify your selections.
	Publication	Consider possible ways to publish your final draft within the guidelines of your task/ topic.	**Choose** the publication strategy and location that best suits your writing and audience.

A Writing Cycle for Teacher Expectations
A Mini-Project of the Writing Process

Beginning Date_____

Ending Date_____

Modes of Writing

A—Narration	E—Explain a Cause/Effect	I—Explain a Solution	M—Poetry
B—Description	F—Explain a Classification	J—Interpretation	N—Summarizing
C—Character Sketch	G—Explain a Problem	K—Compare/Contrast	O—Support an Opinion/Solution
D—Imaginative Writing	H—Explain a Process	L—Personal Letter	P—Miscellaneous

Step	Mode	**Expec- tations	Description of Topic and Teacher Expectations	Points
*1st Draft #1	A	4 ♯s	In the manner of 20th-century short stories we've read, create a narrative satire of a current political or social issue in the news. Half of the points are from your prewriting and half from your 1st draft.	85
*1st Draft #2	K	4 ♯s	Compare and contrast the written and the movie version of a 20th-century short story that we have read.	85
*1st Draft #3	K	4 ♯s	Compare and contrast two short stories of an author we've studied, one we read in class with one you read on your own.	85
Revision		2 ♯s; 10 parts	Enhance 10-12 parts of your selected draft with Jot and Blend (#9).	
			Improve intro and end: Writing Leads (#10) & Writing Closes (#11)	85
			A description of how you used this revision strategy in your 1st draft	
Proofing		80% of errors	Proofreading Triads (#2)	
				85
			The kind of errors and what percent of them you corrected	
Evaluate		85%	Students and teachers complete the mode appropriate Final	
			Evaluation Form.	85
			How close was your estimate or a classmate's estimate of your final grade?	
Publish		Display	Display PowerPoint versions of final drafts in class binder.	
				85
			A description of how you followed the publication plan	

*Includes a completed *Advance Organizer* and 1st draft

**KEY	What students must complete to meet teacher expectations ◎ meets expectations

Another way to present this 6-week timeline is in the form of a custom-made rubric. Combs (2005) presents a *Writing Cycle for Teacher Expectations* (see above) as a wall chart on display for all to see. As teachers move through a 6-week cycle, they add the prompt and their

A *Writing Cycle* for Student Self-Check
A Mini-Project of the Writing Process

NAME _____

Beginning Date _____

Ending Date _____

Modes of Writing

A—Narration	E—Explain a Cause/Effect	I—Explain a Solution	M—Poetry
B—Description	F—Explain a Classification	J—Interpretation	N—Summarizing
C—Character Sketch	G—Explain a Problem	K—Compare/Contrast	O—Support an Opinion/Solution
D—Imaginative Writing	H—Explain a Process	L—Personal Letter	P—Miscellaneous

Step	Mode	**Self-Check	Description of Topic	Points
*1st Draft #1	A	⊙	Satire on the US presidential election	88
			Half of the points are from my prewriting and half from my 1st draft.	
*1st Draft #2	K	+	"The House of Unger" vs. "The Fall of the House of..."	95
*1st Draft #3	K	⊙	Connell's "Most Dangerous Game" vs. "The Umps"	80
Revision	___	⊙	I expanded 8 parts with better images.	
			I wrote a more engaging lead and close.	90
			A description of how I used this revision strategy in my 1st draft	
Proofing		⊙	Proofreading Triads (#2)	
				75
			The kind of errors and what percent of them I corrected	
Evaluate		⊙	Students and teachers complete the appropriate Final	
			Evaluation Form.	92
			How close was my estimate or a classmate's estimate of my final grade?	
Publish		⊙	Display *PowerPoint* versions of final drafts in class binder.	
				94
			A description of how I followed my teacher's publication plan	

*Includes a completed *Advance Organizer* and 1st draft

**KEY	+ exceeds expectations	◎ meets expectations	▭ misses expectations

expectations for each stage of the cycle, creating the scoring rubric as they proceed. Students maintain a corresponding writing cycle, *Writing Cycle for Student Self-Check* (see above), listing each writing task the self-assessing the degree to which they met their teacher's expectations.

The teacher and student version of the *Writing Cycle* present an example from an ELA classroom; however, the *Writing Cycle* fits in classes across the curriculum. Mr. Van Leur's industrial arts students are conditioned to the "write three drafts, finish one" in all of his classes and produce revision without prompting. He states the first day of class that all students must complete a written description of how they will complete each project and hand it in to him before they can start the project in the shop. Once they complete three projects, students select one written draft to revise and submit as a final draft. Ninth-grader Cody submitted this final draft; revisions are noted in bold.

Making a sled

So you want to make a sled? There's nothing better for a homemade present for Christmas, and it's simple. Well, the first things you will need are a 31 inch piece of 1 by 12 and about a 15 inch piece of 1 by 10. Select some stain of whatever color you like, **a permanent marker,** and paint for the scene on the front **of the seat.**

Once you get your boards cut to the appropriate length, you need to take a previously made sled and **use the permanent marker to** outline the runners onto the 1 by 12 and the seat on the 1 by 10. Use a table saw to cut off the large excess wood and cut along the long straight sides of the runners. Then use a scroll saw to cut the more intricate parts **and rounded areas** of the runners and seat. With the excess wood from between where the runners were cut out, trace the shaped piece that is on the front of sled. **It is the steering mechanism and the source of all the fun in a downhill ride.** Use a scroll saw to cut it out.

English students taught by Ms. Haag, North Sioux City, South Dakota, have benefited from the conditioned routine of the *Writing Cycle* for 4 years. Her use of her state rubric shows these results year after year.

Grade	Pretest	Posttest	Improvement
9	60.0	69.0	+ 9.0%
10	70.0	77.2	+ 7.2%
11	70.0	80.4	+10.4%
12	79.6	81.0	+ 1.4%

A typical student selected to *Jot and Blend* details for revising her first draft of a short story. On her own volition, Rachel's writing shows quite extensive revision, not just of amount, but substance and quality of writing.

The Shadow

Who am I? What a good question. **I would tell you if I knew the answer myself, but** I've given up on ever learning my true origin. I had been here for a long time; **since before I could remember.** Even I had **lost track of the exact amount, but it doesn't really matter.** How I got here wasn't important. How I would get out **and what I was going to do with the time I had remaining** was the only significant inspiration to my thoughts. My earliest memory was just of a brilliantly white, dazzling light above me.

Soft voices murmured somewhere near my right side. "What have we done? He won't be safe here. **He won't be safe anywhere. They know about him.** He will always be their target. We should destroy him as we were told," a man whispered. He was frightened. I could feel it. He wanted me gone but was afraid he would remain helpless as he had been his whole life. **I knew this to be true though I can't explain how.**

Rachel's revision empowered her writing with personal style that may have been in her mind as she wrote her first draft, but had yet to appear on the page. The addition of her narrator's prescient, yet uncertain mental power adds dimension to her main character, and the images she added in revision made this imaginative tale gain a life of its own. See Cody's and Rachel's complete drafts at www.eyeoneducation.com. Go to this book's page and follow the links.

As an alternative to the "write three drafts, finish one" routine of the *Writing Cycle*, some teachers prompt students to write three first drafts on the same topic and link the three drafts together in a final draft. The resulting published draft, then, represents a written 1000-word project instead of a 300 to 500-word essay.

Sample Writing Cycle for Courses Across the Curriculum

In every school I visit, I promote frequent writing in every course, writing that permits students time to plan, draft, and most important, return to their drafts to make them more accurate and complete. In a short book like *Empowering Students to Write and RE-write*, the examples of student writing across the curriculum have necessarily been limited. I want to close with solid ideas that I have seen teachers in the core courses of math, science and social students use to reinforce curriculum standards like those required in most states. The following pages include topics and strategies that complete a 6-week *Writing Cycle* as testament of the mastery of course standards in a traditional, yearlong course. Courses on block schedule complete a *Writing Cycle* in 3 to 4 weeks.

How to read the sample *Writing Cycle* (p. 13). In weeks 1–3 of a *Writing Cycle*, teachers prompt students to write first drafts on three different topics to demonstrate mastery of course content. In weeks 4–6, students select one draft to revise, proofread, evaluate and publish.

Student choice allows student to complete one draft out of three first drafts; however, teachers may assist in the selection.

Evaluating includes peer- or self-evaluation followed by teacher evaluation.

Publishing occurs as a culmination of a 6-week project: 1) in-class wall display on a wall from floor to ceiling, 2) a group/individual book (three-ring binder) or 3) oral presentations in small groups.

Sample of a six-week *Writing Cycle for a year-long course*

World Geography

Standards of study serve as basis for *Writing Cycles*. They include physical and cultural geographic features of major regions of the world.

■ Physical and cultural aspects of geography ■ Physical and human systems shaping contemporary 1) North Africa/Southwest Asia, 2) Sub-Saharan Africa, 3) South Asia, 4) Southeastern Asia and Eastern Asia, 5) Europe, 6) Latin America, 7) Canada and the United States, 8) Oceania (Australia, New Zealand and Antarctica Over the years, a *Writing Cycle* may be developed for each section.

Physical and cultural aspects of geography

In all high school courses, supplementary resources become essential. In geography, browse the web for general sites such as virtual atlases and satellite maps: *www.maps.google.com, www.factmonster.com/ipka/A0770414.html, www.geography.about.com, www.geography.about.com/library/maps/blworld.htm,* and *www.members.aol.com/bowermanb/101.html*. More specific sites provide virtual experiences, quizzes and games: *www.sheppardsoftware.com/Geography.htm.* Expect students to consult these sites in producing first drafts of the *Writing Cycle*.

Week	Step of the Writing Process	Mode of Writing	Description of topic prompt for students
1	1st Draft #1	Description	Elaborate on the physical elements of geography based on your research of one geographic region—for example, physical features of the Himalayan highlands.
2	1st Draft #2	Cause/effect	The effects of human settlement patterns and activities on geography
3	1st Draft #3	Support an Opinion	Which defines geography more, physical elements or cultural aspects?
4	Revision	1 of 3 first drafts	**Jot & Blend**—circle 12–15 phrases and expand half of them with vivid details; **Writing Leads; Writing Closes**
5	Proofreading	"	Proofreading Triads
6	Evaluating	"	Peer evaluation with a student-friendly version of a state rubric for writing assessment. Teacher scores with the same rubric.
	Publishing	"	Wall display, three-ring binder, *Author's Chair* in small groups

As described in chapter 6, all first drafts include prewriting that requires brainstorming and vivid, detailed jot lists. This sample sets a minimum expectation for revision of first drafts that includes *Writing Leads, Writing Closes* and *Jot & Blend* rich details throughout the body paragraphs. When students become conditioned to these basic habits of revising the beginning, middle and end of their papers, they will leave for the adult world well-prepared to articulate their thoughts on a variety of topics.

Additional Sample Writing Cycles

See samples of the following courses at www.eyeoneducation.com.

Social Sciences

World History, United States History, Economics and American Government/Civics

Science

Earth Science, Physical Science, Environmental Science, Biology, Chemistry and Human Anatomy and Physiology

Mathematics

Core Math I (grade 9), Core Math II (grade 10) and Core Math III (grade 11)

Alternative to the Writing Cycle

Although the *Writing Cycle* charts work well for schools that adopt the *Writing to Win* framework for teaching writing, a teacher-made framework can work. On the next page you will see two charts: *Writing Tasks for Teacher Expectations* and *Writing Tasks for Student Check.* They illustrate how simple an approach to charting expectations for student self-assessment can be. Notice that every writing task in a class is listed, and students assess their response to every task.

Writing Tasks for Teacher Expectations

Beginning Date _August 24_
Ending Date _December 20_

Date	*Expec-tations	Description of Writing Task	Points
8-18	5 wrds/blank	Framed Draft: Narration—Surprise on the trip	40
8-20	3 ¶s	Story-making kit: a success memory	85
8-25	3 ¶s	Summarize: "Wilma Unlimited," Reading Great Expectations, pp. 308-321	85
9-8	3 ¶s	Summarize one: "Louis Braille," pp. 622-635; "Destination Mars," 524-539;	
		The Seven Wonders of the Ancient World," 428-445	85
9-16		Expand a Sentence: The competitors moved to the line.	40
9-17	2 ¶s	Circle five picture sentences and expand two into paragraphs	85
9-23	80%	Proofreading Triad: capitals, punctuation, spelling, usage	85
9-30	85%	Final Evaluation Rubric for Narration	85
10-7	70%	Benchmark: Unassisted Writing Sample for narrative writing	70
10-14	5 wrds/blank	Framed Draft: Character Sketch—The Trailmaster	40
10-20	5 wrds/blank	Framed Draft: Setting—The Safe Harbor	40
10-28	3 ¶s	Sketch a significant adult at this school: prewriting whole group	85
11-4	3 ¶s	Sketch a hero in the news: prewriting small group	85
11-11	3 ¶s	Draft choice: 1) Favorite character from current short stories	
		2) The setting I see best from current short stories	85
11-18		Slotting for better nouns: The <u>man</u> bought <u>groceries</u> at <u>midnight</u>.	40
12-2	2 ¶s	Circle five picture sentences and expand two into paragraphs	85
12-5	80%	Proofreading Triad: capitals, punctuation, spelling, usage	85
12-9	85%	Final Evaluation Rubric for Character Sketch or Description	85
12-16	70%	Benchmark: Unassisted Writing Sample for expository writing	70

*KEY   What student must complete to meet teacher expectations   ⊙ meets expectations

Writing Tasks for Student Self-Check

Name *Jacob V.*

Beginning Date *August 24*

Ending Date *December 20*

Date	*Self-Check	Description of Writing Task	Points*
8-18	+	Framed Draft: *Surprise on the trip*	
8-20	⊙	Story-making kit: the winning touchdown	83
8-25	+	Summary of "Wilma Unlimited"	95
9-8	⊙	Summary of "Destination Mars"	90
9-16	▭	Expand a Sentence: *The competitors moved to the line.*	30
9-17	⊙	Circled five picture sentences and expand two into paragraphs	85
9-23	▭	Corrected all capitals, punctuation, spelling and usage errors	75
9-30	⊙	Final Evaluation Rubric for Narration	85
10-7	+	Benchmark Sample for narrative writing	100
10-14	⊙	Framed Draft— *The Trail Boss*	40
10-20	+	Framed Draft— *The Safe Harbor*	95
10-28	+	Sketch of Mr. Walker, band director and soccer coach	100
11-4	+	Sketch of LaBron James	95
11-11	⊙	Sketch of Brian Robeson, *The Hatchet*	85
11-18	▭	Slotting: *The man bought groceries at midnight.*	35
12-2	⊙	I circled five picture sentences and expand two into paragraphs	90
12-5	⊙	Corrected all capitals, punctuation, spelling, usage	85
12-9	+	Final rubric for Character Sketch	92
12-16	+	Benchmark: expository writing	95

*KEY   + exceeds expectations   ⊙ meets expectations   ▭ misses expectations

*Teachers enter the final point value for each task after the students have self-assessed their work in the Self-Check column. Teachers simply agree with the self-assessment or adjust it up or down.

A Parting Shot

Teachers of 21st-century U. S. American students need not spend time convincing them that writing is a process and that revision is a recursive feature of each step of that process. Instead, we best use our instructional time to show them both of these truths about the nature of writing in our own writing. As we write along with them from analyzing a topic prompt to evaluating a final draft, we remind them to consider possibilities at each step of the process and make informed choices. We need not burden ourselves with making corrections in the texts of their writing or giving specific suggestions of what choices we might make; we just need to become proficient at pointing them toward and reminding them of the possibilities at each step. Teaching writing and using writing to learn is this simple; it is just not that easy because it flies in the face of traditional teaching and learning in the United States. It even challenges a good bit of what is published in the name of the workshop model for writing that covers the pages of myriad books on teaching and using writing to learn in this century and the last; but it is this simple.

Here's to authentic writing!

Empowering Students to Write and RE-Write
Session Guide #6 for Professional Learning Teams

Responding to

Chapter 15: Stepping back from a mindset for revision

Before joining *Professional Learning Team (PLT) Session #6*

Make sure you have written your response to these topics in your journal.

1. Explain how creating a mindset for revision is really just a matter of helping students.

    a. Consider possibilities at each step of the writing process.

    b. Choose one of them to move forward.

2. Explain what topics you would include in a book on writing to learn based on your work with your students.

Exemplars

Be prepared to analyze the exemplars of student samples and teacher models from the five earlier PLT sessions and to help your PLT create a final collection of exemplars for writing and rewriting.

Discussion questions for PLT Session #6

1. What has your writing about the course content with your students showed you about your understanding of the subject matter you teach (chapter 15)?

2. What surprises have turned up in your writing (chapter 15)?

3. What revision strategies presented in *Empowering Students to Write and RE-write* have not worked effectively with your students (chapter 15)? Describe how you changed the strategy to make it work.

4. Describe the two most effective strategies that have helped your students write to learn from your study of *Empowering Students to Write and RE-write* (chapter 15).

Appendix for Student Self-Assessment

I have promoted student self-assessment from the beginning of my career. Thanks to the conscientious work of Rick Stiggins and the Assessment Training Institute (ATI) team of the Educational Testing Service (ETS), we educators have increased understanding of the power of student self-assessment. While student self-assessment appears in each chapter when appropriate, this appendix accentuates the need for simple, consistent and pervasive student self-assessment. Teachers may adjust the expectations for each level of student performance upward, but I have yet to meet the classroom of students who need the expectations lowered. Increased expectations lead to accelerated student performance.

Chap	Instructional tool or strategy	Expectations 🖿	Expectations ⊙	Expectations +
6	*The Assignment page*	2-3 sentences	4-5 sentences	6 insightful sentences
	Advance Organizer	Roughly 50% of lines filled with vivid word choices	Roughly 75% of lines filled with vivid word choices	All lines filled with vivid word choices
7	*Jot & Blend*	Average of 1-2 words/ sentence	Average of 3-5 words/ sentence	Average 3-5 **vivid** words/sentence
8	*Circling Picture Sentences*	Two additional paragraphs that may not fit; too few additional details	Two additional paragraphs that fit; additional details create word pictures	Two or more additional paragraphs that fit; additional details create vivid word pictures and distinctive voice.
9	*Framing Pictures in a Draft*	Two expansions that may not fit; too few additional details	Two expansions that fit; additional details create word pictures; 1-3 deletions	Two elaborated expansions that fit; additional details create vivid word pictures and distinctive voice; several deletions and moves
10	*Combining Sentences*	2-3 combinations of two sentences	4+ combinations of two – and three-sentence groups	4+ combinations and rewording of sentences for clarity
	Weasel Words	3-5 vague or equivalent replacements	5+ improved replacements and effective deletions	Vivid replacements and effective deletions throughout draft

Chap	Instructional tool or strategy	Expectations		
		▭	⊙	+
11	*Framed Drafts*	3-5 words/blank	5-7 vivid words/blank	5 vivid words / blank and elaborated additions
	Sentence Check Chart	Replacement of half the beginning words and verbs in 13 sentences	Vivid replacement of half the beginning words and verbs in 13 sentences	Vivid replacements of beginning words and verbs throughout draft
12	*Writing Leads*	Two leads completed, may be repetitious and/or formulaic	Two fully developed leads completed; one hooks the attention of an audience	Two or more fully developed leads completed; two hook the attention of an audience
	Writing Closes	Two closes completed, may be repetitious and/or formulaic	Two fully developed closes completed; one provides closure or moves the audience to act or change	Two or more fully developed closes completed; two provide closure or move the audience to act or change
13	*Peer Response Form*	Partial completion of some items	Full completion of each item	Insightful completion each item
	Say It Back	Solicits audience to *say it back*	Takes notes as audience *say it back*	Makes significant revisions based on *say it back*
	Author's Chair	Reads aloud with reluctance	Presents draft for all to hear and enjoy; solicits some feedback	Engagingly presents draft for all to hear and fields feedback from many in audience
14	*First Draft Response Form* (primary trait rubric)	Presents marginal improvements based on teacher comments	Presents significant improvements based on teacher comments	Makes improvements that go beyond the teacher's comments
	Final Evaluation Form (rubric)	Cursory completion of peer/self evaluation	Completion of peer/self evaluation that reflects understanding of stated standards	Peer/self evaluation includes insightful comments added to those provided in the rubric
15	Student-initiated revision	Limited use of one revision strategy	Significant use of 1-2 revision strategies	Widespread use of a variety of revision strategies

Appendix for Administrators

As leader of a Professional Learning Team (**PLT**) studying *Empowering Students to Write and RE-write,* you will find that it is important to facilitate each participant's engagement chapter by chapter. The book is set up to help you do that. At the end of each chapter, participants document their level of engagement by submitting their freely written responses to you. At the end of each section of the book, participants join in an hour session to present their responses to others in their group and react to the presentations of others.

For each chapter: Participants submit their journal entries that identify the value for teaching and learning that they gleaned from the chapter (Looking Back) and the part of their curriculum that invites them to use a concept or strategy from the chapter (Looking Ahead). As PLT leader, acknowledge receipt of the participants' entries, respond and return the entries to them within 48 hours. Use the simple rubric of ⊜ for a superficial or unengaged response, ⊙ for an engaged, but ordinary response and + for an insightful response.

PLT session #1: Participants meet for an hour to:

Look back at chapters 1–4

- ♦ **20 minutes**—Participants share one of their journal entries aloud *verbatim* with others in their PLT.

    - ◇ Members of the PLT identify the strengths of the entries and ask questions of the persons sharing their entries.

    - ◇ The sharing participants jot down the responses of the PLT members to their entries.

- ♦ **20 minutes**—Share what they have tried out from the new knowledge found in chapters 1–4.

Look ahead at the further use of the knowledge from chapters 1–4.

- ♦ **20 minutes**—Plan with members of the PLT specific ways to apply the knowledge from the chapters to learn course content.

PLT sessions #2–#5: Participants meet for an hour to:

Look back at the most recent group of chapters.

   ♦ **20 minutes**—How they implemented the plans from the previous PLT session.

   ♦ **20 minutes**—Share the contents of one journal entry aloud with the PLT.

   ◇ Members of PLT identify the strengths of the entries and ask questions.

   ◇ Participants jot down the responses of PLT members to their entries.

Look ahead to applying strategies from the most recent group of chapters.

   ♦ **20 minutes**—Plan with PLT specific ways to apply this knowledge from the chapters to learn course content.

The timeline rolls out like this. In a one-semester study of the book, the team covers one chapter per week. In a whole year of study, a chapter every two weeks will work. Participants keep their journal writing in a notebook or on a file in their word processor. Plan a routine for reviewing their entries at the end of each chapter. They bring their journal entries to each **PLT** session to share.

Chapter	Looking...	Task	Venue	Date scheduled	completed
1	Back	*What was valuable for you?*	Journal entries	_____	_____
	Ahead	*How can you use this knowledge with your students?*			
2	Back	*What was valuable for you?*	Journal entries	_____	_____
	Ahead	*How can you use this knowledge with your students?*			
3	Back	*What was valuable for you?*	Journal entries	_____	_____
	Ahead	*How can you use this knowledge with your students?*			
4	Back	*What was valuable for you?*	Journal entries	_____	_____
	Ahead	*How can you use this knowledge with your students?*			
1–4	Back	*What was valuable for you?*	PLT session #1	_____	_____
	Back	*How did you try out this knowledge with your students?*			
	Ahead	*How will you use this knowledge moving forward?*			

Once the parameters for working with revision are set in **PLT** session #1, participants begin implementing the strategies that they meet in *Empowering Students to Write and RE-write*.

Chapter	Looking...		Task	Venue	Date scheduled	Date completed
5		Back	What was valuable for you?	Journal entries		
		Ahead	How can you use this knowledge with your students?			
6		Back	What was valuable for you?	Journal entries		
		Ahead	How can you use this knowledge with your students?			
1–4		Back	How have you continued to use the value of chapters 1–4 to maintain a mindset for revision?	PLT session #2		
5–6		Back	What was valuable for you?			
		Back	How did you try out this knowledge with your students?			
		Ahead	How can you use this knowledge moving forward?			

In this section (Chapters 7–9), ask all **PLT** participants to try out a strategy from chapter 7 and one from either chapter 8 or chapter 9. Suggest to teachers with less capable writers that they implement the *Circling Picture Sentences* strategy from chapter 8. Teachers with more confident writers move on to the *Framing Pictures in a Draft* strategy of chapter 9. Be sure that someone tries out strategies from all three chapters.

Chapter	Looking...		Task	Venue	Date scheduled	Date completed
7		Back	What was valuable for you?	Journal entries		
		Ahead	How can you use this knowledge with your students?			
8		Back	What was valuable for you?	Journal entries		
		Ahead	How can you use this knowledge with your students?			
9		Back	What was valuable for you?	Journal entries		
		Ahead	How can you use this knowledge with your students?			
5–6		Back	How have you continued to use the value of chapters 5–6 to maintain a mindset for revision?	PLT session #3		
7–9		Back	What was valuable for you?			
		Back	How did you try out this knowledge with your students?			
		Ahead	How can you use this knowledge moving forward?			

In this section (Chapters 10–12), **PLT** participants who teacher ELA, Reading, ESOL and Special Education students need to try out the *Combining Sentences* and *Spotting Weasel Words* strategies from chapter 10. Other teachers may try a strategy from either chapter 11 or chapter 12. Get commitments from each participant to experience a specific strategy so that the **PLT** hears a report of as many of the strategies as possible.

Chapter	Looking...	Task	Venue	Date scheduled	Date completed
10	Back	*What was valuable for you?*	Journal entries		
	Ahead	*How can you use this knowledge with your students?*			
11	Back	*What was valuable for you?*	Journal entries		
	Ahead	*How can you use this knowledge with your students?*			
12	Back	*What was valuable for you?*	Journal entries		
	Ahead	*How can you use this knowledge with your students?*			
7–9	Back	*How have you continued to use the value of chapters 7–9 to maintain a mindset for revision?*	PLT session #4		
10–12	Back	*What was valuable for you?*			
	Back	*How did you try out this knowledge with your students?*			
	Ahead	*How can you use this knowledge moving forward?*			

In this section (Chapters 13–14), all **PLT** participants need to experience these strategies. Get commitments from each participant to report on a specific strategy so that the **PLT** hears a report of as many of the strategies as possible.

Chapter	Looking...	Task	Venue	Date scheduled	Date completed
13	Back	*What was valuable for you?*	Journal entries		
	Ahead	*How can you use this knowledge with your students?*			
14	Back	*What was valuable for you?*	Journal entries		
	Ahead	*How can you use this knowledge with your students?*			
10–12	Back	*How have you continued to use the value of chapters 10–12 to maintain a mindset for revision?*	PLT session #5		
13–14	Back	*What was valuable for you?*			
	Back	*How did you try out this knowledge with your students?*			
	Ahead	*How can you use this knowledge moving forward?*			

The final chapter begins the task of putting strategies of *Empowering Students to Write and RE-write* into place to provide ongoing support for the curriculum. If you already use *Writing to Win*© instructional materials, the *Writing Cycle* chart is the obvious place for these plans (Combs 2005b). Otherwise, use a teacher-made chart like *Writing Tasks for Teachers Expectations* (chapter 15, p. 23). Ask all **PLT** participants to bring a log of the strategies they have tried during this initiative to contribute to the school-wide plan. Most schools create a *Log of Writing Tasks* for each subject area. **PLT** session #6 launches the creation of these plans. Additional meetings will bring them to closure.

Chapter	Looking...		Task	Venue	Date scheduled	completed
15	Back		*What was valuable for you?*	Journal entries		
	Ahead		*How can you use this knowledge with your students?*			
13–14	Back		*How have you continued to use the value of chapters 13–14 to maintain a mindset for revision?*	PLT session #6		
15	Back		*What was valuable for you?*			
	Back		*How did you try out this knowledge with your students?*			
	Ahead		*How can you use this knowledge moving forward?*			

I welcome your reaction to the professional learning strand of *Empowering Students to Write and RE-write.* Let me know what sections of the book worked best for you and your teachers. I am interested in how you adapted the **PLT** plan to fit your needs. Please offer your suggestions for how we can improve *Empowering Students to Write and RE-write* to meet the needs your teachers and students. Contact me at info@writingtowin.com, on our website, www.writingtowin.com or at our fax number, 706-543-6306.

Here's to authentic writing!

List of References

(appropriate grade levels listed in parentheses)

Anderson, Jeff

2005, *Mechanically Inclined.* Portland, ME: Stenhouse Publishers.

Anderson questions the practice of starting every class with error-filled sentences for students to correct. Then he presents an alternative blend of proofreading and revision strategies with a light touch that cajoles students into an awareness of the strengths and weaknesses in their writing (3-8).

Atwell, Nancie

2002, *Lessons That Change Writers.* Portsmouth, NH: Heinemann.

Atwell presents carefully crafted lessons that take teachers and students through a definitive presentation of the writer's workshop model powered by student-teacher conferences (6-8).

Bishop, Wendy (Ed.)

2004, *Acts of Revision.* Portsmouth, NH: Heinemann.

A collection of essays by published writers and teachers with an emphasis on models of professional writers. For practiced high school writers (9-college).

Combs, Warren

2007a, *Journal for Writing Across the Curriculum, secondary teacher's manual.* 2nd ed. Athens, GA: Erincort Consulting, Inc.

A rich variety of critical thinking strategies for short writing presented in a routine that captures the power of student self-assessment. A standards-based approach to writing to learn across the curriculum (6-12).

2007b, *Monitoring the Progress of Young Writers.* Athens, GA: Erincort Consulting.

2005a, *Sentence Building.* 2nd ed. Athens, GA: Erincort Consulting, Inc.

A full presentation of sentence-combining exercises, the language strategy that posts the greatest Effect Size (ES) on improving writing from the writing intervention research for all three tiers of *Results through Intervention,* RtI (1-9).

2007c, *Working Portfolio for Students.* Athens, GA: Erincort Consulting, Inc.

2005b, *Writing to Win* resource guide, 6-8 and 9-12. 3rd ed. Athens, GA: Erincort Consulting, Inc.

A framework for delivering a standards-based approach to teaching the writing process and using writing to learn across the curriculum. Emphasis on long writing, including the written component of research projects (6-12).

Elbow, Peter

1981, *Writing with Power.* New York, NY: Oxford University Press.

Several chapters on revision, especially appropriate for classrooms in which teachers have established openness among students to revision (6-12).

Heard, Georgia

2002, *The Revision Toolbox: Teaching Techniques That Work.* Portsmouth, NH: Heineman.

A readable presentation of instructional tools for teachers versed in teaching the writer's workshop model (3-8).

Joos, Martin | 1961, *Five Clocks.* New York, NY: Harcourt, Brace and World.

The simplest and most readable presentation of the registers of the English language (6-college).

Murray, Donald | 1991, *The Craft of Revision.* New York, NY: Holt, Rinehart and Winston.

Foundational work for teaching students to revise. Award-winning journalist, professor and writing coach (6-college).

Noguchi, Rei | 1991, *Grammar and the Teaching of Writing.* Urbana, IL: National Council of Teachers of English.

A comprehensive review of the teaching of grammar of American English from its beginning. Clearly establishes the negative effect of instruction in formal grammar on the quality of student writing. Cites sentence-combining practice as the model for teaching grammar that effects writing positively (K-college).

O'Connor, Flannery, Sally Fitzgerald, and Robert Fitzgerald | 1969, *Mystery and Manners: Occasional Prose.* New York, NY: Farrar, Straus and Giroux.

Reaves, Douglas | 2006, *The Learning Leader.* Alexandria, VA: Association for Supervision and Curriculum Development.

One of Reaves' books that presents the research of the 90-90-90 schools. Establishes frequent writing as the common instructional strategy that posted the greatest gains in achievement and equity across the curriculum (K-12).

Reed, Kit | 1989, *Revision.* Cincinnati, Ohio: Writer's Digest Books.

A classic presentation of advice and strategies for teachers and students who want to know how to revise (9-college).

Rowling, J. K. | 1998, *Harry Potter and the Sorcerer's Stone.* New York, NY: Scholastic Press.

Stiggins, Richard, Judith A. Arter, Jan Chappius, and Stephen Chappius | 2003, *Classroom Assessment for Student Learning.* Princeton, NJ: Educational Testing Services.

The definitive course on formative classroom assessment. The rationale and research findings that establish student self-assessment as the assessment that best improves student performance across the curriculum (K-12).